On Kee Thuan Chye and *March 8*

"Kee gets to his point at once. Ar[...]
bone, a basher and a brawler. But, [...]
brains ..."

— Edward Dorall

"Kee is brave enough to make a stand for what he believes. His honesty is to be appreciated even if you don't agree with the man!"

— Malachi Edwin

"Many who have devoted themselves to social consciousness writing in recent times have embroiled themselves in ideological straitjacketing. Kee Thuan Chye's social consciousness transcends that, it is a consciousness that arises from an acknowledgement of the diversity that exists amongst man and his is an evolutionary consciousness, not an imposed one. It includes all and neglects none."

— Eddin Khoo

"One of the first books to document and discuss the consequences of Malaysia's history-making general election in March 2008."

— *The Star*

"This book contains the views of Malaysians of all races and from all walks of life who believe the change is for the good and will inspire a brighter future. It is a toast to the real victors of the 2008 general election — the people who voted for change!"

— *theSun*

"If you've never really cared about the future of Malaysia, then *March 8: Time for Real Change* might just make you want to care about it now."

— *Malaysiakini*

"*March 8: Time for Real Change* is the other voice. It shouts with great passion from across the wide gulf that separates some of us but nevertheless it wants to be heard. We will be doing ourselves a disservice if we turn a deaf ear to our own people."

— *Free Malaysia Today*

"I'm thinking: Everyone should read this book."

— Beth Yahp, *Off the Edge*

NO MORE BULLSHIT,
PLEASE,
WE'RE ALL MALAYSIANS

KEE THUAN CHYE

mc **Marshall Cavendish**
Editions

© 2012 Kee Thuan Chye

Published by Marshall Cavendish Editions
An imprint of Marshall Cavendish International
1 New Industrial Road, Singapore 536196

Cover design and layout by Adithi Khandadi

This publication represents the opinions and views of the author based on his personal experience, knowledge and research, and does not reflect the views of the Publisher or the Printers. The Publisher makes no representation or warranties with respect to the contents of this book, and specifically disclaims any implied warranties or merchantability or fitness for any particular purpose, and shall in no event be liable for any loss of profit or any other commercial damage, including but not limited to special, incidental, consequential, or other damages.

Other Marshall Cavendish Offices:
Marshall Cavendish International. PO Box 65829 London EC1P 1NY, UK • Marshall Cavendish Corporation. 99 White Plains Road, Tarrytown NY 10591-9001, USA • Marshall Cavendish International (Thailand) Co Ltd. 253 Asoke, 12th Flr, Sukhumvit 21 Road, Klongtoey Nua, Wattana, Bangkok 10110, Thailand • Marshall Cavendish (Malaysia) Sdn Bhd, Times Subang, Lot 46, Subang Hi-Tech Industrial Park, Batu Tiga, 40000 Shah Alam, Selangor Darul Ehsan, Malaysia.

Marshall Cavendish is a trademark of Times Publishing Limited

National Library Board, Singapore Cataloguing-in-Publication Data
Kee, Thuan Chye.
No more bullshit, please, we're all Malaysians / Kee Thuan Chye. – Singapore : Marshall Cavendish Editions, c2012.
p. cm.
ISBN: 978-981-4382-01-4

1. Malaysia – Politics and government. I. Title.

DS597.2
320.9595 – dc22   OCN775402794

Printed in Malaysia

DEDICATION:

THIS BOOK IS DEDICATED TO
EVERYONE WHO WANTS A BETTER MALAYSIA,
INCLUDING MY WIFE, LIM CHOY WAN,
AND MY CHILDREN, SORAYA SUNITRA KEE XIANG YIN
AND JEBAT ARJUNA KEE JIA LIANG.

DISSENT IS THE HIGHEST FORM OF PATRIOTISM.
– *HOWARD ZINN*

preface

THIS IS A BOOK COMPRISING EXCERPTS FROM THREE OF MY POLITICAL PLAYS, A COUPLE OF POEMS, TALKS I'VE GIVEN, INTERVIEWS IN WHICH I WAS THE SUBJECT, AND POLITICAL COMMENTARIES I'VE WRITTEN.

I have put it together with the hope that it will serve as some kind of documentation of the times we live in and the kind of politics Malaysians have had to suffer.

I also hope it will impress upon Malaysians the need to speak plainly and openly, without fear of reprisals and persecution.

My style has always been plain and direct — because I believe in calling a spade a spade. I recall my good friend Edward Dorall saying that my writing reflects that of "a basher and a brawler". He probably meant it ain't pretty, but it gets to the point.

That, I admit, is true. I admit my writing tends to be confrontational — and being confrontational, some people will say, is not right for our culture. I, however, don't give a damn. Street protests are also said to be not part of our culture and yet we already had street protests against the Malayan Union more than 60 years ago.

I hope this book will demonstrate that so-called conventional wisdom is not always real wisdom. What matters most is what we ourselves believe.

I have put in these pages my beliefs. Not everyone will agree with them, but that's all right. I welcome differences of opinion.

I am just an ordinary citizen who is concerned about how my country is being governed and where it is heading, and I want to have my say, in my own small way.

I know there are many like me who care. I hope they, too, will come out and speak up, so that a multitude of voices can generate sufficient volume to penetrate the ears — and the hides — of the people who decide our present and plan our future.

Together, we can do our bit for a better Malaysia.

I wish to thank my publisher, Marshall Cavendish Singapore, for sponsoring these pages that carry my voice. And Christine Chong, Deputy Head of Marshall Cavendish Malaysia, not only for helping make this happen but also for her encouragement and assistance throughout my years of association with the company.

For allowing me to reproduce articles and interviews that originally appeared in their website or publication, I wish to thank *Malaysiakini, MalaysianDigest.com, Free Malaysia Today, theSun,* the *Penang Economic Monthly, Kairos* and Oon Yeoh. I also wish to record my appreciation for the work they are doing to create greater awareness among Malaysians.

KEE THUAN CHYE

ALL WE WANT IS AN EVEN CHANCE

New Sunday Times, May 14, 1989

> I wrote 'All We Want Is an Even Chance' in 1989 and it somehow got published in the *New Straits Times*. I heard afterwards there was adverse reaction to its publication from the higher-ups, but due credit must go to the then editor of the Sunday pullout for choosing to publish it in the first place. I include it here because emigration was a big issue with me, and also because Malaysia is now feeling the negative effects of brain drain so many years later.

I used to tell my friends who were thinking of emigrating to instantly drop the idea. Think of the dislocation, I said, the uncertainty. Think of the cultural problems. What would their children grow up to be? Malaysia is home, I always stressed. We should stay back and find ways to surmount whatever problems we face. We should fight for our place, if need be.

We were born here. We've lived here for decades. Where in the world would there be another place which provided such convenience of living, such comfort that comes from being so used to the place; from people we know and are familiar with; from the generally easy-going atmosphere?

What if in the middle of the night, you missed your *char koay teow* or *mee rebus*?, I challenged. What if you needed some good old Malaysian warmth and looked around to find you had left all your best friends behind, and the new friends you've made are not quite the same? Not the back-thumping, casual, *chhin-chhai*, nonsense-talking type?

Sure, there are many things here that are not right. But should we run away?, I protested. Isn't it taking the easy way out? (Some people might even say "the cowardly way out" but I wouldn't go so far as that.)

We have to think of our children, they counter-protested. Their education, their future, and better opportunities for them.

But how can you be sure that you won't end up even worse in whichever country you're going to?, I asked. You'd be a minority, you might be discriminated against, you might be treated as second-class citizens.

At least there would be channels for protest, they said. Over here, you can't even vent your dissatisfaction without fear of getting into trouble. Come to think of it, how many channels are open for this kind of airing?

I couldn't answer them. I searched my mind furiously for some convincing examples but they fell terribly short. So, I resorted to my last defence.

But this country needs you, I asserted, my face almost turning blue. It needs you more than Australia or Canada or New Zealand or wherever. They are already OK on their own. They are already better developed, whereas Malaysia is still struggling to find its place on the map. We can't afford to lose you!

This was usually greeted with a profound pause, as if my point had rightly made its mark. Their faces usually registered a pain that came with an assaulted conscience. For that moment, I thought I had won even if it might have hurt them a bit.

Then slowly, haltingly, came the heart-rending reply: It's true what you say. We know that, too. We have tossed and turned over this. We have weighed it carefully. It's not an easy decision at all. But do you think the country really cares if we go? Do you think the country has stopped for a while and said, wait a minute, what's happening? Why are so many people leaving? What's wrong?

There is so much we have to give, to contribute to its growth, but sometimes, this is not appreciated. Sometimes, there are too many restrictions against our giving, and too many restrictions against our growing. So, we might as well go somewhere else where we may get an even chance.

We have never asked for much, even from this country. Just an even chance. And that's all we'll be asking for elsewhere. We don't know for sure that we'll get it, but we have to take the risk. We have to find out.

I was momentarily stumped by the reasoning. It wasn't so much the emotion behind the words as the fact that they had been so thought-out. No counter-argument came to my rescue; I realised I didn't deserve any. What could I say in reply to a revelation like that?

I uneasily wished them the best of luck.

Since then, I haven't been so sure of my earlier stand. As such, I no longer try to talk people out of emigrating. I still maintain that it's sad to see so many go, and it's even sadder when they are my friends, but now, I can see that they have their point. I am in no position to argue against it. What do I know about how they really feel?

Going away to start a new life in a different country is not something that is done on a whim or impulse. (Unless one has committed a crime and knows he won't get extradited if he runs away overseas, but there are not many of us like that. I hope.)

I hate to say it, and I never dreamt I would say it, but it probably takes a lot of guts, too, to go in search of something one is not entirely sure of.

Perhaps I am too much of an idealist to think about something as conceptually nebulous as "the country needs you". Perhaps it is even too narrow and confining. We are children of the world, are we not? Is it my advancing age that makes me tend to think like a jingoist?

Perhaps we should think in global terms. If an emigrant realises his potential in some other country, it should not be seen as a loss for Malaysia but a gain for the world. "The country" is just a concept created by the political mind; it really bears no meaning to an individual's reality.

What can I say if people want to make a better life for themselves? "The country" is just a land where one settles on to try and make the best living.

Yes, some of these emigrants are selfish; they want their cake and to eat it, too. They secure a permanent residence in some other country while they retain their Malaysian citizenship. If they don't make it there, they know they can always come back. It's not exactly a scrupulous proposition; they are only thinking of themselves.

But who else should they be thinking of? When it comes to the crunch, to whom should we owe our loyalty if not ourselves?

I don't really know the answers, of course, as an idealist. But nowadays, when I think about what my friends said about "an even chance", I think of the taxes I'm paying as a pledge of my loyalty to this country and the pride I feel as its citizen.

And inevitably, I feel that the least I should get in return is nothing less than an even chance.

SHARING A COMMONWEALTH IN MALAYSIA

This was an address I made at a plenary session of the 11th ACLALS (Association for Commonwealth Literature and Language Studies) Triennial Conference on Literature and Language held in Kuala Lumpur in December 1998. I had it published soon after in the Literary Page of the *New Straits Times* and received a memo from the newspaper's editor-in-chief ticking me off for doing so. I was not surprised.

What is meant by "sharing a commonwealth in Malaysia" as pertains to literature? I shall address it from the point of view of the writer. And because I am a writer writing in English rather than Malay, which is the national language, my views will be coloured by that bias.

To me, writers share a commonwealth if they feel they belong to a community that ensures equal rights for all; provides them with nurture, support, even funding; accords them official recognition – in short, makes them feel wanted. In Malaysia, such a commonwealth does exist but for those who write in the national language. Only their works are considered "national literature", as distinct from literatures in other languages, which are termed "sectional" or "communal" literatures. In practice, this means that "sectional" or "communal" literatures do not enjoy support, funding or recognition from official sources, despite the fact that they are no less Malaysian in substance and expression. They are not officially promoted; neither are they recognised for the intellectual and creative contributions that they make to the national culture and imagination.

Dewan Bahasa dan Pustaka, the national literary agency, overseer of Malaysian literature, gives little significance to these "sectional" literatures. There is not even an ongoing programme to translate them into Malay. The Dewan goes to other parts of the world in search of literary texts to translate, and has done so with the works of Patrick White, Sally Morgan, Yukio Mishima, just to name a few, but it has not looked closer to home to the works of English-language writers like Lee Kok Liang, Ee Tiang Hong, Salleh Ben Joned, K.S. Maniam, Wong Phui Nam or Omar Mohd. Noor. There has been an anthology of poetry originally written in English with parallel translations in Malay published by the Dewan 10 years ago, but that seems to have been the first and last of such endeavours. Its Malay title, *Antologi Puisi Pelbagai Kaum*, does not even allude to the poems as being Malaysian; transliterated, it means "Anthology of Poetry by Various Races".

In the giving out of literary awards, none of the national ones has been given out to the "sectional" litterateurs. As for something more international like the S.E.A. Write Award, which is presented annually to writers of Southeast Asia, all the recipients from Malaysia since the inception of the award in 1979 have been those writing in Malay. This is not surprising since nominations for the Malaysian candidate are made every year by the Dewan and the right-wing, chauvinistic literary organisation called Gapena. It has become something of a joke that because of the nature of the selection, the established Malay writers simply have to wait their turn to get the award. If they don't get it this year, they're sure to get it sometime. In neighbouring Singapore, the nomination is rotated among writers from the three major language streams; is that why Singapore has achieved developed nation status while Malaysia is struggling with its Vision 2020?

I do not mean to belittle the national language nor the writers who write in it. I believe in and support the use of Malay as the national language, and I respect writers as writers regardless of what language they write in. It is also to be expected that in a multi-racial society, the desire of the predominant race to safeguard its dominance can overwhelm other considerations.

Even so, it remains to be said that the continued practice of keeping the literary commonwealth restrictive rather than all-encompassing is one that writers surely cannot feel comfortable with — because it goes against norms that writers would uphold rather than reject. It divides rather than harmonises, stirs up feelings of envy, and fosters defensiveness on the part of the privileged and distrust on the part of the marginalised.

To understand why despite its divisiveness this practice continues to prevail, it is necessary to look at the larger social and political context. Since the founding of this nation 41 years ago, divisiveness has been a condition operating at the centre of Malaysian life. The political system is still organised and conducted along ethnic lines. It is a system that lends itself to, indeed actively engenders, the politicisation of issues such as race, language, culture and religion.

It is a system that keeps up barriers when barriers need to be removed. It retards the evolution of a truly Malaysian consciousness through constantly reminding the people that they are Malay, Chinese, Indian and Others. Or Bumiputera and Non-Bumiputera. Malaysian politicians attune their speeches according to the groups they are addressing. Hence, they will talk of Malaysian unity when they address a multi-racial audience, but switch to chauvinistspeak when they face an audience of their own race.

Race consciousness is still at a level where almost every issue is seen, consciously or otherwise, from the perspective of race. What this means for the writer is that his ethnic origin is often considered above the ideas he expresses; and he can be suspected of professing an agenda even if he does not have one. The writer, thus, finds himself confronted with a formidable barrier of prejudice, a barrier that has often prevented him from exposing — with uncompromising honesty — the glaring contradictions that exist in Malaysian society, from criticising the political excesses that have been perpetrated over the last 20 years, and from denouncing the financial and political scandals that have arisen in that same period.

The other big barrier that the writer comes up against is curtailment of free expression. Despite avowals by the authorities that Malaysia upholds democratic principles, there are some things that cannot be expressed publicly. If what is said or written is construed to be a threat to national security, the person responsible can be charged under the Internal Security Act (ISA). This Act, which allows for detention without trial, was a severe measure introduced by the British colonial regime to combat Communism. Today, however, there is no longer the threat of Communism since the Communist Party of Malaya has given up its struggle − coincidentally enough on December 2, 1989, exactly nine years ago to the day − but the ISA continues to be enforced.

To the best of my knowledge, no writer has yet been detained under the ISA specifically for his writing. That is perhaps because we have become adept at practising self-censorship. We learn quickly what to exclude from our texts if we want our writings published. As for playwrights, who have to apply for a permit to have their plays staged, they try not to include anything that may jeopardise their chances of getting that permit. Some years ago, an innocuous play about a man recounting the difficulties he underwent to bury his grandfather was denied a permit. Why this was so remains a mystery. Perhaps, unknown to us, burial is regarded as a subversive activity.

When Sinclair Lewis wrote that "Every compulsion is put upon writers to become safe, polite, obedient, and sterile", he had to have been referring to Malaysia. Given the divided character of the society, Malaysian writers often feel that what they say is not going to reach out to a wide audience, much less influence them. In any case, change in Malaysia usually comes about at the initiative of the ruling authority, not the individual, not even the grassroots. The voice of the writer is one

not appropriate. It should be the Government that decides, not the Umno Supreme Council. I'm sure you know that too.

Interestingly enough, Umno Youth had also been in on the act – one year earlier. The organisation protested against the making of the film even before it was shot. I don't know about you, but I find that shocking. Why has it come to pass that politicians are interfering in the making of culture?

I have dwelt at length on this issue of the banning of *The Last Communist* because I think it says a lot about the kind of society we have become. We are obviously insecure, obviously paranoid, and, far worse, obviously confused. And yet, we are supposed to be embarking on an exciting journey towards developed nation status by the year 2020.

We have seen from this example the narrow agenda and petty fears of politicians and journalists. If you bring in the examples of the films *Sepet* and *Gubra*, both written and directed by Yasmin Ahmad, films that have been reviled for non-artistic reasons, you will meet another set of people who haven't realised that the world is bigger than their coconut shell – I'm talking about racists and religious extremists.

The all-important question, however, is this – do they represent the majority of Malaysians? But then, what do we mean when we say "Malaysians"? And that's when it gets very complicated. Because I know and you know that there are Malaysians who are considered more Malaysian than other Malaysians. And when it comes to the crunch, the Malaysians who are considered more Malaysian tend to have more say. And even if only a handful of them were to express unhappiness over an issue, chances are they would be given attention disproportionate to their numbers. Right or not?

That explains the banning of *The Last Communist*. That also explains the closing down of the KakiKino Film Club that was screening foreign art films at Finas – until a member of the public complained that it was showing pornography. Actually, these foreign art films sometimes contain scenes of nudity but that's as pornographic as the nude women in classic Renaissance paintings. These paintings, by the way, are proudly exhibited in famous museums and art galleries throughout the world but you probably know what our censors do with them when they appear in magazines. They take out their marker pens and blot out the parts that get them wild — either with moral indignation or delight; I'm not sure which. But they're vandals all the same.

Let me now tell you about *The Vagina Monologues* and its fate in Malaysia. *The Vagina Monologues* is a critically acclaimed feminist play written by American playwright Eve Ensler that speaks out on issues important to women, such as rape and violence against them. In 2002, two theatre groups in KL collaborated on a workshop performance of it that ran for five shows. They managed to secure a permit for it from City Hall. Encouraged by the success of the show, the producers decided to extend the run. But this time, when they applied for a permit, did they get it? No. Why? Because when a scholars' association in Kedah read about the workshop in the newspapers, they filed a complaint against it. An objection raised by people all the way from Kedah, who had not even seen the play. Does that sound familiar? It seems to have become a Malaysian habit to denounce something one has not seen, hasn't it?

The Black American writer James Baldwin once wrote: "Ignorance, allied with power, is the most ferocious enemy justice can have." Replace the word "justice" with "culture" and that observation is just as apt. We, Malaysians, are truly in the grip of the tyranny of a minority. This minority is dictating what we can see and do.

The movie *Sepet* presents the multicultural reality in our society by showing slices of Malaysian life and centering on the love between a Chinese boy and a Malay girl, but in Parliament no less, an MP no less, with the titles 'Datuk' and 'Dr' no less, said that the film did not reflect national identity. He criticised the movie for its "*rojak* language" and "inappropriate scenes", one of which is of a young man in his underwear. Do we Malaysians not speak "*rojak* language" in our everyday life, throwing in Bazaar Malay, English, Tamil, Mandarin, Cantonese, Iban and so on? And don't some of us sometimes go about in our underwear at home?

A more important question: What does that MP mean by "national identity"? Well, I think you know the answer to that question.

I suppose the MP would also concur with the Malay press for denouncing *Sepet* also because it has a scene in which the Malay girl meets the boy in a Chinese coffee shop which has a stall selling pork rice. Isn't it enough that the Malay girl doesn't eat the pork rice? Is there a law that says she can't step into such a coffee shop? And if she did, "national identity" would be in serious jeopardy? *Relek la.*

Really, what we already know from this is that there are people who do not want to embrace pluralism, multiculturalism and the idea of Bangsa Malaysia. Well, that's fine. If that's how it is with them, they're free to adhere to their own beliefs. It gets to be a problem, however, when they try to make their beliefs prevail over the activities of others who don't share these beliefs. That is a blatant infringement of human rights. The repercussions of this have a great negative effect on the arts. Because the arts foster what is positive and life-affirming and progressive and democratic.

And it's not only the arts that have been short-changed by this tyrannical minority. As you know, we now cannot discuss Article 11 of the Constitution. The Constitution, mind you. That piece of writing on which our whole nation is founded. And the gag order comes from no less than the Chief Executive Officer of Malaysia. Because, he says, such discussion can cause tension in our society. OK, as authority-fearing Malaysians, we won't say that such an order goes against the spirit of Article 10 of that same Constitution, the Article 10 which guarantees freedom of expression. We won't say that. But then, if we think hard about it, isn't the Government sending out confusing signals? We are all Malaysians but the Government does not seem to treat us equally. We are a democracy and yet, not so. We are mature people and yet, we cannot participate in mature discussions. Is it because one sector is not mature enough? Well, the Government is then continuing to pamper a spoilt child, a child who is given to ranting and raving, throwing tantrums, threatening to erupt in violence. Shouldn't the Government lead them to the mature path, teach them tolerance and rational understanding? We are in a globalised world. We are going towards Vision 2020. At the very least, the Government could tell them, "Look. If you don't agree with this and that but most others do, just respect what they want. Respect the rule of law, the principles of the Constitution. Don't create a fuss, don't act like *samseng*. If you resort to violence, we'll have to take action against you as stipulated by the law."

It doesn't take a rocket scientist to see the simple logic in that. But perhaps a rocket scientist would point out that if the Government actually did that, it might not continue to be the Government. And that's the rub. Nobody wants to bell the cat. And yet, this minority that behaves in such an unreasonable and unruly way needs to be pulled up before it gets totally unmanageable. It's already getting away with posting death threats on the Internet against one of the organisers of the Article 11 forums. What happens if at some time in the near future it gets away with murder?

I have been in the arts for 30 years and I'm appalled that instead of improving, the situation has got worse for artists. The restrictions are still there. Sixteen years ago, I directed a play called *Madame Mao's Memories* that was about Jiang Qing and not at all about Communism, but it was not given a permit. That same paranoia is still here today. In 2004, the play *Election Day* by Huzir Sulaiman was rejected by City Hall because it contained the names of real people like Mahathir Mohamad, Anwar Ibrahim, the lawyer R. Sivarasa, etc. Even the mention of Guardian Pharmacy was not allowed. Why that was so is anybody's guess. Now, apart from these unfathomable restrictions, we artists also have to put up with the new insidious phenomenon of not offending the sensibilities of the tyrannical minority — because all it takes is a complaint from them to shut down our show.

But why pick on the arts? It's not a danger to public safety or national security. A play or a film is not going to cause the audience to run amok or start a revolution. The reach is small, minuscule, compared to the exposure politicians get on national television. That's the real theatre now. The big stage is the political stage, where an event can be telecast live to millions of people and made larger than life. Reality is being theatricalised by the politicians in power every day. They are the big-time actors, their PR consultants are the mega stage managers. They know how to use the medium to theatrical effect. The brandishing of a *keris* and its threatening implications are beamed to millions of homes to ram a message through. If any censoring is required, it should be for something as racially divisive as that. Instead, it was allowed to be a dramatic act on a big scale. No theatre company could have that kind of luxury or be able to afford such coverage. And yet puny theatre companies can have their productions closed down because some member of the public makes a complaint. When huge numbers of the public complained about that *keris* drama, they were told to be silent.

The Prime Minister says we are a nation with First Class infrastructure and Third World mentality when referring to our poor maintenance of public facilities. Perhaps he should extend it to mean the mindset of Malaysians who disrupt activities, including cultural ones, because they feel that their beliefs are under threat.

It is the arts that are under threat. And there is precious little that artists can do to defend their rights; not while the Government and the people give in to tyranny. Recently, we celebrated our Independence Day, symbol of our freedom. But are we really free? Are we free from fear, free from ignorance, free from prejudice?

I don't think I need to tell you the answer. You already know it.

excerpt

FROM THE PLAY
1984 HERE AND NOW

In the '80s, it was virtually impossible (as it is now, really) to write about the political issues of the day and see it published in the media. The natural outlet for me was writing political plays. I include here a scene from my play *1984 Here and Now* in which the characters, who are journalists working for a newspaper, grumble about the constraints imposed on journalism by the political dictator Big Brother. This was written in 1984 and the play was staged a year later. But the issues are still with us today, and the same political abuse is being perpetrated, including keeping the same muzzle intact on the media. In fact, 1984 was the year the Printing Presses and Publications Act was enacted requiring all printing presses to obtain a licence granted by the Home Ministry that would be renewed every year. It gave the Home Minister "absolute discretion" in the granting and revocation of licences, and the power to ban any publication he deems is a threat to national security. And in 1987, an ouster clause was established to prevent the actions of the Home Minister from being called into question by the courts. All this explains why the mainstream media has become so gutless.

Scene 2

(Newspaper office. WIRAN and some colleagues, among them JUMON, are working on video display terminals as the lights come on. CHIEF SUB-EDITOR enters.)

CHIEF SUB: Jumon, have we got a front page lead yet?

JUMON: There's one story here about Leek accusing Kala of making a seditious statement.

CHIEF SUB: You mean Kala's call for Party members to control 45 per cent of the economy?

JUMON: Yes. Going by the Constitution, it is a seditious statement.

CHIEF SUB: But you must understand, Jumon, that Leek is a Prole.

JUMON: And Proles don't count, right?

CHIEF SUB: No, it's not that. You still don't want to understand that our paper has a policy to follow. Kala is a Party member.

JUMON: And, therefore, he can get away with making seditious statements. I'm sure if a Prole had made a similar statement, he would have been arrested.

CHIEF SUB: I don't want to argue with you, Jumon. That's the reality of the situation and you should be aware of it.

JUMON: But we are a newspaper. Our job is to tell it like it is. Call a spade a spade.

CHIEF SUB: You are too much of an idealist.

JUMON: I'm only doing my job.

CHIEF SUB: Yes, just stick to that. In any case, I hear that Big Brother will be moving for an amendment to the Constitution regarding sedition.

JUMON: What? Just like that?

CHIEF SUB: Just like that.

JUMON: To save Kala's skin?

CHIEF SUB: For now, we will use another story for the front page lead — the Inner Party's decision to stop the setting up of a Prole university.

JUMON: But according to the Constitution, the Proles have a right to set up a university.

CHIEF SUB: You want to tell that to the Inner Party?

JUMON: We can tell it to the people.

CHIEF SUB: Let me tell you this, Jumon. The Inner Party runs the country, not the people.

JUMON: That should not be the case in a democracy.

CHIEF SUB: You are an idealist. I'm not going to waste time arguing with you. I'll have to check with the Chief Editor about running the university story as front-page lead. Did you know that yesterday, we ran a public reaction story to the Inner Party's implementation of the Education Policy and one point was considered too critical? Big Brother gave the Chief Editor a shelling, and the Chief Editor took it out on me. The word is, we can't hurt the Inner Party's image. You and I, we just do our jobs.

(CHIEF SUB exits. WIRAN comes over to JUMON.)

WIRAN: You should have known better.

JUMON: Bread-and-butter journalist. You know the latest joke, Wiran? All it takes is for Big Brother or his deputy to fart and he'll get 20 paragraphs on the front page. This morning, the Opposition Party Leader made a reasonable statement about ways of integrating the Proles and the Party members, and I think it should at least be second lead on page two. But the Chief Sub said cut it down to four paras and use it as a cut-off, 24-point heading two lines across two columns.

WIRAN: I know how you feel.

(Suddenly, there is a commotion. POLICE OFFICERS bring in the CHIEF EDITOR and a CARTOONIST. The CHIEF SUB-EDITOR, distraught, follows behind.)

WIRAN:	What's happening?
CHIEF EDITOR:	I want to know what the charges are against me.
POLICE OFFICER:	You'll know soon enough.
CHIEF EDITOR:	I want to call my lawyer.
POLICE OFFICER:	You won't need one.
CHIEF EDITOR:	There must be a mistake. You can't take me in like this.
POLICE OFFICER:	I have my orders.
CHIEF EDITOR:	And why are you taking our cartoonist? He hasn't done anything wrong.

(CHIEF EDITOR and CARTOONIST are hustled out. All in the office begin to whisper to each other, wondering what has been happening. They crowd around the CHIEF SUB, asking for an explanation.)

WORKER 2:	I heard a rumour that the Inner Party is not happy with some of the things the Chief Editor has allowed to be published. Somewhat critical of the Administration.
CHIEF SUB:	We must be extra careful from now on.
WORKER 3:	But what about our cartoonist?
WORKER 2:	He's been too outspoken with his political cartoons lately. Rumour has it he's sympathetic towards the Communists.
WORKER 1:	That's hard to believe. I know him well, he's not like that.
WORKER 2:	Nowadays, you don't know what to believe any more.
JUMON:	We are not getting enough of the truth, that's why.
WORKER 1:	What's going to happen to them?
CHIEF SUB:	If they don't confess their crimes, they could remain inside for an indefinite period of time.
WORKER 1:	Years?
CHIEF SUB:	Yes.

WORKER 1:   I hope it will turn out all right. Perhaps they will confess immediately.

CHIEF SUB: But things will not be the same any more. They will be marked for life.

JUMON: Perhaps they are innocent. Haven't you all thought of that?

WORKER 3:   Are you suggesting that they have been framed? Why would the Inner Party do a thing like that?

JUMON: They have their reasons.

WORKER 3:   Yes, the peace and stability of the nation. They won't arrest people who are not a threat to our safety.

JUMON: They would arrest people who tell the truth.

CHIEF SUB: It's already six, Big Brother is making an important announcement. Switch on the TV.

(Light comes on TV screen. Gamelan music plays as BIG BROTHER makes his appearance.)

BIG BROTHER: Peace be with us. I wish to announce, comrades, a new amendment to the Constitution that has been passed in Parliament today. The Opposition Party has accused the Second Minister of Economy of having invoked racist sentiments in calling for Party members to own 45 per cent share of the economy. In levelling such an accusation, the Opposition Party itself is committing an irresponsible act. The Opposition Party itself is pandering to racist sentiments. It is making political capital of the issue in order to whip up sympathy for itself and instigate adverse reaction to the workings of the Inner Party. It is manipulating the issue into a sensitive one. To prevent this and to assure the races of this nation that there has not been an encroachment on their rights, Parliament has today amended the

Constitution to waive the ruling on sedition on all matters pertaining to the economy provided they do not question the rights and privileges of Party members, as has been guaranteed by the Constitution. The stability of the nation depends on strict observance of the Constitution. The Inner Party will not hesitate to take stringent action against those who attempt to undermine it. Peace be with us.

(NOTE: *"Prole" and "Party member" are two different races.*)

MAHATHIR THE
MESS-MAKER

TO MANY, MAHATHIR MOHAMAD IS THE MOST HATED PRIME MINISTER MALAYSIA HAS HAD SO FAR, THE ONE WHO HAS DONE THE MOST DAMAGE TO THE COUNTRY. I TOTALLY AGREE. I SENSED HE WAS BAD NEWS SOON AFTER HE TOOK OFFICE, AND HAVE SINCE SATIRISED HIM IN MY PLAYS. LIKE MANY MALAYSIANS, I THINK OF HIM AS SOMEONE WITH A SELECTIVE MEMORY CHOOSING TO REMEMBER THINGS FAVOURABLE TO HIM AND TO FORGET WHAT COULD INCRIMINATE HIM. I ALSO THINK OF HIM AS SOMEONE WHO WOULD BLAME OTHERS RATHER THAN ACCEPT RESPONSIBILITY FOR HIS OWN ACTIONS. A GOOD EXAMPLE IS HIS ATTEMPT AT DOWNPLAYING HIS ROLE IN OPERATION LALANG. I THINK OF HIM AS A CHAUVINIST WHO WOULD NOT BE ABOVE CAUSING RACIAL RIFTS, AS IS EVIDENT IN THE THINGS HE SAID AFTER THE MARCH 2008 GENERAL ELECTION AND IN HIS ASSOCIATION WITH PERTUBUHAN PRIBUMI PERKASA MALAYSIA (PERKASA). WHEN HE WAS PM, ONE OF HIS SLOGANS WAS "LEADERSHIP BY EXAMPLE". THAT THE LEADERSHIP OF UMNO AND BN HAS BECOME WHAT IT IS TODAY IS VERY MUCH DUE TO THE EXAMPLE HE SET WHILE HE WAS PM.

THE MAN WHO CREATED A CULTURE OF FEAR

Excerpted from "Change and Hope and People Power", published in the book *March 8: The Day Malaysia Woke Up* (Marshall Cavendish, 2008).

On the issue of governance over all these years of Barisan Nasional (BN) domination, one has to acknowledge that no other Prime Minister has been as autocratic as Mahathir Mohamad, and I'm happy to go on record to say that I've never liked or respected him. And it's not just because of that perpetual sneer on his face. Even when he smiles. Or the fact that he behaves like a bull in a china shop. In the '70s, I saw how academia started to get messed up when he was Education Minister, when Dr Hamzah Sendut was replaced by Hamdan Sheikh Tahir as Vice-Chancellor of Universiti Sains Malaysia, where I was a student. Hamzah was a highly respected academic with liberal views and aspirations for USM, Hamdan was a civil servant.

As a journalist, I've seen how Mahathir gagged the media. We used to joke in the newsroom that Mahathir had only to sneeze and he would get 20 paras on the front page. If he were to fart, he'd get more. But seriously, reporting the news was never the same from the early '80s onwards. He would appear frequently on the front page or at least never beyond Page 3 (unless it was something not too terribly important). You could criticise the ministers (to a certain extent) but not the PM. After a while, criticising ministers also became taboo. The Opposition came to be given little coverage. When there was any, it was usually to paint them in a negative light. The rules were never written down of course, but through practice, it became common knowledge what was acceptable and what was not. This was all the more insidious because editors began to second-guess what would displease the political masters, and to play safe. Many stories came to be spiked as a result, injudiciously. This spawned a culture of self-censorship, which is arguably worse than censorship. Equally bad was the culture of *ampu-bodek* or apple-polishing in the newsroom. Editors forsook the values and principles of journalism and served more to please the political masters. Chief editors who were considered not to have given "110 per cent" support could be and were removed. Spin-doctoring came into the game (although it was not known by that name then as the word had not yet been coined). When A. Kadir Jasin was Group Editor-in-Chief at *New Straits Times* during the Anwar crisis in the late '90s, the front-page lead on at least two occasions was not a news story, as should be the case, but virtually an editorial condemning Anwar.

I need not say more about what Mahathir did to the judiciary; that's already legend. I can say that he created the culture of fear in Malaysia with the unleashing of Operation Lalang in 1987 during which more than 100 people were detained under the ISA. He was a master at political manipulation. Despite having entered Sabah only three years earlier, Umno managed to insinuate itself into a ruling position there in 1994, diluting the power of the Kadazandusun-majority Parti Bersatu Sabah (PBS). This was incredibly fast. And just as amazing is the fact that by 2003, Umno was firmly entrenched and holding the reins of the Sabah Government. Interestingly, Joseph Pairin Kitingan, President of PBS and Chief Minister of Sabah from 1985, was charged with corruption in 1991, a year after he had pulled PBS out of BN which it was pressured to join in 1986. He was found guilty in 1994, the year another state election was due. PBS won by a close margin and Pairin was sworn in as Chief Minister, but he was forced to resign when many of PBS's elected Assemblymen subsequently defected to BN. At the time, money politics was already a term in vogue in the rumour mills.

Mahathir always likes to win. Look at the way he's going on and on about Abdullah Badawi; he won't stop until he gets what he wants. So when it comes to losing, whether he wants to admit it or not, Mahathir is naturally a sore loser. When BN lost Terengganu to PAS in 1999, the state's five per cent oil royalty which is legitimately due to it was taken away and substituted with a lower-quantum Wang Ehsan. Was that right or fair?

Mahathir built Putrajaya, which is now a white elephant, a surreal Disneyland for tourists to gawk at. I've been there at night and seen what a virtual ghost town it is and yet, the place is lit up with money that comes from your pocket and mine. He has always been a champion of *Ketuanan Melayu*. (It was during his stewardship when Abdullah Ahmad coined that term.) And yet he supposedly came up with the concept of Bangsa Malaysia. Look at his recent playing of the race card while addressing a gathering in Johor Bahru. Referring to a Hindraf 5 memorandum, he said to the crowd: "What does it say? Malaysia for Malaysians! This is the reality of the present situation. If we do not speak up, if we choose to keep quiet, we will lose our rights and the other races will take over." How does that gel with Bangsa Malaysia?

A BLACKLY COMIC WHODUNIT

Free Malaysia Today, February 11, 2011

Operation Lalang was a black day in Malaysian history. On October 27, 1987, 106 people were detained under the ISA in one fell swoop. Most of them were from Opposition parties and NGOs. A few newspapers were suspended. It traumatised Malaysians and made them submit to the culture of fear. Some have yet to recover from it.

Whoever initiated Operation Lalang did a strong disservice to the nation. It was a shameful exercise of power. Whatever the reason or reasons may be for invoking the ISA on that occasion on so many individuals, there is no fair justification for doing so.

Perhaps that is why Mahathir Mohamad, who was the prime minister then, has recently come out to say he was not responsible for it. In typical Mahathir fashion — for he is accustomed to blaming others for things he might have done — he blamed it on the police.

In his interview with Tom Plate for the recently published book *Doctor M: Operation Malaysia – Conversations with Mahathir Mohamad*, he said:

> *Well, I would have handled it differently, except that the police wanted to do these things because they say it is necessary ...*
>
> *I actually met all of the opposition members (beforehand) and assured them that they would not be arrested. And you know what the police did? They arrested them. My credibility is gone.*

It's almost laughable — in a scary way — to note that the PM had no control over what the police were going to do on such a large scale and with such disastrous effects. How could the police have been given so much power then? Are they still as powerful today? Does that make Malaysia a police state?

Apparently, in 1987, the police did have that power — according to Haniff Omar, who was the IGP at the time. He has just come out to corroborate Mahathir's finger-pointing the police for launching Operation Lalang.

But more than that, he says he consulted Mahathir before swinging into action, and even though Mahathir was against it, the police took it upon themselves to steam ahead. Whoa! Is this a black comedy? The PM was against it but he had no power to forbid the IGP from carrying it out? Who's the boss? The CEO of the country or the IGP? Well ... "(The police) were independent, at least during my time," says Haniff.

Really scary! Are we safe any more? Who protects us from the police? During Operation Lalang, did Mahathir renege on his duty to protect the people?

Well, most of the 106 were released before the 60-day detention order was up, but at least 40 others were authorised to be detained for two years. This authorisation could only have come from the Home Minister. And the Home Minister then was Mahathir Mohamad.

Wow! The plot thickens! Mahathir tells Tom Plate he was against Operation Lalang and yet he signed the orders to detain at least 40 people for another two years! Where's the logic? Was Mahathir unaware of what he was signing? Did he have his eyes closed? Did he say, "I don't want to know *la*, just let me sign."?

Mahathir certainly has some heavy explaining to do.

He also has to explain the suspension of the three newspapers, namely, *The Star*, *Watan* and *Sin Chew Jit Poh*. Did the police order the suspension too? Of course not! That could only be done by the Home Minister. And who, pray tell, might that be?

By most accounts and from the list of people detained, Operation Lalang seemed targeted at social and political activists critical of the Government and mainly Opposition politicians. Several of them were DAP and PAS members. But Haniff says the police action was not politically motivated.

To be sure, Operation Lalang was the outcome of the racial flare-up sparked by the controversy over the Education Ministry's appointment of senior assistants and principals to Chinese schools who were not Chinese-educated, but why were only certain groups and individuals arrested?

Najib Razak, who was then head of Umno Youth, led a huge rally in Kampung Baru, right inside Kuala Lumpur's Malay heartland, obviously the place to whip up racial sentiments. Did that not qualify for ISA detention? And yet Najib was not taken in.

Umno announced it would hold a rally drawing half a million people. It said the event was to celebrate its 41st anniversary, but given the timing at such a potentially incendiary moment, the real agenda could have been something more sinister. And yet no action was taken against those who mooted it.

Mahathir told Tom Plate he assured the Opposition politicians that they would not be arrested, but DAP supremo Lim Kit Siang, who was among those served with the two-year detention order, has come out to say he never met Mahathir before the big swoop. Neither did Mahathir give him assurance that he would not be detained.

Who is lying – Kit Siang or Mahathir?

Either way, the big-dollar question still pops up: If Mahathir said he gave that assurance, why then did he sign the order to detain Lim (and six of his DAP comrades) for two years?

More so than ever, we can now see how dangerous the ISA can be. Whether it grants power to the police or the Home Minister, it is subject to abuse. Now more than ever, it is clear that such a dangerous law should be abolished. What does the current administration have to say to that?

Ultimately, for Operation Lalang, regardless of who really initiated it, Mahathir, as the PM then, has to take the blame. One can't imagine

Malaysian society — views her father's participation at this event. I'd love to read her column on that.

Perkasa is anathema to progress; subscribing to it is subscribing to a bleak future. What does it preach but narrow-minded concerns? What is it really championing? An old system that has seen Malaysia plunge into the abyss of corruption and rent-seeking. A system that has made the country unattractive to foreign investors, that perpetuates the mediocrity arising from affirmative action that has gone extreme and awry.

Mahathir used to pride himself as being a forward-thinking man; and yet in his speech at the gathering, he asked Prime Minister Najib Razak and the Umno leadership to listen to Perkasa and to return to the old ways of defending Malay rights. This is passé politics. Malaysia should now be looking forward to multi-racialism and globalisation rather than be frozen in a time warp — for whose benefit? Everyone will suffer if we stagnate.

Even Malays are talking of the need to reform affirmative action, chief among them Nazir Razak, Najib's own brother and the CEO of CIMB Group. In an interview with *The Edge* published on March 15, he said, "I spent much of the 1990s listing companies and saw at close proximity arbitrary allocations of shares [made] to individuals in the name of the NEP. Many become rich or much richer overnight, and then we wonder why *bumiputeras* are not competitive."

He advocates that the New Economic Model that Najib will be unveiling at the end of this month must be "transparent and conducive to competition and market forces". This would be the kind of thing Perkasa would object to strongly.

Mahathir, of course, won't acknowledge it but Opposition leader Anwar Ibrahim's idea of an economic model that provides assistance based on need rather than race makes better sense. Why talk of protecting Malay privileges when it is only a small group of Malays who are reaping the rewards of such privileges? Why fight for the NEP that benefits only a small group of Malays with the right connections and helps them succeed in business without really trying? According to

Nazir, "Unfortunately, (these) few may be politically powerful and loud."
Is Perkasa in cahoots with them? If not, why serve their cause?

As for Ibrahim Ali, his speech at the gathering sounded like an Umno
speech. He hit out at Anwar and blamed him for causing the problems
currently faced by the Malay community. What problems, indeed, are
being faced by the Malay community? Does Ibrahim see it as a problem
that there is a split in thinking among the progressive Malays and the
backward ones like him? That, surely, is not a problem. Is it wrong to
want to move forward, to cast off the old beliefs that are proving to be a
burden not only to the community but to the country as a whole?

He hit out at DAP's 'Malaysian Malaysia' concept. He said the
DAP wanted to do away with the Malay rulers, is against Islam and the
Malays. That's irresponsible talk. The objective of 'Malaysian Malaysia' is
bringing together all Malaysians, regardless of race or religion, to "enjoy
justice, freedom, democracy and good governance". How can that be
objectionable? Must unity be exclusive to Malays? Why not extend it to
the whole nation? How would that be detrimental to the Malay rulers,
Islam and the Malay race?

On the whole, Ibrahim's speech was full of bravado and nothing
much else. He even warned political parties not to make an enemy of
Perkasa because they would lose at the elections. And, strangely, among
the resolutions taken at the gathering was one urging the Government
to retain the ISA. What has that got to do with Malay rights?

The event itself was more of a theatre presentation, really. Mahathir
was given a *tengkolok* to wear and a sash to adorn his torso, and he was
bestowed with the 'Bintang Pribumi Perkasa' award. There was a *silat*
performance, for obvious reasons. Ibrahim unsheathed a *keris* and kissed
it, then waved it in the air to the cries of "*Hidup Melayu!*" — an act that
might have made Hishammuddin Hussein proud. There was also a
performance by the Istana Budaya cultural troupe. One wonders if they
are a Government-sponsored troupe and, if so, whether they were hired
as professionals to participate in the event or whether their services were
offered gratis.

Should Perkasa be taken seriously? Or is it just a showcase of tribal emotionalism with more hype than substance? Right-wing groups have not been known to go very far — anywhere in the world. As long as they don't create violence or cause harm to anyone, they should in a democratic space be allowed to vent their *geram*. Nonetheless, they should be roundly rejected by sensible citizens. If Najib has any guts, he would make a strong statement against right-wing thinking and activism. He would staunchly stand by his 1Malaysia concept and make an unequivocal commitment to multi-racialism.

The rest of us might well ask why "*pribumi*" features in Perkasa's name. Ibrahim and his gang are not *pribumi*, surely? Do they represent the Orang Asli? As far as we all know, those are the real *pribumi*. Let's not confuse the meaning of the term with that used in Indonesia. Here, we already have *bumiputera* so let's stick with that. The Registrar of Societies should look into this.

Let me end with a word on Mahathir. It is clear that he should have known better than to associate himself with Perkasa. After this, what credibility is there left for us to still give the old man? He is obviously as guided as Ibrahim is by tribal emotionalism. Pathetic, indeed. At one time, there were non-Malays foolish enough to hold him in high esteem; now they should be disabused of their foolishness.

DAP leader Lim Kit Siang puts it eloquently: "Mahathir has come full circle, from an ultra back again to an ultra (*sic*) — repudiating Bangsa Malaysia and Vision 2020 which he enunciated in 1991. This is the greatest tragedy."

I have to disagree with that last sentence, though. Tragedy, in the original Aristotelian sense, occurs only with tragic heroes who embody nobility and greatness in their character. Mahathir, I must say, is nothing of the sort. A person who does what Mahathir does exudes neither nobility nor greatness. "Meanness" might be a suitable word, but I'm not mean enough to say it.

CLOSER TO COSMETIC SURGERY

Malaysiakini, February 22, 2011

DOCTOR M: OPERATION MALAYSIA — *Conversations with Mahathir Mohamad* by Tom Plate (Marshall Cavendish, 2011)

Gush and glibness spread through Tom Plate's *Doctor M: Operation Malaysia – Conversations with Mahathir Mohamad* like irksome background noise. And rather than show us the former prime minister of Malaysia for what he is, Plate tells us how to picture him.

One of the most fawning comments he makes on Mahathir, whom he generously plugs as a "soft authoritarian", is that "the best doctors are almost always soft authoritarians. They make you take the medicine that's good for you, whether you like it or not." That's hard to swallow, and not just because it's a gross generalisation.

The American career journalist's book of his interviews with Mahathir is essentially gung-ho journalism as entertainment — with the non-self-effacing interviewer appearing as a commentator as well (sometimes as a stand-up comic, too), and the subject airbrushed to look like a hero.

To be sure, we get glimpses into the subject's dark side, but only enough to give the required colouring.

Plate hails Mahathir during his 22 years in office as "arguably the world's single most important practising Muslim national political leader". In typical hyperbolic fashion, he dubs Mahathir "the *ultimate* anti-al-Qaeda" (my italics).

Jews may think he is their enemy, and maybe they are right. But in my view they have got it wrong – tragically wrong.

That's the main thesis of his book, and he goes all out to affirm it. He is amazed – and impressed – that during Mahathir's rule, Islamic terrorism erupted in many parts of the world whereas Malaysia was totally free of violence. That, for him, accounts for Mahathir's prowess as an Islamic leader to be lauded by the world.

Any sensible Malaysian could have told him that this was simply because Mahathir created a culture of fear. He had the ISA and an excellent Special Branch that could nip any trouble in the bud. He did not tolerate public dissent and he muzzled the media.

Plate takes the line that "maybe this place doesn't have as many crazies as Indonesia, but it must have some" and asks Mahathir, "What was it about Dr M's management of Malaysia, his government's management of the Muslims? They were responsible citizens."

Again, any sensible Malaysian could have told him it was because Mahathir gave paramouncy to Islam and Muslims. So why should Malaysian Muslims be disgruntled? And as for Islamic terrorists from outside, why would they target Malaysia, a brother Muslim country?

Plate is barking up the wrong tree. His thesis is flawed. But he appears ever protective of it.

There is even one occasion, as recounted in the book, when Plate seems more protective of his thesis than having the opportunity of portraying what Mahathir really is. This is over Mahathir's assertion that there were hardly any Jews in the World Trade Centre when 9/11 happened.

To himself, Plate admits that this "seemed a borderline scary assertion, factually inaccurate (in fact, there were hundreds of Jews among the fatalities)". But he doesn't correct Mahathir.

Instead, he feels worried that Mahathir might say more, that he might endorse "the ludicrous hypothesis that the government of Israel had secretly orchestrated the 9/11 attacks". And when Mahathir doesn't say more, Plate actually sighs "with enormous relief".

It became one of those rare times in our conversations that I was truly glad to see him pull up, for to doubt his maturity (not to mention his mental health) would not be healthy for the book. Or for my thesis that Mahathir's life and views are of profound relevance today.

Plate notes that a few months later, "after we finished our series of conversations", Mahathir "came out with a lulu" when he said if the US was capable of making the movie *Avatar*, it was capable of staging 9/11. That, as Malaysians know, was one of the most laughable statements ever made by anyone, but Plate merely leaves it as a by-the-by. Obviously, pursuing it would have compromised his thesis.

He is generally gentle with Mahathir. He is seldom confrontational; he asks politely-framed questions, and when an issue looks in danger of getting heated, he eases off.

Thus, when it comes to the issue of some of "Dr M's relatives (being) worth plenty, and that the good doctor himself has funds and shares stashed here and there (and especially in Japan) and everywhere", he doesn't push it. He chooses instead to project Mahathir as the humble wage-earner who, as PM, made less than US$3,000 a month, "like a meagre US journalist's pension".

Mahathir comes out looking like a saint who says he's not greedy and that his "real reward is achievement".

When it comes to Malaysian issues, Plate often does not ask the right questions or press on with relevant follow-up ones. Here's one question he could have asked Mahathir but did not when the latter said he was against detaining the 106 people during Operation Lalang: "Why then did you, as Home Minister, sign the order to detain 40 of them for two years?"

When Plate asks, "Does the government of Malaysia have good control over ISA?" and Mahathir answers, "Yes", he could have followed that up with: "Then why did the government detain an innocent journalist under the ISA in 2008 and even say, stupidly, that it was for her own protection?"

Alarmingly, Plate goes to the extent of justifying Mahathir's management style as "politically efficient corruption". One would have thought corruption was corruption, but Plate prettifies it here: "Dr M kind of bribed the whole country to behave! ... (it) produces something of value that cannot always be quantifiable: getting key elements of a society to buy into the system so as to attain political stability ... it may be the most politically efficient."

This would normally belong in the realm of spin-doctoring, but in journalism these days, you never know!

In any case, Plate's book is not hard-talk, hard-core journalism stuff. It's written for a popular audience, and comes complete with hyperboles, corny bits ("If nothing else, the Proton was further evidence ... of Dr M's protean will") and naïve remarks by the author.

His chapter titles, modelled after the James Bond movies for the laughable reason that Mahathir is a man of action, are not only corny but also strained. A bad-taste example is 'Die Another Way?' for the chapter on the 9/11 deaths.

On the whole, *Dr M: Operation Malaysia* seems closer to cosmetic surgery than dissection. For a more substantial interview, without the pop and the corn and the showman-like sheen, you'd be better off reading Lee Kuan Yew's *Hard Truths*.

excerpt

FROM THE PLAY
THE SWORDFISH,
THEN THE CONCUBINE

I started writing this play in the late '90s, but between then and 2008, when it premiered on stage in Singapore, I kept revising it to get it right. It has since been staged again — in 2011, also in Singapore. The play is based on two episodes of *Sejarah Melayu*, but it's not a re-telling of those stories. It is very much a play about the present. .

   This excerpt is from the scene that begins with a rap performed by the entire cast, accompanied by *gamelan* music. The rap makes light of the fact that Hang Nadim, the boy who saved Singapura from the swordfish (*todak*) attack, would soon be killed. I've left out the part leading up to Hang Nadim's killing — under the orders of the Sultan, at the advice of his ministers — and jumped to the aftermath of it.

GAMELAN RAP

(LOGOD and RIS KAW perform the rap with the CAST ENSEMBLE to the accompaniment of a gamelan troupe.)

LOGOD and RIS KAW:	Little boy, little boy, you are dead.
ENSEMBLE:	Little boy, little boy, you are dead.
LOGOD and RIS KAW:	Little boy, little boy, you are dead.
ENSEMBLE:	Little boy, little boy, you are dead.
LOGOD and RIS KAW:	Little boy, little boy, you are dead.
ENSEMBLE:	Little boy, little boy, you are dead.

LOGOD and RIS KAW:	Little boy, little boy, you are dead.
ENSEMBLE:	Little boy, little boy, you are dead.
LOGOD and RIS KAW:	You're dead, you're dead, you're dead, you're dead.
	The king has said —
ENSEMBLE:	"Off with his head."
LOGOD and RIS KAW:	The king has said —
ENSEMBLE:	"Off with his head."
LOGOD and RIS KAW:	Little boy, little boy, you are dead.
ENSEMBLE:	Little boy, little boy, you are dead.
LOGOD and RIS KAW:	You're dead, you're dead, you're dead, you're dead.
ENSEMBLE:	You're dead, you're dead, you're dead, you're dead.
RIS KAW:	Check it out.

****

(CITIZENS come in.)

CITIZEN 1:	Hang Nadim's blood has not stopped flowing.
CITIZEN 2:	What are we to make of this?
CITIZEN 3:	The boy was stupid. He should have kept his idea to himself. He'd still be alive.
CITIZEN 4:	It also shows that our leaders are so powerful, they can get away with murder.
CITIZEN 3:	How can you say that? Where is your evidence?
CITIZEN 1:	Tuanku says Nadim had to be sacrificed. For the sake of national security.
CITIZEN 3:	Yes, indeed. If he were allowed to grow up, he would start an uprising and cause hardship to everyone.
CITIZEN 2:	God forbid! Our lives would be disrupted.

(*SANG BUPALA comes in. The CITIZENS form a corps of media personnel and swarm around him.*)

SANG BUPALA:	I'll take questions now.
CITIZEN 1:	Yang Amat Berhormat, who ordered the killing of Hang Nadim?
SANG BUPALA:	It was a Cabinet decision.
CITIZEN 2:	Some citizens are planning to organise a forum to discuss the killing. Will they be given the permit to do so?
SANG BUPALA:	There will be no more discussion on the issue. It will cause tension in society. And for the record, the killing of Hang Nadim was for the sake of preserving national security.
CITIZEN 1:	But wasn't it rather drastic?
SANG BUPALA:	Nothing is drastic in the service of the State.
CITIZEN 3:	Couldn't he have been detained instead?
SANG BUPALA:	No. He was not a terrorist.
CITIZEN 4:	Then what was his crime?
SANG BUPALA:	He was a threat to society.
CITIZEN 4:	But —
SANG BUPALA:	Tell the people that.
CITIZENS:	Yes, Yang Amat Berhormat.
SANG BUPALA:	The media should write only about things that bring about harmony. Can that be done?
CITIZEN 4:	Yes, Yang Amat Berhormat.
SANG BUPALA:	(*rapping*)
	It all went well, as I thought it would.
	People understood 'twas for the common good.
	The media was called, their response was great,
	They quickly saw the need to co-operate.

MARCH 8 AND MORE

THE OUTCOME OF THE MARCH 8, 2008, GENERAL ELECTION HAS MADE AN UNPRECEDENTED DIFFERENCE NOT ONLY IN MALAYSIAN POLITICS, BUT IN MALAYSIAN LIFE AS A WHOLE. NOT ONLY DID WE GET A BIGGER OPPOSITION; NOT ONLY WAS BARISAN NASIONAL DENIED ITS TWO-THIRDS MAJORITY IN PARLIAMENT; NOT ONLY DID THE OPPOSITION WIN FIVE STATES; MORE THAN THAT, MALAYSIANS BECAME MORE SENSITISED TO POLITICS. MORE AND MORE MALAYSIANS HAVE SINCE BEEN COMING OUT TO CLAIM THEIR STAKE IN THE DEMOCRATIC PROCESS, INCLUDING TAKING PART IN STREET DEMONSTRATIONS SUCH AS THE BERSIH 2.0 RALLY, AND DISCUSSING POLITICS IN THE NEW MEDIA AND SOCIAL MEDIA. THE YOUNG HAVE BEEN PARTICULARLY ACTIVE IN JOINING CIVIL SOCIETY MOVEMENTS TO AGITATE FOR REFORM. THE FEAR OF ANOTHER MAY 13 IS GONE. PUBLIC DISCUSSIONS OF ISSUES, EVEN THOSE PREVIOUSLY CONSIDERED "SENSITIVE", ARE BURSTING OUT. ALL THESE POSITIVE CHANGES WOULD NOT HAVE ESCALATED WITHOUT MARCH 8. ON THAT SCORE, IT IS ESSENTIAL TO KEEP THE MARCH 8 SPIRIT ALIVE — TO REMIND MALAYSIANS THAT THE FUTURE OF THE NATION IS NOT MERELY IN THE HANDS OF THE RULING PARTY, BUT MORE CRUCIALLY IN THE HANDS OF THE PEOPLE.

MERDEKA ON MARCH 8

First published in the book *March 8: The Day Malaysia Woke Up* (Marshall Cavendish, 2008)

It was like watching a B-movie western in which the bad guys bit the dust one by one. And the audience cheered wildly as they watched it happen. But it was not a movie; it was real-life — it was the 2008 Malaysian General Election.

They were "bad guys" in the proverbial sense. They were associated with a ruling coalition that had let power get to their heads after having enjoyed it for decades, given out contracts to a relatively small circle of cronies that came to be dubbed "Umnoputras" instead of offering them for open tender, played the race or religion card when it suited them, seemingly cared more about remaining in power than the interests of the nation, resorted to lies and cover-ups, promoted judges in a questionable manner ... it was kinda like the Old West.

Barisan Nasional still made up the numbers to hold on to the reins of government, but they were denied the two-thirds majority they have always prized and held for 50 years. They also lost four states and failed to win back Kelantan, where they were badly trounced. If not for Sabah and Sarawak, who came to the rescue yet again, BN might even have lost by a simple majority. Many of their big guns got shot down throughout the country, even those facing total tyros. They comprised ministers, deputy ministers and head honchos of BN component parties. It was all the more cheering that the ones who pulled the trigger were the wised-up voters.

After four long decades, since 1969, Malaysians finally woke up, as if from a spell, cast by the wizard called Barisan Nasional, or from a stupor, induced by the shock of May 13. The people woke up to the need for change. And they were amazingly united in acting on that need. From north to south of the peninsula, they asserted it through their vote. The media called the phenomenon a "political tsunami". Some called it "the perfect storm".

BN won by a landslide in the 2004 elections when the populace felt they wanted to give the newly installed prime minister Abdullah Badawi a chance to consolidate his leadership. He had been a welcome change from Mahathir Mohamad and was seen as being more benign and accommodating. After getting his strong mandate, he set about instituting some reform, including acting against corruption. But after a while, it fizzled out. He promised to be a prime minister "for all Malaysians" but when it came to the crunch, he was powerless to stop the more racist and hardline religious elements, even from within his own party, from riding roughshod over the minority groups. Many came to call him "the sleeping prime minister". So in 2008, a good percentage of those who had endorsed him four years earlier roundly rejected his coalition and voted for the Opposition, made up of Parti Keadilan Rakyat (PKR), the Democratic Action Party (DAP) and Parti SeIslam Malaysia (PAS). This group of parties with diverse ideologies, led by former Umno stalwart and deputy prime minister Anwar Ibrahim who was thrown out of office in 1998 by Mahathir and convicted of corruption one year later, was then known as Barisan Rakyat. Less than a month after its election success, it refashioned itself on – of all days – April 1 as Pakatan Rakyat.

BN went into the 2008 campaign with tremendous advantage. It had the mainstream media solidly behind it. It made use of state facilities, like RTM. It had loads of money. Many of its *ceramahs* were lavish affairs, replete with food and entertainment, possibly to attract people who would otherwise not go since they could already get all the BN propaganda in the Government-controlled newspapers and on radio and TV. The Opposition, on the other hand, had limited funds. Much of it was raised from *ceramahs* where they passed round a collection box among the audience. But the public were willing to give. In my small suburban area of Bandar Utama, the Opposition collected RM10,000 at an evening of dialogue with the residents. The DAP gathering at Han Chiang High School in Penang, which drew a crowd in the tens of thousands, reportedly collected RM130,000.

To borrow a line from the song 'Sink the Bismarck', the BN had the biggest ships, they had the biggest guns. And yet when the results came out, many of these ships were sunk and many of these guns fired blanks. In some instances, BN candidates who were expected to sail through, especially those who were pitted against totally inexperienced neophytes who had never been associated with party politics, surprisingly lost. As someone remarked, "Even if you had put up a cow to stand against BN, people would have voted for the cow." This might sound somewhat unflattering of the candidates but it summed up the anti-BN sentiment.

As the results were coming out through *Malaysiakini* — which announced them faster than any other media body — unless you were a staunch BN supporter or a complete fence-sitter, you'd be shouting with joy each time a BN candidate lost. You'd be all the more ecstatic if a BN Goliath fell, such as Shahrizat Abdul Jalil (who lost to Anwar Ibrahim's daughter, Nurul Izzah) or M. Kayveas (who lost to Nga Kor Ming). And you'd be crying foul that Khairy Jamaluddin, one of the most disliked BN personalities who also happened to be the prime minister's son-in-law, pulled through, especially when it seemed he had initially been trailing.

As for Information Minister Zainuddin Maidin, even if you were a neutral observer, you might have found it hard to stifle a surge of *schadenfreude* when you heard he had lost his parliamentary seat by a huge majority of 9,000-over votes. On March 12, the Australian newspaper *The Age* wrote: "A measure of how complacent the Government had become was its appointment of the inept Zainuddin to the role in the first place. His appalling performance on Al Jazeera television late last year (when he was interviewed about the BERSIH rally, a peaceful march for fair and free elections which was disrupted by the police with water cannons and tear gas) was a very public international humiliation for all Malaysians. Voters did what Prime Minister Abdullah Ahmad Badawi did not have the guts to do: they removed him from office. ... Zainuddin had patronisingly warned Malaysians about false information spread by bloggers. They responded by voting one of the most popular bloggers — Jeff Ooi — into parliament."

These were the appetisers, so to speak. The sweetest, most popular defeat of the day was arguably that of Samy Vellu, the president of the Malaysian Indian Congress (MIC), who had become most unpopular partly because he had been around too long; he had held the Sungai Siput seat in Perak for eight terms and was going for his ninth. Yet, even though he had been head of the MIC for three decades, the perception now was that he had done little for the Indian community which his party represents. The disaffection of the Indians came to the fore when the Hindu Rights Action Force (Hindraf) staged a massive demonstration which resulted in the tens of thousands of Indians who showed up being greeted by the police with tear gas and water cannons, and five of its leaders being detained under the ISA. Samy Vellu was subsequently reviled by his own community for standing by and letting this happen to them. Before and during his election campaigning, he was sometimes pelted with sandals and rotten tomatoes by his own people. So much hatred had been built up against him that when he lost the election, it was cause for rejoicing. Even better, his conqueror was the unassuming Michael Devaraj Jeyakumar, who was standing against him for the third time and had all this while been quietly and steadfastly working to improve the conditions of poor people in the constituency. Hardly anyone had given him a chance, but the fact that he won is a testament of what one can achieve with hard, honest work and perseverance. Several cakes had been brought to the Sungai Siput Convention Hall that night in readiness for a double celebration — a victory for Samy Vellu and the occasion of his 72nd birthday — but it looked like he didn't have the chance to blow out the candles himself. They were already all out.

On the whole, no one expected the swing away from BN to be so severe. When it began to be clearer that something extraordinary was becoming reality, many people got excited; even those who would normally not be turned on by politics. A friend of mine in Penang, Andrew Choong, called me to proudly attest that even though he had been in hospital the day before because of a slipped disc, he made it a point to get out of bed to go on crutches and vote. Another friend, H.S. Teh, called me each time a significant result was confirmed ... the DAP's Teresa Kok securing the biggest majority of 36,492 votes ... deputy minister Chia Kwang Chye, who was one year our senior at university, losing his seat ... the Opposition winning 10 out of the 11 seats in the Federal Territory of Kuala Lumpur ... and so on. H.S. was most ecstatic in reporting that his hometown of Penang had fallen to the Opposition.

The Gerakan Party, which had spearheaded the government in Penang for three decades, was totally wiped out there. Chief Minister Dr Koh Tsu Koon lost his parliamentary seat to the DAP's P. Ramasamy, an academic who was standing for election for the first time.

Despite this, Koh proved to be a gentleman. When it was official that BN had lost Penang, he did not hesitate to call a press conference and admit defeat and ensure that there would be a smooth transfer of government to the Opposition. This was at a time when unofficial news of many other BN losses throughout the country were flying around in SMSes and carried on *Malaysiakini*. Those who had lived through May 13, 1969 — when racial riots broke out in the aftermath of the Opposition's winning two states and denying BN its two-thirds majority — feared the worst. It was also somewhat ominous that the official media machinery, for example, RTM, and even TV3, was announcing official results of mainly BN victories. Its viewers had no inkling that Penang had fallen. In view of the situation, even the Opposition began to get tense. Some of its leaders sent out messages advising supporters to go home and refrain from celebrating openly, in order not to provoke any untoward reaction from supporters of the other camp.

Koh's concession of defeat helped to calm the situation. I would like to think that it was a purposeful signal to his BN colleagues in other states and in federal positions to accept the outcome graciously. Whatever it was, he was setting a sporting example. And for that, he deserves credit. The chief ministers of the other states that BN lost — Perak, Selangor and Kedah — did not concede immediately.

BN was in a daze. You could see it in the eyes and faces of its leaders when in the wee hours of March 9, the Election Commissioner declared BN the winner of the general election by a simple majority. They couldn't quite reconcile with the fact that they had performed the worst in all the elections that had taken place since Independence. How could they have lost four states, failed to win back Kelantan and, worst of all, their two-thirds majority? They were to be in denial for weeks after that before Abdullah Badawi finally admitted responsibility for the debacle.

There were many factors that contributed to the election outcome. In a word, it was the arrogance of BN, especially of its dominant party, Umno, that chiefly led to this. It was arrogance reflected in its failure to listen to the people; in its belief in its own invincibility as evident in Umno Vice-President Mohd Ali Rustam's telling BN partner PPP (People's Progressive Party) to leave the coalition if its members were not happy with their seat allocation; in its continued practices of cronyism and disregard for the law, as seen in the Selangor Assemblyman Zakaria Md Deros' (now deceased) building of a huge mansion in Klang without approval from the local council; in its insensitive handling of issues of grave concern to non-Malays and non-Muslims, like the Lina Joy case which threw up questions about Article 11 of the Constitution which guarantees every Malaysian the right to profess and practise his religion, and Deputy Prime Minister Najib Razak shockingly declaring that Malaysia was an Islamic state and had never been a secular one. Non-Malays were driven to give up faith in the ethnic parties within BN that were supposed to represent their interests. Over the years, it had become evident that these parties, particularly the Malaysian Chinese

Assocation (MCA) and the MIC, were effete in the presence of Umno, which seemed to call all the shots.

For instance, the MCA said nothing about Hishammuddin Hussein's aggressive wielding of the *keris* at the annual Umno Youth General Assembly, an event that was given live TV coverage and, therefore, seen throughout the country. And he did that not once but for three years running. He even said insensitively in 2007 that if he did it often enough, the non-Malays would have to accept it. The very first time he did it in 2005, he struck a war-like pose as he asserted that Umno Youth wanted the return of policies favouring the Malays and would take action against those who opposed its proposal to revive the New Economic Policy (NEP). It was overtly racist and many non-Malays were shocked. Significantly, Abdullah Badawi as Umno president did nothing to rein him in right from the start.

This same Hishammuddin in 2007 issued what he categorically called a "warning" to the president of the MCA, Ong Ka Ting, to stop making the statement that Malaysia is a secular state, and asserted that he would personally "not allow the matter to proceed further". He had the temerity to hurl such harsh words at a BN colleague who was senior to him in ranking. On another occasion, when the Gerakan Youth Chief, S. Paranjothy, spoke sympathetically about the Hindraf rally being an expression of the frustration of oppressed and marginalised Indians, Hishammuddin ordered Gerakan to take action against him or face having its ties with Umno Youth and even BN itself severed. Who was Hishammuddin to dictate to Gerakan, a senior party in BN? Only the BN chief could do that; he was only the Umno Youth chief.

No wonder the non-Malay electorate realised it was common sense that the Opposition proposed when it said to them: Why do you want to vote BN candidates into office when they would be ineffective? Do you think they would speak up for you in BN or in Parliament?

BN's campaigners thought they could use the old tactics and win the game, like using the mainstream media to spin their propaganda and blackball the Opposition. It turned into overspinning and became instead a liability. It sparked a move by civil society groups calling for a boycott of the mainstream media. More tellingly, BN ignored the power of the Internet and the blogs and the SMS in exposing its misdeeds and scandals. As *Newsweek* described it: "To reach voters, the opposition relied on bloggers, YouTube and text messages sent to grass-roots organisers via cell phone: common tactics in places like Indonesia, Taiwan and South Korea but new to Malaysia."

BN thought the electorate was not mature enough, but they were wrong. They used scare tactics as they had done many times before, warning of the possibility of an outbreak of violence if the coalition was not returned to power. On the eve of the elections, Prime Minister Abdullah Badawi was on the front page of every newspaper warning non-Malays that if they did not vote for their ethnic parties, they might end up with no representation in the government. It proved to be an empty threat that the voters were smart enough not to heed. As it turned out, Abdullah Badawi still gave PPP a deputy minister post afterwards even though it had no seat at all in Parliament after its president, M. Kayveas, lost while contesting the party's only seat on March 8. This was done through the back-door way of first making PPP's Youth Chief T. Murugiah a senator. A party with zero seats still gets a deputy minister. No wonder Sabah is upset that it's getting disproportionate reward for the grand results it delivered. In fact, the MIC has only three parliamentarians now but it is being represented by a minister and a deputy minister. Somehow, mathematics doesn't play a part when it comes to selecting who gets in.

BN also resorted to their dirty tricks to stack the odds in their favour, including getting the person they trusted to remain as chairman of the Election Commission (EC) even though he was due for retirement. But the people were not fooled; what could be more obvious than passing a bill in Parliament to raise the retirement age so that this person could continue to perform his role? And when the EC decided to scrap the use of indelible ink, which was to ensure fairness in that a voter could not vote more than once, that was the ploy that broke the public's trust, whatever was left of it.

And so the die was cast. Out of the 222 parliamentary seats, BN won 140, securing only a simple majority to form the government. The Opposition won 82 seats, an improvement of 62 from the 20 they had managed to get in the 2004 General Election. BN's 140 was down 58 from the 198 it won in 2004. Out of BN's tally, 54 came from Sabah and Sarawak. The East Malaysians really came to save BN.

In terms of the popular vote, BN got almost 51 per cent and yet it won 140 seats (about 63 per cent of 222), which is appallingly disproportionate. The Opposition, on the other hand, won almost 47 per cent of the popular vote but only about 37 per cent of the 222 seats. This is certainly something to be addressed in future elections.

Umno had 109 seats in 2004; this time it lost 30 of those. The MCA had its representation cut by half, from 31 to 15. The MIC was hard hit, from 9 down to 3. The hardest hit was Gerakan, which retained only 2 of the 10 they had. And of course, the PPP lost the only seat it had, which meant a 100 per cent drop.

The people made history on March 8. It bears repeating that the election outcome was the people's victory. This was one general election that stirred a lot of people, moved them to do something with that vote of theirs. There are stories of Malaysians coming back from faraway places just for the purpose of doing their part. The writer Beth Yahp, who has been living in Australia for years, came back to vote. More than that, she attended numerous *ceramah*s during the campaign period. My old classmate, Yeap Leong Teik, based in Singapore, told me he made it a point to return to Penang, where he was still registered, to cast his vote and make a difference.

Especially in the final week or so, you could feel the fervour in the air, the sense of destiny. Fence-sitters were starting to shift out of neutral gear. People you never expected to be saying it were saying, "Let's do it. Let's show them." Joseph Lim, whom I came to know when we signed up to be polling-cum-counting agents, said he was motivated to volunteer despite his in-laws' warning against it for fear of May 13. I, too, had never been so actively engaged, never even so much as distributed campaign flyers for any party before, but this time I wanted to be involved. Even my teenaged children, still too young to vote, helped out at a *pondok panas* on polling day apart from joining a candidate on his campaign walkabout. Some days before that, they complained to me about the coverage in a mainstream newspaper of responses to former PKR deputy president Chandra Muzaffar's declaration that Anwar Ibrahim could not be trusted and that it would be an "unmitigated disaster" for the country if he were to become prime minister. They counted more than a dozen stories in that one day's issue each upholding Chandra's opinion and further running down Anwar. The headlines were blatantly disparaging. At a book launch after the elections, P. Ramasamy, by then a deputy chief minister of Penang, pointed out that from what he could gather the day after that smear campaign, many people were incensed and made the decision there and then to vote for the Opposition. This was a classic example of how overspinning can actually cut the other way and benefit its intended victim. Chandra himself was reviled for his action, and deservedly so. It smacked of being a personal attack from an embittered ex-party leader.

Penangites were probably the proudest on the night of March 8. They knew they succeeded in what they had set out to do; they gave the Opposition a virtual landslide victory, concretised in a two-thirds majority in the State Assembly that astounded the winners themselves. My old friend, Tan Kok Hin, a Penang anaesthetist, joined the hordes at the Red Rock Hotel to wait for the Chief Minister-designate to appear for a press conference. When Lim Guan Eng and his colleagues appeared at around 1 a.m., the roar of the crowd was deafening. Said Kok Hin: "And then when Guan Eng, Zahrain (Mohamed Hashim, a PKR state leader) and Ramasamy held their hands together high up in the air, it was a touching moment to relish — as it reminded me of the multi-racial Malaysia I used to know." I can relate to that; Kok Hin and I are contemporaries, and we did indeed grow up in a different time, a different Malaysia, which disappeared after 1969.

And so, when as I got back home at around 5 a.m. on March 9, after having waited for the announcement of the official results of my parliament and state constituencies — won by Sivarasa Rasiah (Subang) and Elizabeth Wong (Bukit Lanjan), both of PKR — after having shed tears of joy intermittently and communed with fellow believers in the cause of a greater Malaysia, never wanting the historic moment to end, knowing we had done our teeny-weeny bit and realising that perhaps we could now look to a brighter future, I took out my mobile phone and wrote an SMS that I then promptly sent out to all the people I had been in touch with via this medium in the days leading up to March 8 and on election night itself, sharing information and sentiments, frustrations and joy.

I ended the message with one word: "Merdeka!"

MARCH 8
TWO YEARS AFTER

Talk given at Assumption Church, Petaling Jaya, on March 4, 2010.

I suspect I was asked to speak tonight because I brought out the book *March 8: The Day Malaysia Woke Up*. I put it together, not only because my publisher asked me if I wanted to do it, but mainly because I felt it was very important to document a milestone of contemporary Malaysian history. More than that, I felt that a book like that would also allow Malaysians to express what they hoped for a better Malaysia. I was very gratified and happy that many Malaysians responded and gave their views freely.

There was a lot of optimism right after March 8. There was a sense that things *would* get better. You all would no doubt remember that significant day, especially those of you who participated in making it happen. I did too in my own small way, by voting as I've always voted — for a truly democratic state to prevail, for a political balance that would not grant any party or faction overwhelming domination. The juggernaut that had dominated our lives for more than 50 years was cut down in its tracks when we denied it the two-thirds majority it had been so used to; when we denied it the control of five states within the peninsula. We did it. We brought about change. We were euphoric.

But has there been much change two years since that day? There was so much to hope for then. I, for one, hoped the idea of multi-racialism would be accepted and manifested in government policies. But instead, we are becoming more divided along racial lines. Right after March 8, Umno embarked on its campaign to strike fear into the Malays and to warn them that they were under threat. Through its propaganda machinery and roadshows in various parts of the country, Umno went all out to spread that message. Ahmad Ismail called the non-Malays "*pendatang*" and was suspended for three years, but his suspension was lifted after one year plus. The Government came to assume a schizophrenic personality — the prime minister talks about 1Malaysia while his deputy says things that are completely contradictory. The Government talks about multi-racial unity while Umno talks about Malay unity.

I had hoped after the elections, both Barisan Nasional and Pakatan Rakyat would set aside their political differences and get down to the business of working for the national interest, of saving this country. Instead, they have been doing their darnedest to do the dirty on each other. Barisan is coming out tops in that effort because it has the media under its control. Both seem to be doing their worst to win the next general election.

I had hoped we would have leaders who would be honest, clean and respectful of us the people, who would not think we were stupid or immature. Instead, most of the time, we hear of more and more corruption — on both sides — and mud-slinging between party colleagues. Quite soon after Najib Razak took over as prime minister, he told a gathering of senior mainstream media editors, "I have no baggage." The editors nearly fell off their chairs. If the number one leader of this country can say something like that, what can we expect of the rest? No wonder Syed Hamid Albar could say that the journalist Tan Hoon Cheng was detained under the ISA because it was for her own protection. And Hishammuddin Hussein could come out to defend the cow-head protestors and actually say "they felt victimised". Really *kesian*. But the best comment on that incident came from Khir Toyo: "There was no religious significance in bringing the head," he said. "The cow is a stupid creature and (the protestors) wanted to point out that the [Selangor] State Government was being stupid." I dread to think that before March 8, he was the *menteri besar* of Selangor.

I had hoped Pakatan Rakyat would turn out to be a formidable force, united and effective, providing a strong opposition in Parliament. But look at the state it's in today. The number of elected representatives who have quit PKR is distressing. Pakatan can't blame the mainstream media for this. Neither can Pakatan blame anyone for its ability to produce frogs. Anwar Ibrahim promised us defections from Barisan to Pakatan on Sept 16, 2008, but it never happened. Now it's happening – but the defectors are *from* Pakatan. In any case, Anwar's attempt to take over the government on September 16 was misguided and merely exposed his true ambition – to be prime minister, above all else.

After March 8, I had hoped the Government would undo the damage that had been inflicted on our country by the man who screwed up our institutions, created a culture of fear, fostered the negotiated contract, invested our money in white elephants and still doesn't know when to shut up. I think you all know who I mean. I don't want to talk too much about him. If I get started, we could be here all night. I just want to say that the Americans could only make *Avatar* whereas he managed to lead a country to the dogs. The point is, the Government has not dismantled the culture he created and restored our faith in the country's institutions.

What we have seen in the last two years is that our leaders are not good enough. There are no visionaries. They are mostly people who are only thinking of their own positions, or taking over somebody else's. Or thinking of their own party, their own people. And they will do anything to ensure that they get what they want. There's talk that there are now at least three factions within Umno, and Najib is not secure. We have seen the recent efforts to undermine his administration. The most worrying faction is the right-wing one. And there is no underestimating their influence. Outside of Umno, the right-wing movement is apparently gaining momentum, and the Allah issue is giving them the common cause. At present, the most prominent group is the Malay NGO Perkasa.

Barisan would cease to have an important organ for the dissemination of its propaganda. *The Star* reaches out to a wide non-Malay, mainly middle-class readership. Barisan can't afford not to reach out to these people. Closing down *The Star* would be like Barisan cutting off its nose to spite its face. The failure of our mainstream media is due to their high tendency to fear the Government and their lack of courage. They should have built on the momentum after March 8 when they somewhat liberalised their coverage. Remember how relatively balanced they were in the months after March 8? Their owners realised that for the sake of public acceptance, they had to temper their pro-Government bias and so they opened the window of freedom by a few degrees. Besides, they had to hedge their bets in case Anwar did manage to take over the government. But then when September 16 didn't happen, there was no need to consider that any more. So the mainstream media stopped being balanced. Months later, Najib took over as PM. He tightened the screws. Thereafter, the mainstream media went back to bashing Pakatan.

It's a shame that *The Star* as a whole has not reflected the boldness of its managing editor, P. Gunasegaram. He has been pushing the parameters with the articles he's been writing, and the stories he's been running in *The Star*'s business pages, which he edits. But now *The Star* would seem more adept at things like running a picture of Rosmah in its pages every day. Never mind if it's newsworthy or not. As I have said elsewhere, no wife of any previous prime minister has had so much exposure. There must be something quirky in the editor's thinking. Surely, buyers of newspapers want to read news rather than gawk at the pictures of PM's wives, no matter how gorgeous they look.

Why does the Government still choose to deny us media freedom when we can read worse things on the Internet? Why does the Government say and do things that are illogical, even stupid? And not realise that the public is not as stupid as they think it is? To recall the Government's dubious actions, we just have to go into the A-G's office and ask what has happened to the Lingam case, the PKFZ case, the RMAF case, the Hasbie Safar case, the Al-Islam reporters case, and whether the people who placed wild-boar heads in the two mosques have been arrested. Or recall what Najib said when he was asked if action would be taken if people protested against the Allah issue — "Oh, we can't stop people from protesting," he said. What a change from before, when the Government used to say protesting was not in our culture. But maybe Najib is right. After all, they couldn't stop thousands of protestors spilling onto the streets on August 1, 2009, to protest against the ISA. Even though they used tear gas and water cannons! Hey, even Lim Guan Eng is a genius. He claims that the word "Penang" belongs to the State Government. Penang! It's not enough that they own the state — for now, at least — they also want to own the word! So, how now? I'm from Penang. Can I still say I'm a Penang boy without first getting permission from him? So, who needs reality TV? Every day, we Malaysians are getting reality comedy.

In view of all this, can we say that March 8 has not been of any use at all? Can we say that it was just a flash in the pan? Is there anything positive that has emerged from March 8?

Fundamentally, I think Malaysians are becoming more courageous. More and more are speaking up. Fewer and fewer are kowtowing to the people in high places. We are struggling to shake off the culture of fear and I think we are succeeding. Look at the turnout at candlelight vigils and protest marches. When we were protesting against the ISA detention of Tan Hoon Cheng, Raja Petra and Teresa Kok, I was amazed to see people I never expected would show up at such gatherings. Three years ago, such people would not have dared come near these perilous activities. A very dear friend of mine thought many times, consulted with his wife, consulted with me, experienced cardiac palpitations when he was about to post his very first comment on a blog. That blog, incidentally, was Haris Ibrahim's *The People's Parliament*. Not long after that, he was joining me in an anti-ISA protest march right in the city centre. Another instance of courage is that of the young woman who was so angered by the pro-ISA march staged by Pewaris in November 2008 that she yelled at the protestors. She couldn't *tahan* the fact that they were turning the ISA issue into a racial one. Some of the marchers chased her. She got punched a couple of times. Luckily for her, the police escorted her to her car. But as she drove off, the protestors mobbed and kicked her vehicle.

There is a new spirit of defiance now, and we have models of defiance to show us the way — among them Anwar Ibrahim since the *reformasi* days, Raja Petra Kamarudin, P. Uthayakumar, Nizar Jamaluddin and his Perak band, *Malaysiakini*. Instead of giving in to authoritative pressure, they stood tall. And that's how it should be. Because if we always bow down to them, they will kick us in the face. But if we stand up to them, we can at least look them in the eye.

Another positive — Malaysians are no longer afraid of another May 13. The spectre of racial riots has been exorcised. The recent Allah issue reinforces that. Despite the puny efforts of a few to start a fire by attacking a *surau* and depositing wild-boar heads in mosques, there was no racial riot. The political battlefields of Malaysia are no longer marked by Malays versus non-Malays. From the time of *reformasi* in the late '90s, the split within the Malay community has been evident. In the 1999 GE, it was the non-Malay voters who saved Barisan from possibly losing its two-thirds majority. Compared to the 1995 GE, Umno's votes in 1999 dropped by 8 per cent. Najib nearly got voted out of the Pekan constituency. He scraped through with a majority of only 241 votes.

In fact, as long ago as the mid-'70s, it had already been predicted that a time would come when the major political strife would be between the Malays. The failure of the NEP to evenly redistribute wealth among the Malays has accelerated this. A class fight is settling in between the Malays who have not and the Malays who have a lot. The real issue now is corruption. Many Malays have come to realise that the people who join Umno these days are largely doing so not because they believe in helping their own community but because they want to get rich. Umno still tries to sell the idea of *Ketuanan Melayu*, but to the Malay have-nots, what is the meaning of that *ketuanan*? As one of my Malay friends puts it, "The Malays are divided. On one side are the feudal Malays of Umno who are backward-thinking and their grassroot supporters who are mainly not well-educated or cannot properly evaluate their own leaders. On the other side are the civil Malays who do not support Umno as they are more civic-conscious and aware." Even so, when push comes to shove, anything can happen. Much will depend on how effectively Umno plays the racial game. While it is unwise to look at the Malays as a monolith, it is equally unwise to ignore the tribal instincts of a community. Especially when it's constantly being told that it's under siege.

Looking forward on a more optimistic note, however, we have to acknowledge that March 8 has given us something precious for the next GE, and hopefully for longer into the future — choice. Now we have two different sets of salesmen knocking on our doors, bending over backwards to win our custom. In this duopoly, we can expect better deals, better packages, maybe even better products. It may be difficult to trust some of the old hands in the Opposition team, or to put much faith in some of their newbies, or to be certain that their company won't fall apart because their ideologies are different, but if we want to retain this situation of two coalitions battling to our benefit, we have to nurture it. It sure beats having a monopoly.

We have to keep the March 8 spirit alive.

If people were to ask me how I'd vote at the next GE, this is what I'd say — why vote in the people who have been taking us for a ride and robbing us blind? They may actually bring about a slew of reforms just before the elections in order to win our hearts and minds ... well, let them. We can accept that, like some voters who accept money, and still vote them out. Why not let in a new group of people and see what they can do? At least at the beginning, they will be so bent on winning our approval, they will bring us a further slew of reforms — until they get corrupted or prove to be incompetent. If that happens or if they don't come up to our expectations, and the other set of salesmen clean up their act, we can choose anew at the following GE.

That's a simplistic way of looking at it, of course. More importantly, I think we need to get in a fresh government because the old one has

There is talk going round that if there is a change of government at the next GE, the consequences might be violent. Power might not be handed over in a gentlemanly manner. But then, when the March 8 results were being announced, we also feared that there might be another May 13. Our fear proved to be unfounded. So when the next general election comes around, it might be appropriate to recall the words of Franklin Roosevelt: "The only thing we have to fear is fear itself."

Choice is what we have now. That has been the gift of March 8. We should exercise that choice — for the betterment of our country. And exercise it without fear.

THE DAY SARAWAK WOKE UP?

MalaysianDigest.com, May 18, 2010

The writing is on the wall. The people want change. And it now extends to the people of Sarawak as well.

A few days before the voting in the Sibu by-election, DAP supremo Lim Kit Siang had said it would be a miracle for DAP to win it, but on May 16, polling day, the miracle did happen. Wong Ho Leng garnered 18,845 votes to beat the Barisan Nasional candidate, Robert Lau, by a majority of 398. BN's Fortress Sarawak has been breached.

Never mind if it's only Sibu, which is an urban area with a majority of Chinese voters — the message has gone out loud and clear. People are as mad as hell and they're not going to take it any more. (With apologies to the 1976 movie *Network*, starring Peter Finch and Faye Dunaway.)

It's also clear from this experience that you can't always buy people, at least not *all* the people. Najib Razak and his forces promised millions to the people of Sibu; and Robert Lau was not expected to lose because of the wealth and influence of his family that encompasses a substantial part of Sibu — but it all came to no avail.

While addressing the residents of Rejang Park, Najib came across more like a salesman than a prime minister. Talking about the need to solve the flood problems that have been plaguing the area, he said to them: "I want to make a deal with you. *Boleh tidak?* Can we have a deal? Can we have an understanding or not? The understanding is quite simple — I help you, you help me."

It sounded like the tune he sang in Hulu Selangor when he told the school in Rasa and the Indians to whom he gave the land that their temple had been illegally built on that in return for what he would give them, he expected them to vote for BN.

To the people of Rejang Park, Sibu, he offered RM5 million to repair their drainage and sewerage system with this proviso: "If you deliver me Robert Lau on Sunday, on Monday I will ask [for] the cheque to be prepared ... *Lu mahu lima juta, kan? Gua mahu Robert Lau menang. Boleh tak? Lu tak payah keluar duit. Gua kena keluar duit.*" (You want 5 million, right? I want Robert Lau to win. Can or not? You don't have to pay anything. I'm the one who has to fork out the money.)

The language is graceless and not what one would expect from someone holding the highest office in the land. Moreover, the jibe about his having to fork out money calls attention to his claim that the money is his to give, as if it came out of his own pocket. On a more serious note, lawyer and DAP chairman Karpal Singh has come out to say that Najib's offer to make such a deal "is a clear violation of the Election Offences Act" for which he could be thrown into jail.

The Rejang Park people did right by not falling for the ploy. They still came out and voted for the DAP. I would like to think this wasn't because Rejang Park is considered a "black area" for BN but because they knew that the RM5 million should not have come only when there was a by-election and the Barisan Nasional wanted to buy their votes. Why wasn't the flood problem attended to long before? Aren't the people of Rejang Park entitled to proper public services like good drainage — at any time, not only when their votes are called for?

Of course, now that Robert Lau has not been voted in, the promise may not be delivered. But even if it were, there should be no one saying that the Rejang Park residents must be grateful and beholden to the BN. Why must they when they would be getting only what has long been due to them?

The Sibu fiasco is going to bother BN an awful lot. The by-election result may not be the beginning of a total swing against the ruling coalition, but it will have an effect on the voting pattern in the near future. BN cannot afford to be faced with this if it is determined to win the next general election. It needs to ensure that Sarawak will continue to come to its rescue and keep it in government. It also needs to ensure that this new rejectionist spirit will not spread to Sabah, another of its guarantors for Putrajaya.

What's more, the Sarawak state elections have to be called by mid-2011. That's about a year at the most for the state's BN leadership to reassess its position. They will need to do a serious reality check. Taib Mahmud has been in power for 28 years and grumbles of discontent about 'Pek Maw' (white hair), the Chinese nickname for him, are getting louder among the electorate.

For too long now, Sarawakians have been tolerating the poor governance, the poor management of the economy and the unchecked amassing of wealth by the well-connected and the powerful. They have seen how selective the development in the state is, and how a few people have prospered while most of the ordinary folk are neglected. For these shortcomings and his perceived attempt to create a political dynasty, the white-haired Rajah might even turn out to be a liability.

The DAP and its Pakatan Rakyat partners will no doubt capitalise on this as they build up their arsenal to take on the Sarawak BN behemoth. If they can take the message of Sibu and transmit it to all parts of the state, including the deep interior, and convince the people of the need for change, they could have a chance to win more than they ever have.

Then, May 16 might turn out to be the day Sarawak woke up.

THE BEGINNING OF CHANGE IN SARAWAK

MalaysianDigest.com, April 18, 2011

There was no tsunami in Sarawak. Barisan Nasional (BN) is still firmly rooted after winning 55 seats out of the 71 in the state elections last Saturday.

It lost seven from its haul of 62 in 2006, but that's only an 11 per cent drop. Parti Pesaka Bumiputera Bersatu (PBB), helmed by Taib Mahmud, who continues to be chief minister after a 30-year reign, won all the seats it contested. The main BN casualty is the Sarawak United People's Party (SUPP), whose president, George Chan, also lost his seat and, thereby, his position as Sarawak's deputy chief minister.

Predominantly Chinese, the SUPP lost its hold on the urban areas, conceding further to the Democratic Action Party (DAP), which doubled its seats from six in 2006 to 12 this time. This clearly indicates that when the Chinese are discontented, they will stop voting for BN, even for the Chinese-based parties within the coalition. It happened in the general election of 2008 with the Peninsular Malaysia Chinese; now it's happening with the Sarawak Chinese.

They've realised — at last — that it's useless to vote for any Chinese party that is within BN, because it will have little power to stand up for the community. In Peninsular Malaysia, the MCA is eclipsed by Umno, and in Sarawak, the SUPP has been a yes-party to Taib and PBB.

The MCA should take note of the Sarawak election outcome. It's bewildering that the party seems to think it can recapture its former glory by remaining in BN, despite being publicly insulted left, right and centre by Umno leaders. Minister in the Prime Minister's Office Nazri Aziz recently called the MCA "the neglected wife" who "keeps complaining to outsiders that she has been detained, sexually abused and denied food by her husband, but she refuses to divorce", and yet the party is shamelessly clinging on.

Interestingly, before the Sarawak elections, MCA Deputy President Liow Tiong Lai said the SUPP's performance would be a barometer of how the MCA would perform at the next general election. Well, now that the barometer indications have turned out negative, what will the MCA do?

Many Opposition supporters are disappointed with the election results — not only did the tsunami not happen, but BN's two-thirds majority remains intact. Prior to polling, expectations had been raised that a big change was coming, especially in view of the mammoth turnouts at Opposition *ceramahs* in urban centres and the dissatisfaction expressed by Sarawakians themselves with the overstaying Taib. But the outcome is not commensurate with the expectations.

Some are asking: If the Sarawakians wanted Taib to go, why did they continue to vote for his party?

The answer probably lies in the physical vastness of Sarawak and the lack of communication access between the rural interior and what we would call "the outside world". If in the last 30 years the ruling regime has done little to improve connectivity between the two realms, it could be that such a situation actually works in its favour. Those in the interior are not brought up to speed on political goings-on and so have little interest in politics. They are not provided with amenities like electricity that will give them access to television. Well, even if they had that, the TV channels churn out government propaganda, anyway.

Their concern is with their daily lives and struggles. So when election time comes around, they are not tuned in to the issues of Sarawak, let alone national ones. The ruling regime keeps them where they are so that their votes are ensured. At election time, goodies, including those in the form of money, are dispensed. It has become the norm. Non-partisan observers on the ground reported: "In rural areas, whoever spends more, wins. It's amazing not a few people in such areas seem to expect something in return for their vote." This corroborates what the Opposition reportedly alleged – that BN agents gave cash handouts to voters, ranging from RM100 to RM2,000 per voter.

Opposition supporters are disappointed that Parti Keadilan Rakyat (PKR) managed to win only three seats when there was so much hoopla before polling that it would do much better from the 49 it was contesting. That's a success rate of only six per cent. But if they were to view it from another angle – that PKR is relatively new to Sarawak, that it had won only one seat in 2006 and now has three, which is a 200 per cent increase – there is some cause for hope. Add to that other factors like limited funds, difficulty of penetrating the rural areas, lack of mainstream media coverage, and attempts by the police to break up its *ceramahs*, and the hope for future expansion appears brighter.

Of note is the fact that despite the odds, PKR still managed to garner 17 per cent of the popular vote. The 17 per cent translates into 117,100 ayes, which when compared to PBB's 192,785 (28.7 per cent) sounds pretty encouraging. PKR was not a washout, unlike the Sarawak National Party (SNAP), which got a paltry total of 15,663 votes (2.33 per cent).

The party should take heart from the elections and be inspired to rejuvenate itself. It should now stop its party infighting and squabbling, and reorganise to become a credible force for the general election. It should work even harder to establish itself in Sarawak with Baru Bian, who wrested the Ba'Kelalan seat from BN, spearheading the enterprise. The current political scenario being what it is, PKR should touch base with longhouses that had been instructed not to let the Opposition visit, and try to cultivate their support.

Pakatan Rakyat as a whole – even though the DAP, PKR and PAS have local branches and their candidates are Sarawakian – might consider finding Sarawak parties to ally with as these will be better received by voters who are suspicious of parties that originated in Semenanjung. Indeed, many may have voted for Taib's party this time round for fear that if it lost or won poorly, Umno would seize the chance to rush in. Like it did in Sabah.

Meanwhile, what will Prime Minister Najib Razak honestly make of the Sarawak election results? He had hoped that BN would win big to keep up its momentum of winning the last few by-elections, motivating him to *turun padang* together with his deputy, Muhyiddin Yassin, and spend six days canvassing for votes throughout the state, reportedly spending RM500 million. But has the result of his efforts been satisfying? Did he manage to ensure that Sarawak is still BN's safe deposit?

Well, he cannot be sure of the Chinese support now. And George Chan's post-election comments are rather damning of his own coalition. He blamed the state and federal governments for not listening to the people and for doing "too little too late" to correct "unfair and unjust policies", and warned that BN cannot presume that Sarawakians would continue to support it. Coming from such a senior party leader, this is revealing.

The support of the rural populace will still be substantial, but will this be enough for Najib to call for a general election soon? The way it looks, the BN momentum seems to have been stalled. On top of that, Taib will still be a liability to BN unless he steps down, but he has brazenly announced that he will stay on for another two to three years. What will Najib do next to pacify voters regarding Taib? How indeed will he handle Taib himself? For starters, expect more money and development to be pumped in soon.

The state elections may be over, but things are just beginning to hot up in Sarawak. The DAP must assess the situation wisely and work at a constructive politics from now on. Instead of continuing to campaign for Taib to go — when his staying on might actually work better for the Opposition — its newly elected assemblymen should show the electorate their seriousness in bringing about positive change through hard work. The party would also benefit from finding indigenous leaders to come into its fold, and from working with its political partners to penetrate the rural areas.

Baru Bian himself has said that the elections indicate "the beginning of change for Sarawak" and a good start for a two-coalition system in the state. "Judging from the voting pattern, it looks like there is a clear choice now for people to vote for Barisan or Pakatan Rakyat," he said.

If that's truly the case, and if the Opposition capitalises on it, a tsunami may still be waiting to happen. It could come in full force in BN's next nightmare.

excerpt

FROM THE PLAY
THE SWORDFISH,
THEN THE CONCUBINE

Nurhalisa is the eponymous concubine of the play. The daughter of finance minister Sang Ranjuna, she is smart and feisty, and she is an activist. But she has no choice but to be a concubine of the sultan. This sultan, Iskandar, is the successor of the one who agreed to the execution of Hang Nadim (in the earlier excerpt).

(RANJUNA brings NURHALISA to ISKANDAR. They wait as ISKANDAR is not there yet.)

RANJUNA: Nurhalisa, I have failed you.

NURHALISA: Ayah, you could not say no without being disloyal. If you did, our whole family might all be dead by nightfall.

RANJUNA: You should be more than what you will become. But I have no power to let you fly.

(ISKANDAR enters.)

RANJUNA: *(sembahs)* Tuanku, may I ... at Tuanku's order ... my daughter, Nurhalisa.

ISKANDAR: Sang Ranjuna, why is your voice quivering?

RANJUNA: She is most precious to me, Tuanku.

ISKANDAR: She will be to me soon.

NURHALISA: I want to make one thing very clear —

RANJUNA: Nurhalisa —

ISKANDAR: Sang Ranjuna, you may go.

(NURHALISA bids her father goodbye. He goes.)

NURHALISA: Let me make this clear. I'm here because you have the power to do to us whatever you wish, but you do not have the power to possess me completely.

ISKANDAR: Not once in your speech did you address me as Tuanku. And when I came in, you did not *sembah*.

NURHALISA: So punish me.

ISKANDAR: And begin our relationship with bitterness? It's stressful enough being Sultan. Having to meet all those demands. And knowing that anyone in my inner circle could assassinate me at any time. Sometimes, I secretly welcome that. Yes, I'm weak. You can see that, can't you? And I'm isolated. The system of warlords, cronies and rent-seekers — it's impossible to change that. It's corrupt as hell. And I get mad just thinking about it.

NURHALISA: Even if you say it's impossible, you should still do something to change the system.

ISKANDAR: Tell me about it!

NURHALISA: Show your people justice. Start by apologising to Tok Guru for what your father did to his son, Nadim.

ISKANDAR: What will that serve except make a public display of my own weakness?

NURHALISA: Accepting responsibility is not weakness. You want to show you're strong? Expose your ministers who are corrupt and prosecute them.

ISKANDAR: That's scary. They have grassroots support. They have thugs, spies, and the means to buy people or blackmail them. They're worse than the Mafia. They're the ones running this kingdom!

NURHALISA: What kind of a sultan are you then?

ISKANDAR: Don't worry your pretty head over that. I just want to have a good life. I'll give you one, too. I've wanted to do that since the first day I met you. Give me your love. And give me an heir.

NURHALISA: Get your royal consort to give you an heir.

ISKANDAR: (laughs) She's still a virgin. I've never once touched her. She pisses me off. It's been like that since I married her. And the marriage was planned when I was only five years old. Five years old. You see how much freedom I have?

(NURHALISA doesn't know what to say.)

ISKANDAR: Come. Come and be with me. I'm lost, and screwed-up. I have no-one I can trust. You could be my only hope.

(LOGOD, RIS KAW and ENSEMBLE enter, rapping. During this, ISKANDAR gradually leads NURHALISA out.)

LOGOD and RIS KAW: Pretty maid, pretty maid, you are dead.

ENSEMBLE: Pretty maid, pretty maid, you are dead.

LOGOD and RIS KAW: Pretty maid, pretty maid, you are dead.

ENSEMBLE: Pretty maid, pretty maid, you are dead.

LOGOD and RIS KAW: Pretty maid, pretty maid, you are dead.

ENSEMBLE: Pretty maid, pretty maid, you are dead.

LOGOD and RIS KAW: Pretty maid, pretty maid, you are dead.

ENSEMBLE: Pretty maid, pretty maid, you are dead.

LOGOD and RIS KAW: You're dead, you're dead, you're dead, you're dead.
               The king has said —

ENSEMBLE: "Come to my bed."

LOGOD and RIS KAW: The king has said —

ENSEMBLE:	"Come to my bed."
LOGOD and RIS KAW:	Pretty maid, pretty maid, you are dead.
ENSEMBLE:	Pretty maid, pretty maid, you are dead.
LOGOD and RIS KAW:	You're dead, you're dead, you're dead, you're dead.
ENSEMBLE:	You're dead, you're dead, you're dead, you're dead.

NAJIB THE SALESMAN AND FLIP-FLOPPER

NAJIB RAZAK BECAME PRIME MINSTER IN APRIL 2009, AFTER ABDULLAH BADAWI WAS FORCED TO STEP DOWN, PRIMARILY FOR THE 2008 GENERAL ELECTION FIASCO. JUST BEFORE HE STEPPED INTO THE NATION'S NUMBER ONE JOB, NAJIB HAD PROVEN HIMSELF TO BE A RUTHLESS MANIPULATOR BY STEALING PERAK BACK FOR BN. RIGHT AFTER THAT, HE HAD A TOUGH TIME TRYING TO CLEAN UP HIS IMAGE. HE RESORTED TO BLATANTLY BUYING VOTES BY OFFERING CASH AND OPPORTUNITIES. HE SHOWED HIS SALESMAN TACTICS MOST OBVIOUSLY AT THE HULU SELANGOR AND SIBU BY-ELECTIONS, AND BY HIS WOOING OF THE INDIAN COMMUNITY WITH A DELUGE OF PROMISES.

OF HIS PLANS FOR MALAYSIA:
- 1MALAYSIA — SUPPOSED TO BE INCLUSIVE BUT NOT TRULY SO.
- ECONOMIC TRANSFORMATION PROGRAMME (ETP) — LARGE PROJECTS UNDERTAKEN CRITICISED AS PROVIDING OPPORTUNITIES FOR UMNOPUTRAS AND CRONIES TO MAKE MONEY BEFORE MALAYSIA BECOMES BANKRUPT.
- MALAYSIA TO ATTAIN HIGH-INCOME STATUS BY 2020 — MOST ECONOMISTS SCEPTICAL OF SUCCESS BECAUSE OF THE DEARTH OF MUCH-NEEDED EXPERTISE CAUSED BY THE BRAIN DRAIN FROM MALAYSIA OVER THE DECADES.

- GOVERNMENT TRANSFORMATION PROGRAMME (GTP) — INSTEAD OF TRIMMING THE BLOATED CIVIL SERVICE COMPRISING A STAGGERING 1.4 MILLION PERSONNEL, NAJIB THREW MONEY AT THEM IN THE FORM OF HIGHER SALARIES AVOWEDLY TO MAKE THEM IMPROVE THEIR SERVICE BUT IMPLICITLY TO WIN THEIR VOTES.

NAJIB HAS COME TO BE KNOWN AS THE FLIP-FLOP PM FOR MAKING NUMEROUS ABOUT-TURNS IN ACTION AND POLICY DECISION-MAKING. AMONG HIS FLIP-FLOPS:

- A FEW DAYS AFTER HE SET UP A PARLIAMENTARY SELECT COMMITTEE TO COME UP WITH ELECTORAL REFORM, HE ANNOUNCED THAT THE NEXT GENERAL ELECTION COULD BE HELD ANYTIME AND WAS NOT BOUND BY THE FINDINGS OF THE COMMITTEE;
- A FEW DAYS AFTER HE OFFERED BERSIH 2.0 THE OPTION TO HOLD ITS RALLY FOR ELECTORAL REFORM IN A STADIUM, HE RENEGED ON THE OFFER AND BLAMED BERSIH 2.0 FOR CHOOSING STADIUM MERDEKA;
- A FEW DAYS AFTER HE SAID THE GOVERNMENT WANTED TO DO AWAY WITH BUMIPUTERA QUOTAS, HE DENIED HE HAD MEANT THEY SHOULD BE ABOLISHED;
- HIS GOVERNMENT SAID SUBSIDISING FUEL WAS BECOMING UNSUSTAINABLE AND CAME UP WITH A TWO-TIER FUEL SUBSIDY SCHEME SYSTEM TO ADDRESS THE PROBLEM, BUT IT WAS SCRAPPED WHEN IT RECEIVED NEGATIVE PUBLIC FEEDBACK;
- HIS GOVERNMENT WAS PLANNING TO INTRODUCE THE GOODS AND SERVICES TAX (GST) BUT THEN DECIDED TO HOLD BACK WHEN OBJECTIONS WERE RAISED BY THE PUBLIC AND SOME SEGMENTS OF UMNO.

THE LIST GOES ON, SHOWING EVIDENCE OF NAJIB'S CONCERN FOR WINNING VOTES ABOVE ALMOST ALL ELSE WHEN MAKING POLICY DECISIONS AND TURNAROUNDS.

THESE ARTICLES, PLACED IN THEMATIC RATHER THAN CHRONOLOGICAL ORDER, RECORD MY PERCEPTIONS OF HIS PERFORMANCE AS PM, AND OF HOW LOW-CLASS HIS MENTALITY CAN BE FROM THE WORDS HE SPOKE.

PEANUTS, NOT
SWEEPING REFORMS

Free Malaysia Today, September 16, 2011

Peanuts. That's what Prime Minister Najib Razak's so-called "sweeping reforms" are. They hardly amount to a political transformation.

While it's cheering to note that the Internal Security Act (ISA) will be repealed — finally, after our many years of waiting — and that the Emergency proclamations are to be lifted — a decision that is decades overdue — it's disturbing to be told that they will be replaced by two new laws aimed at preventing subversion and safeguarding public order.

And even though the detention period under these new laws may be shorter, with further extensions to be made by court order, the Home Minister is still the one to decide who gets detained on suspicion of being a terrorist.

This means, theoretically speaking, that although Najib has given the commitment that "no individual will be detained purely based on political ideology", there is no stopping the Government from branding a political opponent a suspected terrorist, whether or not he is one. Just to lock him away.

And why must there be two new laws to replace the ISA? It's like 'sell one and get two free'! It also sounds suspicious. We might end up with even more restrictions. Why didn't Najib come right out and give us a better idea of what these two new laws would be? Is he holding back some nasty surprises?

Another so-called "reform" is scrapping the requirement for publications to renew their printing licences annually. This, also, is nothing to crow about. It still means that publications have to obtain a licence that the Home Minister may or may not grant. It still means the Home Minister has the absolute power to suspend or revoke a licence at any time. And his decision cannot be challenged in court. He does not even have to give a reason.

It also means the Home Ministry can still call up newspaper editors and cow them into submission for publishing something the ministry finds objectionable. Like what happened recently to *The Star* when it ran the heading 'Ramadhan delights' for an eating-out supplement that was not totally devoted to *halal* food.

The ministry can still practise the double standards it has been practising — turn a blind eye to the race-baiting and rabble-rousing of *Utusan Malaysia* but come down hard on the minor transgressions of other publications. So where's the change?

If the Government were truly sincere and had the political will, it should repeal the Printing Presses and Publications Act (PPPA) and no longer require publications to obtain a printing licence. That would be in keeping with the spirit of what Najib talked about instituting in Malaysia when he announced the "reforms" on September 15 — a "democratic system based on the universal philosophy of 'of the people, by the people and for the people'."

None of the newly announced "reforms" fully cohere with this spirit. On Section 27 of the Police Act, Najib said there would be a review to take into consideration the provisions under Article 10 of the Federal Constitution which guarantees Malaysians the right to freedom of speech, freedom of assembly and freedom of association. But in the same breath, he said police permits would still be required for street demonstrations, subject to certain criteria.

If freedom of assembly, which should be a right of all citizens, is still curtailed in this fashion, what is that rubbish talk of Najib's about forging a democratic system "of the people, by the people and for the people"?

He did say, however, that "permission to assemble will be given in accordance with procedures to be fixed later that will take into account international norms". But this sounds vague. What international norms did he mean? And when is "later" going to be?

And speaking of Article 10, why doesn't the Government address the other impediments to freedom of speech, such as the Official Secrets Act (OSA), the Sedition Act, the Universities and University Colleges Act (UUCA), the Multimedia and Communications Act, the Public Order (Preservation) Ordinance?

No wonder Home Minister Hishammuddin Hussein was smirking and applauding when Najib made his announcements. His absolute powers remain intact.

Let's not be fooled, people. The changes Najib announced are merely cosmetic. And, of course, they will have to be passed in Parliament first before they become effective.

Meanwhile, Articles 149 and 150 are still there to provide Parliament with the power to pass laws that do not have to be consistent with the freedoms guaranteed in Articles 5, 9, 10 and 13, and to allow the Cabinet to declare an emergency. The Emergency proclamations may go, but Article 150 is still around. We, the people, are still vulnerable.

Some of us may say that we cannot expect the Government to make such truly sweeping reforms in one go, and that we should be thankful for the small mercies we are now getting. Some may say this could be just the beginning, and more reforms could come.

That's well and good. But at the same time, we should give credit where it's due for this beginning. It's not Najib we should thank. What we are getting is what has been due us for a long time, what any concerned government should have given us even without our having to pressure them to do so.

We should instead acknowledge that the March 8 effect lives on, and therefore the credit for these changes should go to us, the *rakyat*, for voting as we did on March 8, 2008. We voted in a stronger Opposition, we denied the ruling party the two-thirds majority that it had abused to increasingly curb our democratic rights over the decades. We sent them the message that enough was enough.

These "reforms" have now come about because Barisan Nasional (BN) wants to stay in power, and it has realised that we have the power to decide whether that will happen. The "reforms" are meant to win back our votes. Ever since Najib took over as prime minister, he has been doing things merely to ensure that BN's goal is fulfilled, not because he is altruistic or benevolent in spirit. We have seen his meanness in numerous other ways.

Watching him speak on September 15 when announcing these "reforms" as part of his Malaysia Day address, we could have contrasted it with his speech to 6,000 Umno members and Malay NGOs at Putra World Trade Centre (PWTC) a couple of days after the Bersih 2.0 rally, and called him two-faced.

At that PWTC gathering, he was far from being the prime minister who cared about reform and the good of the entire country. He was a truculent thug who roused the crowd with the boast of Umno's ability to round up a million members to "conquer Kuala Lumpur". He was a contemptuous chauvinist who exhorted the Malays to unite in order to teach the Bersih 2.0 protestors a lesson and "show them whose country this is".

No doubt, he has since realised his mistakes in his handling of the Bersih 2.0 rally and is now making amends. His ratings have dropped and he's trying to make them go up again. Hence, these "reforms". But let's be wary of his sincerity and be clear about his real purpose.

Let us keep sight as well of the many more ills that the Government has not comprehensively addressed, such as corruption, rent-seeking, wasteful spending, Umnoputraism, our pathetic education system.

Let us demand more reforms, especially those pertaining to our institutions, such as the judiciary, the police, the Attorney-General's Office, the Election Commission, the Malaysian Anti-Corruption Commission (MACC).

There is still a long road ahead. Unless and until the reforms are truly sweeping and the restrictive laws abolished, we should not put our trust in Najib and BN. Make them sweat, make them work, and don't let them take us for granted. Never again.

JUST ONE EMPTY SLOGAN?

First published in the book *Najib's First 100 Days: No Honeymoon* by Oon Yeoh (GerakBudaya, 2009)

For a while, we thought Najib Razak's appointment as Prime Minister would be on April 1. What a joke that might have been. But he was eventually sworn in on April 3. Now the joke's on us. We have a PM who distinguished himself for being a ruthless manipulator when he wrested Perak from Pakatan Rakyat by means generally regarded foul, and who has not parried away the Sword of Damocles that hangs over his head and goes by the name of Altantuya.

In the days following his taking-up of office, it was clear that he wanted to win hearts and minds. He introduced the 1Malaysia concept. Sloganeering is one thing, making it real another. Dr Mahathir Mohamad had his *Bersih, Cekap dan Amanah* but his regime turned out to be one of the most corrupt and cronyistic; Abdullah Badawi said *Work with Me*, which was all very well for him because he turned out to be the sleeping partner.

The 1Malaysia concept has so far been wishy-washy. Its rhetoric makes the claim of uniting Malaysians, but, to pacify the ultra-nationalist groups, Najib has had to explain that it's not the same as the DAP's Malaysian Malaysia on the ground that the latter goes against the Constitution. That specifically means that 1Malaysia upholds the special position of the Malays, which therefore begs the question: Can a nation be truly one if there are citizens who are more equal than others? Isn't that a major contradiction in his 1Malaysia concept?

As if to reinforce this contradiction, on the same day Najib publicly unveiled the 1Malaysia logo, his deputy, Muhyiddin Yassin, said, at another event, that Umno would fight to the last drop of blood to protect Malay rights, and urged the Malays to unite in protecting these rights. Doesn't this sound more like 2Malaysias? And what about Najib's interest in having unity talks with PAS for the sake of Muslim unity? Doesn't that sound like business as usual rather than 1Malaysia?

Najib obviously needs courage to push through what former deputy prime minister Ismail Abdul Rahman advocated. In Ismail's own words: "I felt that as more and more Malays became educated and gained self-confidence, they themselves *would do away* with this 'special position'. In itself, this 'special position' is a *slur on the ability* of the Malays and only to be tolerated because it is necessary as a temporary measure to ensure their survival in the modern competitive world." Perhaps Najib doesn't think that the time is ripe yet, but without addressing this, his 1Malaysia is mere window-dressing.

This matter aside, it has to be said that since taking office, he has not been on a strong wicket. To win Indian hearts and minds, he freed the Hindraf leaders who had been detained under the Internal Security Act (ISA), but when P. Uthayakumar, the most fiery of them, refused to sign a conditional release and to appear before an advisory panel at Kamunting afterwards, it was a sore test of the new administration's standing. Home Minister Hishammuddin Hussein had to come up with an excuse for not taking action against Uthayakumar's defiance. The Government got caught out and it further empowered the Indian community.

Just as feeble was the excuse made by Najib for not fielding a Barisan Nasional candidate in the Penanti by-election. He said it would be a waste of public funds to do so, but the public, who had felt swindled of billions of ringgit for the last couple of decades by the Umnoputras in power, saw right through the spin. As a consequence, the spin did more harm to BN — and Najib. People saw the subcutaneous colour of the vulpine fixer who had earlier purloined Perak from Pakatan Rakyat, and wondered what kind of advice his advisers were giving him.

Of late, he's been trumped by the royals. First, his proposed third bridge to Singapore got rejected by the Sultan of Johor who didn't even give a reason for objecting. Then the Conference of Rulers decreed that the proposed amendments to three bills on the matter of religious conversion had to be referred to the state religious authorities first – and this on the eve of their being tabled in Parliament. From the layman's perspective, Najib's attempts at pleasing the non-Malay, non-Muslim populace have either been less than wholehearted or a long way from fruition. When he announced that there would be a new category of government scholarships to be awarded based on merit, non-Malay parents were not jumping with joy, no doubt because they sensed that the old category favouring one race would probably continue in parallel.

On top of everything, the Altantuya albatross hangs around Najib's neck. The taxi driver taking me to the airport a few weeks after Najib's inauguration expressed his concerns about the case. There were too many unanswered questions, he said, and Najib had done nothing to clear the air. "Why didn't the questions of motive and who gave instructions to the two policemen come up in court?" he asked, echoing my own exact thoughts.

It hasn't helped Najib's cause that in mid-April, the Government sent out a gag order to Media Prima's TV stations preventing them from reporting that Najib and his wife, Rosmah Mansor, were allegedly linked to the murder. Since then, even the police have threatened to charge with criminal defamation and sedition anyone who mentions Altantuya together with Najib and Rosmah.

Three days after he became PM, Najib, in addressing the Malaysian Press Institute, called on the press to perform their duties "without fear of consequence". The gag order to Media Prima, however, contradicts that. Another three days later, the Chinese online daily *Merdeka Review* was barred from Najib's press conference to announce his new Cabinet line-up. And my friend, who writes a column for a mainstream newspaper, had his piece critiquing the line-up spiked.

On the whole, it does look like business as usual under Najib. Until he gets down to the real men's stuff of tackling issues like revamping the police force, reinstating the separation of powers that will grant the judiciary independence, establishing an inter-faith commission, setting the media free by repealing the Printing Presses and Publications Act, abolishing the New Economic Policy, repealing restrictive laws chief of which is the ISA, he will not be able to restore the faith of Malaysians in our institutions and, thereby, unite the people.

Then 1Malaysia would only end up being just another empty slogan.

NAJIB SPEAKS WITH FORKED TONGUE

Malaysiakini, Oct 18, 2009

Najib Razak contradicted himself in his speech last Thursday at the Umno General Assembly. He spoke of the all-embracing 1Malaysia concept on the one hand and he spoke of the need to retain the New Economic Policy (NEP) on the other. The Native Americans in old cowboy movies might have said of his speech that it came from a forked tongue.

How can you have the NEP and at the same time say that we are all 1Malaysia? The NEP is exclusive to a particular group of people; such exclusivity sets them apart. There is no 1Malaysia then; there are 2Malaysias. I say it again for emphasis: There are 2Malaysias embedded in that policy.

Does Najib not see that or is his 1Malaysia idea merely salesman talk or PR spin or marketing label?

This central contradiction is what makes many non-Malays sceptical of what he is touting. The only non-Malays who will buy it are those who are not discerning enough or who are easily bought. I'm almost tempted to include the Bagan Pinang voters in this category but their decision to support so strongly a politician with a corruption record in that recent by-election could be due to other concerns.

Why continue to have an affirmative action programme that is still based on race? Haven't we moved on since March 8, 2008? How much different is Najib's defence of the need for the NEP from that of his cousin Hishammuddin Hussein's pre-March 8 *keris*-wielding pledge to defend it against adversaries? It's merely less militant, that's all.

Najib slammed the Malays who say they no longer need "crutches" and called them arrogant. He asked, "What about the Malays who still require help? Is it fair if the group who still need crutches are denied help?" Why hasn't he thought of providing help to people of all races who need "crutches"? Wouldn't that be more in line with 1Malaysia? All he needs to do is look at the Malaysian Economic Agenda proposed by Pakatan Rakyat. Go back to the basics — have an affirmative action programme based on need. Isn't that the original intent of the NEP?

It looks like Najib was invoking the NEP at the assembly expressly to play to the Malay gallery, to ensure that his regular customers will remain faithful. Meanwhile, the non-Malay customers can wait. He will find some other occasion in the future to throw them small gifts and lure them to buy his merchandise.

That's the kind of ploy we've been used to through the decades, but hasn't it exceeded its sell-by date? Shouldn't we reject it instead of fall for its trickery? Leaders of race-based parties like Najib must resolve their central dilemma — pander to their own race or be truly multi-racial. They can't have it both ways. This time around, Najib has chosen to stick with tradition. He must be held accountable for the doublespeak. Similarly, we have to insist that Ong Tee Keat stick to his promise of resigning as MCA president now that a no-confidence vote has been taken against him.

At the Umno assembly, Najib also said that the Malays are not racist. He is absolutely right; they are not. But what about Umno? He said it is not.

If Umno is not racist, why did it organise forums after March 8 at which Malays were warned that Malay power was being eroded and that Malay land had fallen into non-Malay hands?

If Umno is not racist, why does it maintain an indoctrination agency like the Biro Tata Negara (BTN) which inculcates in young Malay minds the idea of *Ketuanan Melayu* and wariness of the other races? (For more on the BTN, read Dr Azly Rahman's chapter 'On the Problem of

Ketuanan Melayu and the Work of the Biro Tata Negara' in the book *Multiethnic Malaysia*.)

If Umno is not racist, why does it allow the newspapers it owns, particularly in the Malay language, to run stories and commentaries that could easily be deemed seditious? Don't tell me that it's because Umno believes in the independence of the media and therefore does not intervene. I've been in journalism for more than 30 years and I know that's a lie.

Najib also said that Malaysia does not practise apartheid. Sure, Malaysia does not practise apartheid like the National Party of South Africa did. But why do non-Malay parents have to work so much harder to send their children for tertiary education? Why is there a restrictive quota for the intake of non-Malay students into our public universities? Why are there educational institutions that are strictly for Malays? And why was there so much hue and cry against Selangor Menteri Besar Khalid Ibrahim's suggestion for Universiti Teknologi MARA to offer 10 per cent of its places to non-Malay students?

Why is only a small percentage of government scholarships granted to non-Malays? Why do some non-Malay students who top their class not get such scholarships? Do the non-Malays not pay taxes?

Why is the Malaysian Civil Service so understaffed by non-Malays? And of which race are the overwhelming numbers of high officials in the Civil Service, universities, police force, army and so on?

Is it not just a subtler form of apartheid that Malaysia practises? And is it not a fact that ours is one of only a few countries in the world that institutionalises racial discrimination? So, what is Najib talking about? Whom is he trying to fool? What nonsense is this 1Malaysia?

IF IT'S A PROBLEM, DON'T RECOGNISE IT

Malaysiakini, September 22, 2010

Idris Jala is a good speaker. If you listen to him and you don't watch it, he will sell you an idea.

That's what he did — or tried to do — when he gave the keynote address at the 'We Are Malaysia' event hosted by University College Sedaya International (UCSI) on Malaysia Day.

He spoke of 1Malaysia and its aims, and how national unity can be achieved. One of the central aims of 1Malaysia is upgrading the diverse population's attitude towards one another from tolerance to acceptance and, eventually, the celebration of diversity. And one of the central strategies of achieving that is the recognition that, in Idris' own words, "in life, there are only two types of issues".

Sounds rather pat, as if coming from a self-enrichment guru. But as I said, Idris Jala is a seller of ideas.

What are these two types of issues?

Problems and polarities. A problem, expounded Idris, is something that can be solved. A polarity is something that cannot be solved but must be managed. The examples of polarities he gave are old and young, urban and rural, good and evil, rich and poor. Like the North and South Poles, they cannot be removed; therefore, a balance must be struck between them.

To illustrate further, he gave the example of his wife and him. She is fastidious in wanting him to place his socks in a proper basket for

Look also at Clause 5, which states that Article 153 "does not derogate from the provisions of Article 136".

What does Article 136 say?

It says: "All persons of whatever race in the same grade in the service of the Federation shall, subject to the terms and conditions of their employment, be treated impartially." This is another limit to the scope of Article 153.

If the Government follows the rule of law and interprets the Constitution as it should be interpreted, we wouldn't have a racial problem. Yes, *problem*. Let's call a spade a spade. The racial problem we have now is mostly the result of what the Government has done and not done.

It has not followed the rule of law. It has not told Perkasa to grasp the proper provisions of Article 153. Instead, it has been affirming that Perkasa's doing the right thing. Only a few days ago, Deputy Education Minister Puad Zarkashi said Perkasa was championing the people's rights as spelt out in the Constitution. Perhaps Puad hasn't read beyond Clause 1. Perhaps he doesn't understand it fully.

In terms of what the Government has done, it has chosen to take sides to formulate policies that are contrary to the spirit of the Constitution. For instance, is the discount for Bumiputeras purchasing property constitutional? If so, where is it written in that sacred document?

The Government favours one race and marginalises the other races. With regard to the civil service, it has not upheld Article 136 of the Constitution, which calls for impartial treatment for civil servants of all races. Over the past four decades, the promotion of civil servants to the highest positions has been almost totally confined to those of one particular race. Is that impartial treatment?

As for religion, it is again the Government that has created problems. Just to name two, one is its action to deny Christians the right to use the word "Allah"; the other, and more far-reaching, action is declaring Malaysia an Islamic state, as Najib did in 2007 when he was deputy prime minister.

"Islam is the official religion and we are an Islamic state," he said.

He must surely have read Article 3 of the Constitution but chose to ignore what it says: "Islam is the religion of the Federation; but other religions may be practised in peace and harmony in any part of the Federation."

Nowhere is it stated that Malaysia is an Islamic state.

But by his declaration, Najib caused fresh anxieties to surface and made the issue of religion more contentious. In extreme situations, the provisions of Article 3 have been disrespected. A recent example is Perkasa's lodging of a police report against a church in Shah Alam for planning to stage a Christian play during Ramadhan on the grounds that it was seditious and insulting to the Sultan.

That police report became a problem to the church. How would it be solved? In an ideal Malaysian setting, the Government would have stepped in and told Perkasa to respect Article 3. But of course, it did not. For the church and other Christian groups, these problems will continue to crop up in future and there will be no solution in sight if the Government stays silent.

Is the Government silent because it now believes it can call such a problem a polarity? And with a polarity, which cannot be solved, the less said about it, the better? Similarly, in the case of the Johor school principal, who allegedly made racist remarks, is it better to let the issue be until the public forgets about it?

If so, 1Malaysia is not about taking a radically honest approach towards national unity and the celebration of diversity. It seems to shy away from calling a problem a problem and solving it. Calling it a polarity merely adds a new twist to the propaganda.

So, if Idris Jala comes to your neighbourhood and tries to sell you that idea, be sure to ask him some difficult questions. He's a good speaker and can easily mesmerise his audience. His words may sound pretty until you probe them for substance. If you do, you might find that they amount to nothing more than public relations prattle.

TURN 1MALAYSIA INTO AN ACTION PLAN

MalaysianDigest.com, October 21, 2010

The Economic Transformation Programme (ETP) "is not a plan, it is an action-based programme". This is what its overseer, Minister in the Prime Minister's Office Idris Jala, has been repeating to the point of overstatement. By this, he means a goal is identified, the action plan to achieve it is proposed and an end-result is expected. Key target areas are tackled and objectives spelt out.

Why not extend this to 1Malaysia? Why not turn what is now virtually a nebulous concept into an action-based programme — a programme complete with the identification of goals and action plans to realise them?

How else does Prime Minister Najib Razak expect Malaysians to understand what 1Malaysia is? More important, how else does he expect to realise the aims of 1Malaysia?

After two years since Najib first gave us 1Malaysia, it still exists merely on the level of talk. Despite its declared intent of unifying the people, racial tensions have actually intensified. Politicians and civil servants have been guilty of making racist remarks, publicly and behind closed doors. Read comments in blogs and social media and you'll see educated Malaysians of all races vying for the Racist of the Year Award.

Lately, some quarters have been seeking clarification of what 1Malaysia truly means. Among them are the Umno clubs of California and Moscow.

Tengku Razaleigh Hamzah, in a recent interview with the Chinese daily *Sin Chew*, said people still did not know what 1Malaysia means, and this had created confusion. He also said it "misleads the people into believing that [achieving unity] is a matter of simply repeating a slogan".

Unless for some reason Najib wants to maintain the confusion, the sensible thing for him to do would be to spell out 1Malaysia in concrete terms. Given Idris's experience in formulating the ETP, Najib could consider asking him to do the same for 1Malaysia and turn abstract rhetoric into an action-based programme.

So far, Najib has made a few mentions here and there about the aims of 1Malaysia but he has said virtually nothing about how he intends to achieve them. As a citizen, I know precious little about the concept beyond what I heard from Idris Jala, when he addressed the National Congress on Integrity organised by UCSI on September 16.

He said 1Malaysia was about moving towards "accepting and celebrating our differences", not just "tolerating" them. The key to achieving unity is the celebration of our diversity. He gave this formula:

$$Unity = Diversity + Inclusiveness$$

He said 1Malaysia called for society to undergo "behavioural changes" to move from tolerance to the celebration of diversity, and for us to "exhibit 1Malaysia values in our everyday lives".

But how do we exhibit 1Malaysia values in our everyday lives when we are not sure what those values are, apart from their having to do with accepting differences and celebrating diversity? Even in intellectual terms, "accepting differences" and "celebrating diversity" are open to huge, intangible possibilities.

Idris gave one example from the world of football. He said the black British footballer John Barnes distinguished himself as an England player but the English did not put him on a pedestal, whereas the Dutch lionised Ruud Gullit even though he was of mixed ancestry.

This was not a good example, actually. Barnes was an excellent player but he wasn't great. He was certainly not in the same league as Bobby Charlton or Bobby Moore or Gordon Banks. As for the celebration of Gullit as a Dutch icon, that's just a simplistic illustration of achieving unity through such a means. Yes, it's a start to look beyond race when we hail our heroes, but more than that, achieving national unity surely calls for a more concerted programme.

1Malaysia could certainly be an action-based programme if it identified problems like racism and set a related goal to eliminate it, complete with an action plan to bring racists to book, including mass media that invoke racial hatred.

On the constructive side, it could set a goal to build racial unity, complete with an action plan that details measures that would bring the different races together to learn about one another so they can accept their differences, and also to live and work together.

It could entail (I'm merely quoting possibilities):

- the creation of a single-stream education system;
- a reform of the entire education system in order to depoliticise it;
- the complete removal of the category of 'race' in all forms, official and otherwise;
- the closing-down of single-race agencies and institutions;
- the opening up of equal business and employment opportunities to all races;
- the organising of projects to educate the masses on the celebration of diversity.

Whatever fits the principles of acceptance and diversity.

Also important would be an action plan to educate the 1.4 million civil servants to embrace the programme so that they exhibit the concretised 1Malaysia values in the daily dispensation of their official duties.

If these, and more, could be formulated — and implemented — we should see a real transformation. We should see Malaysian society undergoing behavioural changes.

But without a programme, 1Malaysia will end up just a slogan, like the other slogans that came before it, such as Vision 2020, Bangsa Malaysia, Malaysia Boleh.

Vision 2020 was not an action-based programme. It merely enumerated nine challenges that Malaysia would have to overcome to become a fully developed nation by the year 2020. Just looking at two of the stated challenges should convince anyone that it was painted with broad strokes:

> *The first of these is the challenge of establishing a united Malaysian nation with a sense of common and shared destiny. This must be a nation at peace with itself, territorially and ethnically integrated, living in harmony and full and fair partnership, made up of one 'Bangsa Malaysia' with political loyalty and dedication to the nation.*
>
> *The seventh challenge is the challenge of establishing a fully caring society and a caring culture, a social system in which society will come before self, in which the welfare of the people will revolve not around the state or the individual but around a strong and resilient family system.*

Vision 2020 wallowed in abstract rhetoric. No wonder even its proponent, Mahathir Mohamad, said last month that from the way things are going, it may not be achievable. He tried to blame the current government for not employing the right strategies, but the real pitfall is, Vision 2020 had no action plan to begin with.

If Najib wants to avoid the same trajectory for 1Malaysia, he should make it an action-based programme. But this, of course, would call for supreme boldness on his part. And it would depend on how sincere he really is about 1Malaysia.

Does he really want to transform society? Does he really want to make us One? Does he have the will to overcome the obstacles that he knows he will encounter if he decides to push his programme through? The proof of the desire is in the doing. To sum it up in one word — Action.

A GAMBLE THE GOVERNMENT LOST BADLY

MalaysianDigest.com, June 28, 2010

So, it's finally final. No legalised sports betting. After all that vacillating and humming and hawing, Prime Minister Najib Razak has come out to say the Ministry of Finance has withdrawn the approval it had initially given to Ascot Sports Sdn Bhd.

He even admitted that approval was indeed given — but only "in principle" — confirming something he had sought to evade on June 15 when he said no licence had been awarded to Ascot Sports.

Revoking the approval is bad form, of course. What we would call *buruk siku* — taking back after giving. It doesn't augur well for the Government as the public will view this as another of its flip-flops. In the last couple of years, the Government has been flip-flopping so often, it cannot be seen to be in total control.

Why, one must ask, was it so hasty in granting the approval in the first place? Why did it, in these volatile political times, agree to legalising sports betting when an issue like that would inevitably raise a hue and cry in public?

Did Najib and his Barisan Nasional colleagues not weigh the odds and realise that the issue would be politicised? Did they not foresee that the Opposition would latch on to it for political gain and threaten to stage a mammoth rally against this endorsement of gambling? That it would cast BN in a negative light, especially among the Muslim electorate? That even a party like the DAP would use it to win Malay-Muslim hearts?

Had BN become too confident about its having won back adequate Malay support that it could gamble on something like this? Or was BN trying to win non-Malay support since legalised sports betting would have been meant only for non-Muslims? Even ministers like Nazri Aziz and Rais Yatim were going around touting that legalising it would be showing respect for the rights of non-Muslims – even though you'd swallow what they said with a cupful of salt.

Surely, it was not just the World Cup tournament that triggered the move to legalise sports betting even though the foreseen pickings might have been substantial. Was the Government desperate for the revenue it could derive from the legalisation because the nation's coffers are dwindling? And if so, did it not wonder about how it would look to be profiting from non-Muslims through an activity that Muslims would frown upon? On that score, wouldn't the issues of religion and morality inevitably crop up?

Now that the whole thing's been called off, most people would probably not lament that Ascot Sports is the party that has been hard done by, given that its owners have been subject to much criticism, especially in political blogs and online news websites. But the fact remains that the public image of the Government has taken a beating with this *faux pas*. And the fact remains that the company that had been promised the deal has been unfairly treated.

It doesn't matter what the company is; the point is, reneging on a deal already concluded is unbecoming, especially if the party that has failed to keep its end of the bargain is the Government. How does one have faith in a party that actually breaks its word?

The Government has recently prided itself on being one that gets public feedback first before implementing any policy or going ahead with a project. If that's the case, why did it not get public feedback first before proceeding with giving the approval to Ascot Sports?

It has also not helped the Government's cause that it offered half-truths when the controversy was raging. On June 12, Ascot Sports publicly revealed that it had already got the approval from the Minister of Finance, i.e Najib. But on June 15, when he was questioned by the media, Najib said no licence had been issued.

Without splitting semantic hairs, we have to say that an approval is an approval, and even if Najib was not wrong in saying that no licence had been issued, he could have admitted that the approval had already been given but the issuance of the licence was still pending. By being equivocal in his statement, he kept the public in suspense, thereby further fuelling the anxiety and confusion that was already building up.

In hindsight, we might say that it was obviously a damage-control measure. As the issue was out in the open and the feedback was negative, Najib had to be cagey in case the issue turned sour. He was also playing for time to see which way public opinion would eventually go. In other words, he wasn't steadfast in his ruling. This looked like a case of leadership uncertainty.

As it turned out, even with coalition partners MCA and MIC coming out to defend legalising sports betting, it took the bigger voice of Umno to call the shots.

What really must have hurt Najib was the first salvo fired by Johor Umno, which issued a categorical objection on June 13. This was later followed by Umno of Kedah and Perak. Umno Youth, although it uncharacteristically took some time to decide, also joined the fray.

A telling indication from this entire episode is that Najib is not in full control of the party he heads. Neither does he enjoy its full backing to do what he wants.

What is even more demeaning for him is that the final decision for revoking the sports betting approval was made by the Umno Supreme Council. Considering that it was the Government, as represented not just by Umno but also other BN partners, that had given the approval, it should have been the Government that made the decision. Since it was not so, the message that comes through is clear.

BN is not really in charge of the Government. Umno is. And as it looks from here, neither is Najib.

ANTI-EXTREMISM BEGINS AT HOME

MalaysianDigest.com, October 6, 2010

I totally agree with most of what Prime Minister Najib Razak recently said at the United Nations General Assembly, especially about the attempts in some parts of the world to demonise Islam and spread Islamophobia.

I find it alarming to see so many e-mails and videos being circulated warning people of the dangers of Islam and propagating the fear that, with the Muslims multiplying at the current rate, they would one day outnumber people of other faiths and take over the world.

This kind of fear propagation reminds me of that practised by Mahathir Mohamad when he warns Malays that they would lose power to the non-Malays, especially if Pakatan Rakyat takes over the government. It's destructive.

It appals me that even Malaysians are instrumental in spreading Islamophobia by forwarding these e-mails. When I get one, I often reply to the sender to tell them not to disseminate such hatred. I tell them this problem has arisen because of misunderstanding of history, and that these e-mails don't tell the other side of the story, which is the plight of Muslims who have suffered because of the historical events fashioned by imperialists.

Some of the e-mails reek of ignorance and bigotry. One that irked me no end was of an American serviceman answering questions about whether a Muslim could be a real American. These are just some of his answers:

Religiously — no. Because no other religion is accepted by his Allah except Islam.

Socially — no. Because his allegiance to Islam forbids him to make friends with Christians or Jews.

Philosophically — no. Because Islam, Muhammad, and the Quran do not allow freedom of religion and expression. Democracy and Islam cannot co-exist. Every Muslim government is either dictatorial or autocratic.

These answers are so distorted, blinkered and untruthful that they are not worth rebutting. The danger lies in e-mails such as this being received and accepted as the truth by millions of people who don't know what Islam is about.

I am not a subscriber of organised religion, but I believe in the right of all religions to exist. I also believe no religion should throw mud at another and claim to be truer than any other.

The only way to resolve the differences in the world today is to get all sides to sit down at the table and discuss. Perhaps the US should even sit down with al-Qaeda and thrash it out, peacefully. Why not? These two are the major causes of the mess the world is in today. If they can talk, instead of fight, we might get some peace.

This is the same line taken by Najib at the UN when he said: "We must choose negotiations over confrontation. We must choose to work together and not against each other."

He also said, "We must choose moderation over extremism." Which I readily agree with. But then why doesn't he deal with the racial extremists in his own country?

Nothing has been done about the school principals in Johor and Kedah who allegedly made racist remarks. And this despite the calls from several quarters, including the MCA, for action to be taken immediately. Hasn't the lack of action dragged on for too long?

Ironically, as Najib was calling for moderation at the UN, a Biro Tata Negara (BTN) assistant director named Hamim Husin was reported to have made racist remarks at a meeting with Puteri Umno members. His reported reference to Indians as "the Si Botol who only knows how to go up and down Batu Caves" is more than derogatory; it's venomous. It reduces the Indians to utter worthlessness.

He now claims he did nothing wrong because it was a closed-door meeting, but any sensible mind would figure out that this is not an excuse. He was not talking to friends. He was talking in an official capacity in an official situation. In any case, it's not a matter of closed-door or public. He has to be responsible for what he says. Racism is racism, whether it is in the public sphere or over the dinner table with your family members. So, what action will be taken on this matter?

Of course, we know that Najib was talking about religious extremism at the UN, but, outside that and to be consistent, he should hold the same standard for racial extremism. Especially in his own country.

He said we should "work together to combat and marginalise extremists who have held the world hostage with their bigotry and bias". So why doesn't he apply this to the extremists who hold Malaysia hostage with their bigotry and bias? Why does he let an NGO like Perkasa oppose what needs to be done for his New Economic Model and Economic Transformation Programme? Why does he accommodate their objections even when he knows that they stand in the way of a brighter Malaysian future?

At the UN, he said the world had "allowed the ugly voices of the periphery to drown out the many voices of reason and common sense". Isn't that what is happening in Malaysia as well?

Almost every day, we hear "the ugly voices" of Perkasa denouncing this person or that person for saying something it dislikes, including people like MCA President Chua Soi Lek. Every now and then, Perkasa would run to the police station and make a report against someone for making a seditious statement. And the odd thing is, the police would usually take follow-up action and call that person in for interrogation.

But when Perkasa says and does anything that could be deemed seditious, no action is taken against it. A week or so ago, some Perkasa members protested outside the venue where the Chinese rapper Namewee launched his debut album, and burned posters of him. They challenged him to come out and meet with them. They said they just wanted to talk.

If all they wanted was to talk, why did they burn those posters? And why did they call themselves "*hulubalang Melayu*" (Malay warriors) and "*panglima perang*" (commanders of war)? And why did they vow afterwards to hound Namewee wherever he went?

This was obviously a racially motivated act calling for "war". If it wasn't a threat to public peace, what is? But the police did nothing about it.

Well, so much for Najib's call at the UN to "reclaim the centre and the moral high ground that has been usurped from us". When he comes home, he'll have to get down to the ground and reassess his moral position. Or he might find his own position usurped by forces going out of control.

'ANTI-NATIONAL': RIGHT WORD, WRONG COALITION

Malaysiakini, December 8, 2010

What Najib Razak said at the opening of the Barisan Nasional convention on December 5 reflects a mind of the lowest common denominator. It is not the kind of mind one expects of a prime minister.

He stooped really low in taking swipes at the two-family dominance of the DAP (Kit Siang's and Karpal's) and "nepotism" in PKR, forgetting that he, too, is the son of a former prime minister, and that Mahathir Mohamad also has a son who is a deputy minister with ambitions of becoming bigger.

Instead of taking on the Opposition on ideological grounds and maintaining prime ministerial decorum and dignity, he resorted to name-calling. He called Pakatan Rakyat (PR) "anti-national" and "very dangerous". He said their activities were "despicable". Some media organisations reported it as "evil".

These are cheap words that anyone can utter. If by "anti-national" and "despicable" he means that PR has been "bad-mouthing" Malaysia abroad, as he says it has, it would not have been about the country but the government, which deserves to be bad-mouthed anyway. And the Government deserves that for all the ills it has committed over the last three or four decades, and for leading Malaysia to the economic, social and moral morass it is in today.

Let us get one thing clear once and for all, for the sake of all Malaysians — the country and the government are separate entities. Governments come and go, the country is eternal (unless it is destroyed or fragmented).

was the same public reaction when Ling Liong Sik was charged a few months before over the Port Klang Free Zone (PKFZ) scandal.

Toyo had been in the news for a long time over his multi-million-ringgit home. The MACC had been urged again and again to investigate him, but it is only now that the moment has become opportune to haul in the man that the people love to hate. Yet even so, the people are not convinced. After what they've seen of other somewhat similar cases, how could they not be cynical about it? Let's see if the verdict will come before the next general election. Even though the maximum Toyo can get is only two years' jail and a fine.

But election ploy aside, the fact that a prominent Umno man is being charged with corruption speaks ill for the party, especially in these times when the cost of living is rising as prices of essential goods go up and up.

Last month, there was an increase in the price of petrol which Domestic Trade, Cooperatives and Consumerism Minister Ismail Sabri Yaakob said would probably be the last for the year. But only a few days ago, it was raised again. And the story was buried on page 16 of *The Star* with, to add insult to injury, a positive heading!

The people should feel incensed that they are paying more for their daily needs while there are politicians in the ruling coalition, including one who was once a *menteri besar*, alleged to be corrupt. Not to mention the money spent on wasteful projects and on making the Government look good, like the RM36 million spent on McKinsey & Co. And the hiring of the undeserving Samy Vellu as an envoy with ministerial status.

It doesn't add up. Why are we paying to upkeep BN's image and line the pockets of its leaders? Are they the nationalists who uphold the people's interests?

So, the next time Najib wants to use a word like "anti-national", he might want to be sure he knows its true meaning and apply it to the right people. Otherwise, he might appear like a two-bit spinmeister. And that's not becoming for a prime minister — especially one who's not been duly elected.

IT'S A SMALL CUP AFTER ALL

MalaysianDigest.com, January 2, 2011

The Prime Minister declared a public holiday. Just because the national football team won the AFF Suzuki Cup, involving ASEAN nations.

The Youth and Sports Minister said financial incentives would be given to the members of the team.

The MIC president asked for a datukship to be given to K. Rajagopal, the coach.

The mainstream media went to town with its coverage of Malaysia's victory over Indonesia in the final, with newspapers devoting pages to the news, including their front page, hailing the players as "heroes".

Muzium Negara is going to hold an exhibition showcasing the team's success in winning the Cup.

Please! We are going overboard!

Our football team did well and deserves to be congratulated. We should commend everyone who played a part in its victory and tell them they did a good job, and wish them future successes.

They should be praised for their courage in the second leg of the final for facing a hostile Indonesian crowd in Jakarta and losing by only 1–2.

And then we should move on.

What is the real agenda in declaring a public holiday? We didn't win the World Cup; we merely won a tournament featuring the nations of ASEAN, a small regional grouping in the context of the big world out there.

Only eight teams participated in the AFF Suzuki Cup 2010 — the highest-ranked among them according to FIFA (International Federation of Association Football) was Thailand, at the 121st spot. Another participant, Laos, was the lowest among them, at number 167. Out of 203 footballing nations.

Malaysia itself is ranked number 144.

So what's the big deal in winning the Cup to warrant the declaration of a public holiday? If Malaysia had won the Asian Cup, that might have been something more to crow about. Although that still would not warrant a public holiday.

We sound like a desperate footballing nation clutching on to a small trophy and declaring it a blue ribbon. To outsiders looking in, we must appear a laughing stock.

Declaring a public holiday for a low-level achievement is sending out the wrong message and inculcating the wrong values.

It's saying we don't have to bother about standards, so we can celebrate mediocrity. The values cultivated from this are obviously negative: we don't have to do really well in order to be rewarded handsomely. Hasn't this been our national malady in the last few decades?

It's also important to consider that one swallow does not make a summer. Our team's victory this time in a competition involving Asia's football minnows is not an automatic sign that bigger achievements are in the offing. As it is, we didn't even qualify for the Asian Cup 2011.

By all means, we should give due encouragement to the team and build on their Suzuki Cup success, but big-scale celebrations are certainly premature. The rewards for now should be modest and proportionate to the achievement.

Giving a datukship to the coach would cheapen the value of such titles, if they are not already questionable in some cases. Let Rajagopal take Malaysia to the second round of the World Cup finals, then talk about giving him a title. That would be some achievement; although even to qualify for it is, at this point, unimaginable.

So why do we want to swell the heads of our footballers? Hasn't it been the Malaysian hubris to laud sportspeople as heroes before their time has come? And then when they perform the next time on a bigger stage and falter, would it really be their fault if they failed to live up to our expectations?

So, instead of giving substantial financial incentives to the players, why not use the money to provide better training facilities?

Was Prime Minister Najib Razak acting responsibly in declaring a public holiday? Football is big in Malaysia, and especially among the youths, and he knows that. From the way it looked, he exploited the victory to score points and raise his popularity ratings, which could translate into votes for his party at the next general election.

But this time around, he took a cheap shot. And came out looking like an opportunist. Whichever Blue Ocean strategy he employed, it isn't one that comes with moral considerations.

Leadership means imparting what's right, not attempting to be populist. In fact, politics in this country has become so dirty that our leadership has lost sight of what it means to impart the right values. The most obvious example of dirty play is BN's takeover of Perak from Pakatan Rakyat.

If that's leadership by example, it's no wonder that the people have also been influenced to play dirty. That's what was manifested during the first leg of the Suzuki Cup final played in Kuala Lumpur — when Malaysian football fans flashed laser lights on the faces of the Indonesian players to distract them from playing properly. That was, to say the least, a despicable act. From whom did our football fans learn to play so dirty?

Addressing this moral issue is more important than winning tournaments. And it is this that Malaysian leaders should be doing rather than placing priority on the winning. They should be asking whether the Malaysian value system has deteriorated — and if so, why. They should be asking how it can be salvaged, and improved. And whether we have become so corrupt that we don't know what's right and wrong any more.

Coincidentally, as the Cup final was going on, news broke of a Wikileaks disclosure about a government cover-up of a rape allegedly committed by a senior Malaysian Cabinet minister on his Indonesian maid three years ago. Could all this football hype be intended to distract Malaysians from that issue?

Conspiracy theorists believe it could be. If they are right, it would confirm how morally low we have sunk.

SPAMMED BY THE PRIME MINISTER!

MalaysianDigest.com, February 1, 2011

No less than the Prime Minister has just spammed me! In an e-mail wishing me Happy Chinese New Year.

I'm not pleased. In fact, when I got the e-mail, I freaked out. How did he get my address?

I take strong umbrage against whoever gave it to him. It is an invasion of my privacy.

Najib Razak (or rather, his assistants) reportedly sent out that e-mail to 1.5 million people. *The Star* reported that many were happy to get it — in a report quoting only three people. And two of them had Muslim-sounding names! From the tweets I've seen, it seems many Muslims have been getting the e-mail too. Some tweeters considered the greeting "insincere", some suggested reporting the matter to Cyber 999 and even the police.

Many questioned how Najib or his assistants got their e-mail addresses. There's a theory going round that it came from the database of a media conglomerate. If this is true, the practice is, of course, not right. It contravenes the cyberworld law of data privacy. Whoever gave the data to him showed that they did not respect that privacy.

My wife got a CNY greeting from Najib too — via an SMS. Did her telco give her number to Najib and Co? Is that a proper thing to do? And, by the way, who is paying for the SMSes? Najib or the *rakyat*?

Only last week, it was revealed that there is now a new division in the Prime Minister's Department called FLOM — for First Lady of Malaysia — manned by a staff of six. And it looks after the operational needs of Najib's wife, Rosmah Mansor.

Never in our history has there ever been such a division. It reeks of nepotism and other things besides. Why should the PM's wife have a division all to herself? Are there institutionalised provisions for such a thing? Who is paying for the upkeep of this division?

We need to snap out of our distracted state and pressure Najib to justify the setting-up of FLOM. Let's see how his public relations advisers will respond to that. For CNY, they came up with spam; for FLOM, will they come up with flam?

Just for fun, here are two *Urban Dictionary* definitions of 'flom': (1) To untie someone's shoe lace while they aren't looking, so they get pissed off and have to retie it (e.g. "Hey, stop it! This is the fifth time you've flommed me!"); (2) To do something sexual to someone of the opposite sex.

Either way you look at it, it sounds naughty!

Afterword: *Soon after the existence of the FLOM division was discovered and made public by some media, the information regarding it disappeared from the website of the Prime Minister's Department.*

CAN UMNO CHANGE OR COWS FLY?

Penang Monthly, January 2012

Umno is beyond redemption. At its general assembly in December, the message it sent out was suspicion of others and hatred for them, and a desperate desire to win the next general election.

Its president, Najib Razak, once again proved what many of us have long suspected — that he is a dissembler. He exposed the ultimate lie behind his 1Malaysia slogan by saying things that would divide the races rather than bring them together. He set the trend for delegates at the assembly to harp on the threats to Umno from other races. It was disgraceful coming from the prime minister of the country. It was supremely irresponsible.

Worse, two days after the assembly ended, he appealed to the right-wing NGO Pertubuhan Kebajikan dan Dakwah Islamiah Malaysia (Pekida) for support. This has to be the final nail in the 1Malaysia coffin.

To cap it all, Umno showed its partiality to cronyism by defending Wanita leader Shahrizat Abdul Jalil over the scandal surrounding her family's business, the National Feedlot Corporation. One or two colleagues called for her to step down, but the overwhelming majority stood by her and castigated the Opposition for exposing the scandal.

This begs the question: Can Umno change? As the major party in the Barisan Nasional (BN) government, can it truly stand up for other races as well, and work for their well-being? Can it stay clear of corrupt practices? Can it stop dishing out favours and projects to party leaders and their cronies? Can it save Malaysia from financial meltdown or will it rather bleed our coffers dry?

The online news website *The Malaysian Insider* sums it up eloquently: "Umno looks set to win the polls in the next general election but yet looks woefully ill-equipped to lead a multi-racial country. ... One expects delegates to articulate a vision to continue its previous success but that did not happen. Instead, delegates harped on age-old themes of having their culture and faith eroded by political foes taking over the country. That they are the only guarantee of faith and culture. What about the economy? What about the reforms? What about Malaysia? ... Everything is centred around Umno. ... But they didn't articulate the vision for continued success. ... Instead, everyone is at fault except those in Umno."

And yet Najib could tell Pekida: "If we miscalculate and choose the wrong side, our country could very much end up like Greece." Surely, he must mean that the wrong side would be BN. The way it has been going — awarding projects to cronies who have no track record; continuing to allow overpriced purchases by government departments, despite what the Auditor-General uncovers year after year; giving out money like there's no tomorrow in order to win votes, such as the substantial pay rise for civil servants — BN is more likely to lead us down that way.

The civil service is bloated, with 1.4 million employees, but Najib criticised Pakatan Rakyat (PR) for suggesting it should be trimmed. According to his top public service official, 1.4 million is "the right size". How this is so puzzles me. Japan has a population of 127 million and its civil servants number just over a million. We have a population of 28 million and our civil service is as large as Japan's. It seems to me that trimming down the civil service is more likely to save us from going Greek.

And so I think we should not take any more risks with Umno. Especially now that we have an alternative. PR has shown itself capable of running the four states under it and earned positive ratings from the Auditor-General and a few others. It's time to see whether they can bring reform to the country.

Najib, of course, insists that PR will lead us to our doom, but what are his words worth anyhow?

At the Umno general assembly, he presented a grossly untruthful picture of the DAP to strike fear into the hearts of the Malays. He accused the party of being anti-Malay, anti-Islam and anti-royalty.

But after PAS won Terengganu in the 1999 general election, who stopped the state that is 90 per cent populated by Malays from getting its oil royalties and substituted it with the lesser Wang Ehsan? Was it the DAP?

Who created a constitutional crisis in 1983 and curtailed the powers of the Malay royalty? Was it the DAP?

In 2008, who protested against the Terengganu sultan for not accepting Idris Jusoh as the *menteri besar*, and insulted His Highness with the word "*natang*" (animal)? Was it the DAP?

Who gave away citizenships overnight to immigrants, legal and illegal, in Sabah to ensure they kept Umno there in power? Was it the DAP?

So where is the truth in Najib's warning that if BN did not continue to be the government, the Malays would be under threat? Who has proven to be the real threat?

But still, he called on Pekida "to defend the current government" — to guarantee the special position of the Malays, the dignity of Islam, the preservation of the Malay royalty. He thumped his chest and yelled, "We are warriors!" and "We will not surrender even an inch!" He led the crowd in cries of "*Hidup Melayu!*"

Someone was moved to comment on Facebook, "Listening to what Najib said, it feels like we're at war."

A knowing friend warns me: "Do you know what Pekida is about? They are like gangsters. They have secret codes, like particular handshakes or the way they hold their cigarettes. They have 2 million members. These are the people we should worry about."

Indeed, when the film *KL Gangster* came out in 2011, Pekida objected to its portrayal of secret codes and use of words like "*abang long*" and "*ayahanda*" that apparently cut too close to reality.

This prompted blogger Ibnu Hasyim to ask, "*Apakah benar kononnya filem itu membuka 'kod rahsia pertubuhan' Pekida? ... Terkejut kita, apakah pertubuhan dakwah itu pun mempunyai ciri-ciri pertubuhan bawah tanah atau gangster? Pekida adalah Gangster Melayu? Perlukah pertubuhan itu disiasat polis? Mana ada dakwah dan kebajikan pakai 'kod rahsia' pertubuhan?*" (Is it true that the film apparently exposed 'secret organisational codes' of Pekida? ... We are shocked, does this missionary organisation have the characteristics of an underworld or gangster organisation? Pekida are Malay Gangsters? Should the police investigate this organisation? Why would missionary and welfare organisations use 'secret codes'?)

Najib's appeal to Pekida and his words at the Umno assembly spell desperation. That's clear to see because Umno has no case left to make for its continued rule. News of its corruption is bursting out. Soon after the general assembly ended, the Singapore *Straits Times* reported that ex-*menteri besar* Abdul Hamid Pawanteh was involved in the Alstom bribery case. He has, however, denied it.

Earlier, questions had been raised about Defence Minister Ahmad Zahid Hamidi allegedly flying to Saudi Arabia for his *haj* in a private jet, and about "ridiculously overpriced" rural development projects in Sabah allegedly linked to senior BN politicians. The worms are crawling out of the can.

Umno cannot defend itself. So it lashes out at enemies. It fabricates untruths about its enemies. Sadly — and sickeningly — Umno resorts to rousing tribal emotions and harping on the issues of race and religion. After 54 years in power, it still plays those explosive cards.

As the blogger Sakmongkol AK47 (at the time of writing, an Umno member himself) puts it: "Umno gets on by making Malays believe that they are being besieged, attacked, assaulted and victimised. That's how Umno can survive. How does it do that? By fabricating lies and manufacturing stories. The Chinese are going to eat you up. The Chinese are going to Christianise you. They are going to wipe out the sultans, ban the use of Bahasa Malaysia, and abolish Jawi and so forth. You feed on people's irrational fear. You want to maintain stupid and mute people. Can you sustain whole people like that, turning people into xenophobes? I say this is a recipe for destroying Malays, not cultivating them to become self-confident people."

Umno has been doing that for decades. It has not evolved. So how can it change? How can such a party still be allowed to rule multi-racial, multi-religious, multi-cultural Malaysia?

If we continue to vote for it at the next general election, what would that make us? Dumb and dumber?

(NOTE: *Sakmongkol AK47, whose real name is Mohd Ariff Sabri Abdul Aziz, has since left Umno and joined the DAP.*)

excerpt

FROM THE PLAY
1984 HERE AND NOW

The institutionalisation of racial discrimination is one of the central themes of the play. It is stated baldly, because in the '80s that was, to me, the only effective way to express it. I only stopped short of naming the races and chose to call them Party members and Proles, both terms derived from George Orwell's novel *1984*, which inspired me to write the play.

Scene 3

(Out in the streets. Night time. WIRAN is going home after the day's work. He appears deep in thought. A couple of women covered from head to toe pass him by. One of them has a pair of spectacles peeking out, with a little bit of forehead shown. WIRAN looks at them for a while. Music starts in the background: 'Somebody's Watching Me' by Rockwell.

WIRAN comes across three Party members crouching stealthily behind a hedge. He stops at a distance to watch. Suddenly, they lurch forward, the man with the torchlight switches it on, and all three drag a courting couple out from the other side of the hedge. The woman is also one of those covered from head to toe except that her shawl has come down, exposing her face. The couple break free and run off. The three men pursue, shouting, "Sinners! Sinners! Catch them!"

WIRAN walks on. He comes across newspaper posters screaming headlines: 'Newsmen detained for threat to peace', 'Students abroad recalled for violating Party policies', 'Party members nabbed for desecrating Prole place of worship', 'Infighting among top leaders of Prole party'. A little distance on, WIRAN sees a Prole mother dragging her young son.)

MOTHER:	You doan play widem, hnarh. I doan like. You play wit our kind.
SON:	I wan, I wan.
MOTHER:	You hear wat I say or I beat you.
SON:	Wy I carn play widem?
MOTHER:	Dey all party member.
SON:	But dey got nice toy.
MOTHER:	I doan care. Dey all Party member. You come back.

(*WIRAN watches them go off. 'Somebody's Watching Me' fades off. Approaching sound of drums and festivity. A short while later, a group of Proles enter, watching a tiger dance being performed. Then a policeman comes by, blowing his whistle. The Proles ignore him at first.*)

POLICEMAN: Stop! Stop!

(*The dance comes to a stop.*)

POLICEMAN: Do you have a permit for doing this?

(*The performers look at each other, then one speaks up.*)

PERFORMER:	No.
POLICEMAN:	You know you can't do this without a permit, don't you?
PERFORMER:	Wy you all wan to make it hard for us? Wy mus take permit one?
POLICEMAN:	Don't argue. Stop this at once and go home.
PERFORMER:	You tink we scared aah?
POLICEMAN:	I'll have you arrested if you don't stop.

(*Reluctantly the group disbands, shouting abuse as they leave.*)

POLICEMAN: These Proles. Sometimes they are too much. They act as if they own this nation. (*Goes off.*)

(*WIRAN walks on. He comes across a group of Proles playing* mahjong. *The setting can suggest that of a coffee shop.*)

PLAYER 1:   Dam bad luck laa. Never get der card I wan. Mus chane place la.

PLAYER 2:   Wy you worry? Nex game, der wind will blow your way laa.

PLAYER 1:   Wind from your backside la, like der Party.

PLAYER 3:   Haiya, doan tok about der party now la.

PLAYER 4:   Ya, bring more bad luck only. I awso cannot game. Look at my card, all split.

PLAYER 2:   Like our Prole party lah. Weak like anyting. Everyting Big Broder say, OK. Like balls shaking in der pants, man. And now, quarrelling some more, der leaders. Wan more power, wan top post. Firs, dey should be more strong to bring our problem to Big Broder. Instead, every time big Prole party meeting, big quarrel. Trow chair some more. No shame la, dese people. Meanwile, our people suffer. Our chiren carn get place in university. Every year, only so many people can go in. Not fair la. Ay, ay, wait, wait! I wan der card. Doan lah play so fas!

PLAYER 3:   Ay, doan tok so much la. Chuck your card. Wafor you tok so much? Wa can you do?

PLAYER 4:   Cannot do anyting lah. Wat to do?

PLAYER 1:   Every day, jus come gamble, pass der time, enough lah.

PLAYER 4:   Ya, man. Wy boder? We can still do a bit of business, can have mistress, can jolly. Aiya, life is short la, wy worry so much, man?

PLAYER 2:   You doan care aah if your son cannot get job in Gahmen office?

PLAYER 4:   Cannot get, find oder job lah. Not say cannot get. You got brain, you got arm, you got leg, cannot die one la. Haisay, beautiful card la. Bes in der world!

HOLY COW! MINISTER DEFENDS PROTESTORS!

Malaysiakini, September 6, 2009

What a farce the cow-head incident is turning out to be. The handling of the case so far demonstrates clearly that all that talk about 1Malaysia is mostly cow pie.

Firstly, the police have been slow to act. They concluded their investigations last Tuesday and handed them over to the Attorney-General. Now we have to wait further for the august A-G to decide whether action will be taken. In this regard, one can't help but be reminded that nothing has yet come out of the V.K. Lingam case, so long after the Royal Commission of Inquiry ruled that there were grounds for the A-G to take action.

Secondly, Home Minister Hishammuddin Hussein goes out of his way to meet with the protestors, the very people who had committed what is apparently a seditious act by bringing a cow's head to their protest and spitting at it and kicking it. All because they didn't want a Hindu temple to be relocated in their area of residence in Shah Alam.

Would Hishammuddin have done the same if it had been Hindus protesting against the relocation of a mosque in their housing estate? Imagine what the reaction of the authorities would have been if that had been the case.

What's worse, after the meeting, he spouted the most diabolical doublespeak and politicospeak when he told reporters that the protestors could not be blamed as "they had no intention at all" to invoke racial sentiments or cause tension. He even said they felt victimised. He defended their illegal protest (they had no permit) by saying they kept the number of protestors to a small number.

Well, Minister, some people have been arrested for protesting in an even smaller number.

As expected, he blamed the Selangor Government, saying it had made "a poor decision" in relocating the temple. And then he made a statement that he should from now on be forever held accountable for: "In this day and age, protests should be accepted in this world, as people want their voices to be heard. If we don't give them room to voice their opinions, they have no choice but to protest."

Well, that's straight from the Home Minister's mouth, folks. Public protests are A-OK. So keep your tear gas, water cannons and whatnot at home, cops.

To cap it all, Hishammuddin said this was not the first time an animal's head had been used in a protest. He revealed that there was a time when a pig's head, wrapped in an Umno flag, was thrown into Umno's headquarters.

This is most disconcerting, especially coming from a minister who is charged with ensuring peace and harmony in the country. What was he trying to imply? Yes, he was exonerating the cow-head protestors, but wasn't he also sneakily trying to blame another community by bringing up the pig's head? If so, isn't that mischievous? And, surely, he must be aware that two wrongs don't make a right. So why bring up the earlier wrong to justify the cow-head one?

The day after this infamous press conference, Hishammuddin does a virtual about-turn and announces that the cow-head protestors should now be hauled to court because what they did could not be tolerated. He says he never justified their action in the first place. Is he suffering from amnesia? Has boss Najib ticked him off for the things he said the day before?

As usual, he puts the blame on others and says it was bloggers who had made it seem as if he was condoning the cow-head protest. What a genius we have for a minister! Did he learn this from the master, Mahathir Mohamad?

To exacerbate the situation and make the ruling party look desperate, the Malaysian Communications and Multimedia Commission (MCMC) comes out and instructs *Malaysiakini* to remove two videos from its archives — one of the cow-head protest itself and the other of Hishammuddin's shameful press conference.

There is no cause for that. News is news, and what has been recorded is now part of our history. It is insensible of the MCMC to ask that they be removed, as if to erase history like Communist Russia did in the 1940s.

And why remove the Hishammuddin video? I can only fathom one reason for it — to save him from embarrassment. If that is so, the MCMC is not doing him a favour. He has to grow up and be a man. He has to admit his mistake for saying what is recorded in that video. This is his rite of passage. Let him go through it. If he can't be man enough, how can he be considered for future prime ministership? (That is, if Malaysians would allow it to happen.)

All this clearly shows that there are still 2Malaysias, and that in word and deed, our national leaders affirm that.

This can't be good for Prime Minister Najib Razak who seems to be trying to win non-Malay hearts and minds with his 1Malaysia slogan (I say slogan because that's just what it is so far — full of words and little action). The cow-head incident would have set his efforts back substantially. The Bagan Pinang by-election is coming up and there are 20 per cent of Indian voters for that State seat. How will they vote?

Judging by what has been happening the past few months, Barisan Nasional has not been giving a good account of itself. In fact, it has mostly been shooting itself in the foot. And this without the help of Pakatan Rakyat whatsoever.

Just look at the kind of candidate they fielded for the Permatang Pasir by-election. And the current work-in-progress of Najib saying one thing while his deputy says the opposite.

As Najib goes about promoting 1Malaysia, Muhyiddin Yassin has been playing to the Malay gallery. He called Opposition leader Anwar Ibrahim a traitor to the Malay race; defended a provocative article in the Malay press calling on the Malays to stop being cowards and rise up; and on the same day that the 1Malaysia logo was publicly unveiled, he asserted that Umno would fight to the last drop of blood to protect Malay rights.

Meanwhile, race-baiting goes on almost daily in the Malay mainstream media, concerted in its aim to threaten, frighten and divide. That these media organisations are owned and controlled by Najib's own party underscores the conundrum. The messages sent out by these media organisations and the messages he himself is sending out are totally at odds with each other. Whom are we to listen to? Whom are we to trust?

Is there a game plan behind it all? Are we, the *rakyat*, mere pawns in the game? When the game is over, will we be played out?

I certainly hope not.

WHAT WILL THEY DO ABOUT RACISM NOW?

Free Malaysia Today, August 19, 2010

Let's wait and see what action will be taken against Siti Inshah Mansor, the principal of Sekolah Menengah Kebangsaan Tunku Abdul Rahman Putra, Kulai, for the racist remarks she allegedly made at the Merdeka celebrations in her school.

The police will be concluding their investigations soon, under Section 504 of the Penal Code. If they have a case, Siti Inshah could be charged with provocation, which carries a maximum imprisonment of two years, a fine or both.

Meanwhile, DAP supremo Lim Kit Siang has called for her to be sacked. MCA president Chua Soi Lek calls for her to be transferred to a desk job and given counselling. How generous of Chua.

If she did what she is said to have done, she should instead be drawn and quartered, like in the good old days. Or have her head put in a cangue — you know, like in the Chinese movies, where the head and hands are locked up within a square wooden contraption. Or she should be given the Japanese treatment — force-fed water while someone jumps on her bloated tummy, or hung from a tree by her thumbs, and displayed publicly for all to see that this is what happens to racists.

Of course, I'm being facetious, but this must surely be the fantasy of anyone who feels disgusted by any racist act. All the more so if it is committed by someone who is a principal of a school, who should be spreading the message of racial unity instead of — God forbid! — racial hatred.

Siti Inshah is alleged to have said that Chinese students are not needed in the school and can go back to China or Sekolah Foon Yew (a private Chinese school in Johor), and that the prayer strings Indian students wear on their neck and wrist make them look like dogs, and only dogs would be tied this way.

If the allegation is true, what could have possessed her to make her say such things? That is something that must be ascertained. Even if she had been provoked for some reason or other, it is still not her place to react this way to the students. She has a huge responsibility as a school principal to restrain her racist impulses.

Given the seriousness of the situation, if the allegation is true, how then can she be allowed to get away with it? If she were to be exonerated, imagine the damage she could further cause given her influential position. If it is true that she behaved like a racist, her name should instead be remembered in the Hall of Shame.

So far, however, among the Barisan Nasional parties, only the MCA and the MIC have criticised the action. Has any Umno leader come out to say anything against it? And if so, why not?

Siti Inshah is also alleged to have called her non-Malay students *penumpang* (passengers or tenants) in this country. First, we had Umno politician Ahmad Ismail calling non-Malays *pendatang*, now there's *penumpang*. What will they think up next?

These racial slurs are getting out of hand. And that's worrisome. It's symptomatic of the times. We are getting more divided along racial lines than ever before.

That's what you get when you allow the mainstream newspapers to go to town scaring the Malays into believing that the non-Malays are a threat and will soon take over the country. When someone like Zaini Hassan can write irresponsibly and mischievously in *Utusan Malaysia* about a "large-scale war" breaking out that will be bigger than that of May 13, about an alternative constitution being written that will abolish the special position of the Malays and Islam. What rubbish!

That's what you get when you allow newspapers and individuals to go around telling non-Malays they must be submissive, grateful and not speak up for their rights, or go home — to China or India.

That's what you get when you allow organisations like Persatuan Pribumi Perkasa Malaysia (Perkasa) to go on their high horse and slam every reasoned argument made against their credo. So now, for every little thing they don't like, they run to the police station to make a report.

That's what you get when you give them so much face, to the extent of granting them a publishing permit virtually overnight; when you cut them so much slack by saying nothing when they challenge government policies that seek to address the nation's fall from economic competitiveness.

And then, no less than the Deputy Prime Minister invokes the ghost of May 13, pulling the perennial Umno stunt, to tick off Chua Soi Lek for asking for more non-Malay participation in the economy.

Not only is Muhyiddin Yassin behind the times in that regard, he actually warns that this could anger the Malays and it could produce a spark similar to that which ignited May 13. Who is stoking the racial fire here? If a personage like the DPM says it will make the Malays angry, some people might be bound to take that seriously and really feel angered. If the DPM mentions May 13, that might put ideas in some fanatics' heads.

Why must Muhyiddin say something potentially flammable like this? As the nation's No. 2 leader, he should instead avoid bringing up such a thing.

But then, that's what constitutes the central problem of this country. Politicians will make capital of anything without thinking of its consequences. They are short-term players looking for short-term gains. And this short-term playing has been extended for decades in the sick politicisation of race.

Do we have to keep reminding them of the dangers of this game and still see nothing done about it even when the cows have come home? By then, it will be too late. The wound caused by racial discord might have become so infected that it can no longer heal.

The treatment has to start now. And if the people who are in charge of administering it are not up to it, if instead they are exposing the wound to even more bacteria, then we should be looking for an alternative cure.

to give in to the Japanese while other Malayans took the easy option of collaborating with the enemy? And although there were valiant Malays and Indians in the MCP, who were most of its members if not Chinese?

Of course, the fact that the MCP provided patriotic resistance against the Japanese is not known by many Malaysians. It has been expunged from our history books.

The current History syllabus at SPM level is clearly written by the victors, i.e. BN, mostly Umno. Just look at the Malaysian section of the textbook and you will see how the subjective selection of what goes into it serves to manipulate the truth.

Now that it has been decreed that History is to be a must-pass subject at SPM, you can bet the new syllabus will be constructed to further serve the victors' cause. Malaysians would be naïve to believe that "history is history and we cannot concoct something that is not history", as said by Deputy Prime Minister Muhyiddin Yassin. While they may not concoct, they can nonetheless construct.

History is a construct. It is not objective; it can be manipulated. How it is told depends on who is writing it. If Muhyiddin does not know that — which is unlikely — we, at the least, should be aware.

MCA President Chua Soi Lek could have been more explicit and to-the-point when he responded to Ahmad Zahid's statement.

He could have mentioned Chin Peng and the MCP.

He could have mentioned the sacrifices of Yap Ah Loy and his band of 87 miners who were the first to set up a mining camp at the confluence of the Klang and Gombak rivers, 17 of whom died within the first month from malaria. That became the base from which Kuala Lumpur grew.

He could have mentioned the late Tan Chee Khoon who worked tirelessly to promote non-communal politics in Malaysia, and who fought against attempts to pervert the Constitution.

It is not enough for Chua to make general statements saying that the Chinese remained loyal to the country during the Japanese Occupation and the Indonesian confrontation, to illustrate the patriotism of the Chinese. He needs to give concrete examples.

His party has expressed concern about what the content of the new SPM History syllabus will be. Will the MCA do all it can to ensure that the new construct will include truths from various sides? Will it do all it can to ensure that the new syllabus reflects the patriotism of Malaysians regardless of race?

M. Kulasegaran, the MP for Ipoh Barat, made an important and pertinent point when he reminded Malaysians that non-Malays had headed the armed forces before, citing the excellent example of Rear-Admiral K. Thanabalasingam, who was appointed the first Malaysian chief of the Royal Malaysian Navy in 1967.

How many Malaysians know that? Would that be reflected in the new History syllabus?

There was a time when an Indian could be the chief of the country's navy. When will that ever happen again? Meanwhile, is there any wonder that non-Malays are not keen to join the armed forces?

Ahmad Zahid, why don't you tell us the truth?

UMNO'S RACIAL RA-RA-RA!

Malaysiakini, October 27, 2010

Every time an Umno general assembly rolls into town, the mainstream newspapers will be filled to overflowing with coverage of the event. Pages and pages will be devoted to the speeches and debates as well as photographs of the gathering.

But if you were to dig up your old newspapers of up to at least the past two or three decades to refer to the reports on the Umno general assemblies over that period, you'd find that the basic issues and the exhortations of the Umno leaders are virtually the same every time.

At each assembly, the things that are said appear to be variations on the same themes — the Malays need to work harder and improve themselves; they need to be on guard against external threats; their rights will never be taken away from them; Umno will forever protect the Malays; at the same time, the Malays must understand that they live in a multi-racial society so Umno will also see to the interests of the other races ...

There is always a heavy emphasis on the issue of race, and of the Malays in relation to the other races in Malaysia. Somehow, even though it is the dominant party in government, Umno can't seem to get past that and focus instead on national issues that affect the entire population or discuss intelligently the issues of the day from a broader perspective.

Its president would utter some platitude about Umno having to show leadership and be sensitive to the other races, and then stridently champion the Malay Agenda. As the president has also always been the country's prime minister, you'd have to look at the assembly as theatre, the president as an actor, to suppress any suspicion of schizophrenia. Imagine this happening in Singapore, with the ruling party there championing Chinese supremacy. Or the ruling party in Australia championing the whites. Not so easy, is it?

The Hokkiens might say of the 2010 Umno General Assembly proceedings that it was all *"kong lai, kong khee, kong siang mi knia"*. (transliterated: Talk come, talk go, talk same things.) This is something Umno's permanent chairman, Badrudin Amiruldin, can probably relate to; after all, when he told MCA President Chua Soi Lek, "Please don't disturb the 30 per cent which belongs to the Malays", he did so in Hokkien.

More than that, his remark aptly summed up the theme and tenor of the assembly — the party's fixation on the 30 per cent. It didn't matter to all present that Badrudin should instead have said that the 30 per cent belongs to the Bumiputeras. The significant difference was significantly overlooked, but hey! when they're all imbued by the same party spirit, who cares about the details?

Going by the quality of this year's debates and the proposals of some delegates, Umno has not changed a bit. If a party member had been transported from the 1980s into the 2010 assembly, he would have felt quite at home.

Mohd Shafie Apdal said some sensible things about the need to be inclusive and not be jealous of the success of others. So did Khairy Jamaluddin when he expressed the need to appreciate the feelings of the other races for whom Malaysia is also their home and their country. "We often hear grouses about the civil service being dominated by Malays," he said. "Are we to believe that there are only a few non-Malays who are qualified to hold senior civil service positions?"

Many at the assembly, however, took the non-inclusive stance and in so doing provided some entertainment, albeit unwittingly. Salleh Said Keruak said there should not be open tenders for government projects. Instead, contracts should be given to Umno leaders' followers.

And this must be ensured by the setting-up of a system. Talk about institutionalising cronyism!

Ayub Jamil wanted affirmative action included in all the Economic Transformation Programme (ETP) initiatives announced by the Government. If that were done, how would the private sector be attracted to invest in them? What about foreign investors? Wouldn't they prefer countries that don't impose such a condition?

Hasnor Sidang Husin actually blamed the non-Malays for the failure of the Malays to achieve the 30 per cent — by not providing the Malays help in this regard. But was that ever part of the deal? Hey! Since it's not, why don't we write a new "social contract" and put that clause in?

Reezal Merican Naina Merican called for Barisan Nasional (BN) component parties to show Umno fairness and justice. Now, that was sumptuous. Fairness and justice from these powerless partners who can't say anything that Umno doesn't like without being told to shut up? How have they been unfair and unjust to Umno? Oh, is it about Chua Soi Lek questioning the 30 per cent? It's always about the 30 per cent, isn't it? That's not just what the Umno General Assembly revolved around; it seems the whole world does, too. Questioning the 30 per cent is unfair and unjust. Cut it out!

Jalaluddin Alias blamed Umno's partners in BN for the coalition's poor showing in the 2008 general election. To him, Umno was above blame because it managed to win 68 per cent of its seats. It was evidently immaterial to him that in 2008, Umno lost 30 of the parliamentary seats it had held before that. Those losses must have been the fault of the component parties as well.

For the next general election, he urged the Umno leadership to take away the seats lost by its coalition partners in 2008 and give them instead to Umno candidates. This, he said, would ensure a BN victory. Hallelujah! Yes, indeed! Yet even as he showed no quarter for the component parties, he acknowledged that "if MCA doesn't support us, we cannot win". So, let's get this right — take away their seats and still ask for their support? What do you call someone who comes from Klinggong and who exhibits a twisted logic?

Numerous other delegates defended the Government's recently announced projects. They seemed to speak through more than one orifice. Among these was Razali Ibrahim who said mega-projects like the proposed 100-storey Warisan Merdeka tower would help Malaysia become a high-income nation because they would attract funding from the private sector and thereby help the Government save money, which it could then use to solve the people's problems. Brilliant! And would he be the one who will guarantee the participation of the private sector? And also see that the money saved is channelled towards the needy?

Let's save the best for last. This year, Umno President Najib Razak came out strongly to defend the rights of the Malays. He assured them that their rights were enshrined in the Federal Constitution, and these could not be easily taken away from them because any amendment to the related article would have to get the consent of the Rulers. He said the chapter on the rights issue was now closed and there should be no more questioning of it.

To be sure, there is absolutely no mention of "rights" in the Federal Constitution. So it was another significant difference that was significantly overlooked, but hey, when the actor is in the mood for a theatre performance, who cares about the details?

All this is really old hat. The surprising element is that what Najib said about defending Malay rights totally contradicts his 1Malaysia concept and the inclusiveness it advocates. Hey! But it's theatre, and he's performing to a Malay audience. Why not, eh? Why is there a need to be consistent, anyway? Especially when you are the leader of the most powerful party in the country?

And while you're at it, why not use strong graphic language to rally party members to maintain control of the government after the next general election, no matter what: "Even if our bodies are crushed and our lives lost, brothers and sisters, whatever happens, we must defend Putrajaya"?

to protest the issue would be deemed illegal and action would be taken against the perpetrators. He missed that opportunity and thus, he and Najib appeared wishy-washy, even sporting double standards. Now their infirmity could come back to haunt them.

The arsonists have also presented Najib a problem. The bombings could so incense the Christians of Sabah and Sarawak that come the next general election, they could withdraw their support for BN, something that is now evidently crucial if BN is to stay in power. The bombings would also have further alienated the non-Malays whom Najib has been trying to woo back with his 1Malaysia peddling. How should Najib proceed now?

Ironically, something positive seems to have emerged from the Allah issue, the bombings and the protests.

Although the raising of such a sensitive religious issue could have led to ethnic clashes, it did not happen, further reinforcing the post-March 8 belief that the May 13 bogey has effectively been exorcised.

Those at the mosque protests advocating violent action, like the individual in Shah Alam who yelled at the crowd to "*bakar gereja*" (burn the churches), reportedly met with silence. This individual also threatened that "appropriate action" would be taken if the Court of Appeals does not decide in favour of Islam. One wonders why he hasn't been arrested for sedition.

It certainly helped that sensible Muslims did not agree with the protestors and said so publicly. Although a Facebook group formed to oppose the use of the word "Allah" by non-Muslims has drawn almost 200,000 members, the relatively thin turnout at the mosque protests indicates that Malaysians will not simply take up any cause irrationally.

In fact, most reassuring for our multi-ethnic, multi-religious polity was the emergence of Muslim individuals and groups to condemn the bombings. And the initiative of one Dr Mohamed Rafick Khan bin Abdul Rahman to collect donations to rebuild the bombed premises gives a sense of hope amidst the tumult.

The Christians have not missed the opportunity to come out smelling like roses either, with the leaders of the damaged Metro Tabernacle Church saying they forgive the arsonists for what they have done. Heartfelt though that may be, it's still good public relations.

The church's pastor summed it up aptly when he said: "It is a very sad day for Malaysia but a great day to know that most Malaysians do not think like (the arsonists)." He would have been referring to people like Marina Mahathir, who has made one of the most sensible comments on the whole episode — that Muslims have to be strong in their own faith, so that they can rise above a mere issue like the use of a word.

In the aftermath of the bombings, we have, it seems, arrived at some kind of threshold. The sensible people of Malaysia may yet be the ones to lead us forward. At the very least, their numbers can only increase. Now we need to open the door and cross the threshold towards better understanding among the different faiths. It's a great step to take. We should be positive and take it.

THE CHRISTIANS WIN,
BUT FOR HOW LONG?

MalaysianDigest.com, April 4, 2011

In their stand-off against the Government over the Bible issue, the Christians have won. Especially those in Sabah and Sarawak. Not only will the Bible in any language, including Bahasa Malaysia, be allowed to be imported; it can now be printed locally and in the indigenous languages of the Sabah and Sarawak natives. This shows that when you stick to your guns, you'll get what is rightfully yours. In this case, the right to practise your religion freely, as is guaranteed by the Federal Constitution.

The Christians have to be admired for standing up and not giving in. But lest they think they had God, Najib Razak and Idris Jala on their side, they might do well to realise that what decided the issue in their favour and even beyond their wildest expectations was obviously the upcoming Sarawak state elections.

This is a politically expedient decision through and through. Otherwise, it would not have been made at such super speed. Prime Minister Najib desperately wants the Christian vote in order for his coalition to win big in Sarawak. The outcome of the state elections there could be a harbinger of the next general election. He needs a morale booster. He cannot afford a break in Barisan Nasional's momentum after its recent spate of by-election victories. He wants to keep up the public perception — no doubt as advised by his well-paid public relations consultants — that Malaysian support for BN is returning. He also wants to ensure that Sarawak remains a safe deposit for BN. And Sabah, too, where the Christian populace, like that in Sarawak, is substantial.

The Christian uproar over the Bible issue must have scared him. The huge turnout at the Kuching prayer rally last week — to express Christian unhappiness with the Government and to send out a call for religious freedom — was unprecedented.

Given the dire situation, Najib must have realised that it would not have been enough to just agree to release the 30,000-plus copies of the Bible impounded by the Government, so he added a sweetener — the Bible can now be printed in Malay and indigenous languages locally. It took many people by surprise.

This means that the word "Allah" — which appears in the impounded Bible copies and has been a bone of contention between the Home Ministry and Christian publications — can now be used by Christians without restriction. The one thing that can crush it is if the Court of Appeal overturns the decision made by the High Court in December 2009 that granted Christians the right to use "Allah".

However, no date has been fixed yet for the Court of Appeal to hear the appeal, even though it was filed by the Home Ministry more than a year ago, in January 2010. Why, indeed, is this so? What is it waiting for? Is the Government holding on to the case as if it were a trump card it would unleash only when the time was right, for its own political purpose?

And since the case is pending appeal, the question needs to be asked: What will happen to the Bibles in Malay and indigenous languages if the Court of Appeal should eventually overturn the High Court decision and declare that Christians cannot use the word "Allah" after all?

As we know, this saga concerning the use of "Allah" and the prohibition of the AlKitab, the Malay name for the Bible, is not recent. It has been unfolding since 1981, when the AlKitab was banned under the Internal Security (Prohibition of Publications) Order. Is there any assurance that it will not start afresh when the Sarawak state elections and the next general election are over?

This is where Malaysians can derive a moral from the whole saga: That it is hazardous to give the Government too much power through a strong mandate. It is always safer to keep the Government on the back foot and under pressure so that it will listen to the people. Once they have too much power, they are bound to get arrogant and ride roughshod over everyone.

The people of Sarawak might want to consider this important point and vote accordingly.

As for the Christians in Peninsular Malaysia, they might well wonder why the new ruling discriminates against them. While there are no conditions imposed on the Sabahans and Sarawakians over the importation and local printing of the Bible in all languages, why must there be one for Peninsular Malaysia publications, which have to carry the words "Christian Publication" and the cross sign on the front covers?

Is this 1Malaysia? How can it be when it transgresses the principle of inclusiveness that is at the core of Najib's concept?

The reason given for these double standards is that the Government has to consider the interest of the larger Muslim community in Peninsular Malaysia, but it only serves to expose the central flaw of the 1Malaysia concept and the questionable sincerity of its architect. It shows that 1Malaysia is half-hearted, and it lacks the will and the courage to overcome the status quo of divisive practices and prejudices. It is to be applied only when it is politically safe and convenient to be applied. Having a different standard for Peninsular Malaysia over the Bible issue shows even more clearly that the Government's new decision is merely to win the votes of the Sarawak Christians.

The way forward now is to test the Government's sincerity. It has come out to pledge that it wishes "to work with the Christian groups and all the different religious groups in order to address inter-religious issues and work towards the fulfilment of all religious aspirations in accordance with the Constitution, taking into account the other relevant laws of the country". That's according to Idris Jala, the Minister in the Prime Minister's Office who has had to handle the AlKitab issue by dint of his being a Christian even though the Home Minister should be the one doing the dirty job. (Poor man! There were occasions during the stand-off when he was viewed by his fellow Christians as a Judas Iscariot.)

To see if that pledge is true, the Christian groups should next press for easier Government approval to build churches instead of having to wait years for such approval to come, as has been the experience of some. They should ask for *real* churches to be built, like those in the old days with church-like design and the cross prominently featured on their facades, instead of like those that are not supposed to appear like churches and are housed in warehouses or shophouses, as has been the case in recent times. They should ask for churches to be located in appropriate vicinities instead of in industrial areas among factories, as has also been the case in recent times. After all, in the context of 1Malaysia, churches, mosques, Buddhist temples, Hindu temples and all manner of religious buildings should stand alongside one another to proclaim the religious freedom and tolerance of worship that our founding fathers envisioned.

That's just for starters. There must be a litany of other grouses the Christians have been harbouring over the decades concerning the unfair treatment they have been receiving, most of it without regard for their rights as enshrined in the Federal Constitution. But now is the time to make Najib walk the talk. They have to strike while the iron is hot. Because when the time for political expediency is over, God knows whether the Government will be as amenable and anxious to please.

I'm sure there are many others out there — ordinary citizens — who will make that declaration with readiness and sincerity. Perhaps if our leaders won't take the lead, we ordinary citizens should do it, ironic as it may sound. Perhaps we should show our leaders how to walk the talk. Why not?

Let's band together and exercise our right, our power, as the *rakyat*. Let's show Malaysia — and the world — that if our leaders will not take the lead, we the people will take up that responsibility. We will not be doing anything wrong. In fact, we will be doing what is good for our country. We will be bringing about the real 1Malaysia.

How about it? I am a Malaysian first and a Chinese second. What about you?

PEACE, PROGRESS, PROSPERITY

This is a poem I wrote in the early '80s. I think it still speaks about the present.

Be silent.
That's the passport for peace.
The country belongs to those who shut their minds,
learn to unlearn what they once believed,
apply their PhDs to save their own skins.
The country still thrives,
with little yes-men trying to act big —
"no, this cannot; no, that is too sensitive,
shut up, you're a dog barking at a hill!"
In years to come, we may completely lose our voices,
but our skins will be just as thin.

Be complacent.
That's the programme for progress.
The country belongs to computers, not ideals —
command, execute, no questions asked;
beyond the pre-set codes, terminals blink a blank.
Thus the system thrives,
dictating what is right and what is good —
touch the wrong button and that's a bad key;
toe the on-line or you terminate.

In years to come, we may learn only to agree,
then we might lose our right to choose.

Be mundane.
That's the path to prosperity.
The country belongs to mercenaries,
they make their money and their titles,
go home to their palaces and playthings.
In fantasy they thrive,
with mistresses in booty shorts —
"Waa, you saw or not how sexy the men are in *The Vampire Diaries?*"
"So your daughter shook the PM's hand aah, very good, very good."
In years to come, we may exist in tinsel retreats,
with values culled from a bulk of pulp.

TWEEDLEDEE MCA

AFTER THE 2008 GENERAL ELECTION, IT BECAME CLEAR THAT THE
MALAYSIAN CHINESE ASSOCIATION (MCA), SENIOR PARTNER IN
BN BUT MOSTLY IN NAME, HAD BECOME ALMOST IRRELEVANT.
HOPELESSLY OVERSHADOWED BY UMNO, THE BIGGEST PARTNER,
THE MCA HAD BEEN REDUCED TO LITTLE MORE THAN A RUNNING
DOG THAT COULD BE ELOQUENT IN BLAMING THE OPPOSITION
FOR THE ILLS OF THE COUNTRY BUT DELIBERATELY BLIND IN NOT
SEEING UMNO'S WRONGDOINGS.

SHOULD MCA LEAVE BN TO REGAIN RELEVANCE AND DIGNITY?

MalaysianDigest.com, September 8, 2010

It has become an issue of public debate: Should the MCA remain in Barisan Nasional (BN)?

The question struck a poignant chord last month when MCA President Chua Soi Lek spoke up for the Chinese business community and was immediately ticked off by the Umno top brass.

Right after the MCA-organised Malaysian Chinese Economic Congress, Chua called on the Government to, among other things, gradually remove the NEP's 30 per cent Bumiputera equity in all sectors of the economy. Immediately, Umno Deputy President Muhyiddin Yassin retorted and warned him against making statements that could anger other races. He told the MCA not to undermine BN when fighting for the Chinese community. He even invoked the spectre of May 13.

Umno Vice-President Hishammuddin Hussein reminded Chua to "stick to the struggles of BN". He did not specify what that meant, but those who know would form their own conclusions.

Prime Minister Najib Razak was on leave at the time but when he came back, he did the normal thing — remind BN leaders they had to be careful when issuing statements. He did nothing to reassure Chua publicly, even though Najib was himself a main speaker at the Malaysian Chinese Economic Congress, and he had used the occasion to urge the Chinese CEOs present to spearhead his New Economic Model.

What this shows is that Chua and his party have no one they can fall back on when it comes to standing up for issues they are expected to champion. A few days after Muhyiddin's chiding, Chua became defensive, saying in an interview with *Berita Minggu* that he was not questioning the NEP but merely making a suggestion to improve the country's competitiveness in order to help Malaysia become a high-income nation.

In the eyes of the public, that episode showed even more clearly the dilemma the MCA is in.

Then just the other day, like a faithful party man, Chua praised the Government for giving academic awards worth RM2.25 million to United Examination Certificate (UEC) students. He said it showed that "the Government is giving more weight to the UEC, and the role of the Chinese independent schools".

Set against what Muhyiddin, as Education Minister, had said in June that the Government does not recognise the UEC because it does not follow the national education syllabus, Chua's overenthusiasm may be justified. As the saying goes, one has to be thankful for small mercies.

"Small mercies" would seem to be the most accurate description for what the MCA can manage to get these days. Even though it is a senior partner in the ruling BN, it is being seen as an increasingly impotent partner. When it comes to speaking up for the big things, it can be told by its big brother to shut up and that would be the end of the matter.

The Chinese community that the MCA is meant to represent perceived that the party would become increasingly compromised. So they pulled out their support for the party at the 2008 general election. Now, with more evidence surfacing to reinforce this perception, they have become even more convinced that whatever the MCA says in the interest of the Chinese will count for nothing.

If the situation carries on this way, the MCA will probably lose more seats at the next general election.

Chua is keenly aware of this. When he rebutted Muhyiddin and Hishammuddin for their admonitions, he eloquently expressed his party's predicament: "The MCA is aware of its role within BN, but we have a role to play as a Chinese-based party so that we can continue to be relevant."

However, because of the Catch-22 the MCA is in, that relevance will continue to diminish. You can see it in the fact that the MCA these days is reduced to watching the Opposition parties like a hawk and crying out whenever the latter do something it deems contradicts their credo. One obvious example is over the gag order issued by the DAP to stop its members from quarrelling over the Ronnie Liu issue. The MCA yelled that it went against the DAP's avowed principle of transparency.

Unfortunately, when the MCA stoops to serving such a function, it comes off sounding like the pupil in class who, in wanting to gain brownie points from the form teacher, repeatedly cries out, "Teacher! Teacher! Annuar is talking!" or "Teacher! Teacher! Siew Siang is disturbing Veloo!"

That's not the kind of politics that will be useful to anyone. Attacking your opponents merely to smear their reputation is a tactic that indicates political immaturity. Pakatan Rakyat does that a lot too, and it's as deserving of censure. Besides, it doesn't really work. More often than not, it serves only to make supporters of the group that's being smeared more upset, more hardened, and more anti the group that did the smearing. Besides, it's exhausting for the electorate, if not the politicians.

The MCA is no longer a political force. After the farce it went through to oust its former president, Ong Tee Keat; after the charging of another of its former presidents, Ling Liong Sik, for cheating the Government in regard to the Port Klang Free Zone (PKFZ) scandal; after this latest put-down by Muhyiddin, it is clear that the party needs to do something radical to regain its dignity.

That may be something as drastic as pulling out of BN.

If it does that, it might be able to prove its worth. It might be able to convince the Chinese that it still cares for them, to the extent that it was willing to make the sacrifice. It might even win back some votes.

It will, however, take guts to pull out of BN, mainly because the MCA has been used to being in a position of power — or, rather, the shadow of power — for more than 50 years. It knows no other role. It has never been in the Opposition at federal level. If it pulls out, some of its leaders and members, who are still satisfied with the scraps they enjoy by being in the coalition, may be upset that even these will be taken away.

Another consideration is provided by history. In 1969, after the Alliance's poor showing at the polls, the MCA, which had also suffered significant losses, decided to pull out of the Government but remain in the coalition. May 13 broke out.

Can it at least be argued that the Chinese community could lose respectability and even protection if the MCA was no longer part of the Government by pulling out of BN? Would it exacerbate racial antagonism? Would Umno become more rightist if it no longer had the MCA as a partner?

Pulling out may thus not be as easy as it seems. But then, staying is not easy either. The MCA is losing face, and there's no telling how much more it will lose in the near future. As it stands, Umno can prevail over the MCA anytime, which makes the latter's position untenable. Najib seems to get on well with Chua, and Chua is often seen boosting Najib, but even Najib's hands are tied.

The MCA now has 15 Parliamentary seats and 32 State seats, less than half of what it had prior to 2008. Come the next general election, how many will it be left with?

This has to be a cause for great concern. How the MCA leaders address it and what action they take in consequence will be a true test of their mettle.

OPEN LETTER TO CHUA SOI LEK

MalaysianDigest.com, January 12, 2011

Dear Soi Lek,

You are a highly educated person and one with the ability to think. As such, you are probably aware that the welfare of this nation rests on more than just the MCA winning its share of seats at the next general election and remaining in the coalition that holds the power to decide the fate of Malaysia.

You are probably aware that the way forward for Malaysia is renouncing the way of the Barisan Nasional (BN), led by Umno, falling back on an outdated decades-old formula. And that if you and the MCA continue to collude with the other parties in BN to retain power, you are subscribing to practices that could lead the nation to racial rifts and economic ruin.

Would you not agree with me that at this point in our history, as we stand at this crucial crossroads deciding which is the best path to take, national politics should no longer be race-based?

If you do agree, what then is the rationale for the MCA to continue to exist as an ethnocentric party? What is the rationale for you and your party members to stick with Umno which avowedly fights for the Malays and the MIC which avowedly fights for the Indians?

How long more do you see this ethnocentric equation taking hold of the lives of Malaysians, causing strife from time to time when disputes arise over who should get what and how much? We've had 53 years of that; isn't it enough?

Which is more important for you and your MCA colleagues: To stay on in BN in order to reap the rewards of being in government positions, or to do something that will ensure the honour and integrity of your party and of yourseves? I cannot tell you what that thing is which you could do to gain rectitude. You have to find it yourself.

But as you search for an answer, perhaps you would like to reflect on how strong the MCA's position really is within the BN coalition for the party to achieve its aims. Are you, for instance, contributing to inter-racial understanding and harmony? How could that be when you have to speak up against any threat to the position of the Chinese? How could that be when Umno must speak up against any perceived threat against the Malays?

It's a game full of contradictions, isn't it? You can't have one *and* the other, can you? In fact, your attempts over the past several months to speak up for the Chinese — indeed, for the country as a whole — clearly illustrate this.

Last August, after the Malaysian Chinese Economic Congress, when you called on the Government to gradually remove the 30 per cent Bumiputera equity in all sectors of the economy, you were immediately jumped upon by Umno Deputy President Muhyiddin Yassin. He even warned you about May 13.

A few days later, in your interview with a Malay-language newspaper, you had to soften what you had said, clearly showing your vulnerability.

Even Umno Vice-President Hishammuddin Hussein told you to "stick to the struggles of BN". What are they? Do you know?

You were even a target of criticism at the Umno general assembly last October. A delegate slammed you for saying that the social contract should not be discussed openly.

Then at the BN convention last month, you called for a ban on the use of the term "*Ketuanan* Melayu", and you told Umno it should not be approving government policies during its supreme council meetings. But straight away, Hishammuddin said you had upset many BN leaders, including those in the MCA.

This boggles the mind. What you said was absolutely right — how could Umno take it upon itself to decide on government policies when it is only one of the component parties of BN? Does the MCA have no say? So how could MCA leaders be upset by what you said? Have they become Umnofied themselves? Have they become slaves of their masters? Or, as former Perak *menteri besar* Nizar Jamaluddin said, "running dogs"?

If so, what dignity is left in them? And in you, if you continue to serve the MCA within the BN fold?

Isn't it obvious, too, that what you say doesn't count for "doodley-squat", as the American novelist Kurt Vonnegut would call it?

To be brutally honest, what good is your speaking up when you are still within the same cabal and your partners not only disagree with you, they don't respect what you say?

As you have probably been informed, people outside don't give much credence to your speaking up, anyway. They think it's just a *sandiwara* act to merely give the impression that you are standing up for what is right. But it's just an act.

I admit that going by the issues you have been bringing up recently, you are highlighting the fact that things are not being done right, and that your political partners should be held accountable. I might even hazard that you are at least concerned. What I fail to see, though, is your commitment.

For instance, at the MCA general assembly last October, Umno President Najib Razak told your party right within your own premises to be less communal and less demanding. Did you have an answer to that? Did you tell him in return to ensure that Umno would be less communal too? Did you tell him that the MCA was not being more demanding, that it was merely asking for what is guaranteed all Malaysians?

You see, I believe you know what is right for the country, but you are not willing to go all the way to ensuring that what is right prevails. If you were, you would not continue with the current regime. You would press for reform.

Surely, you would not disagree with me if I said the judiciary needs to be independent, that it needs to regain the trust of the people? The same with the police, the mainstream media, the civil service?

Surely, you would not disagree with me if I said our education system needs to be totally revamped to institute quality and regard for merit?

Surely, you would not disagree with me if I said that the way we award government projects needs to be transparent to eliminate cronyism? Or is that too tough a call after your appointment as Penang Port Commission chairman, a move that raised many eyebrows?

Above all, surely you would not disagree with me if I said we need a government that is clean; tells the truth; follows the rule of law; uses public funds for the people's sake rather than for its own; and upholds the country's institutions rather than abuses them for its own advantage?

Do we have such a government today?

If we did, you would not have said what you said last December 5 — when you called for each BN component party to have an equal voice and to share power "genuinely"; when you said BN had to change to be inclusive, multi-racial and to put the people first.

I know how to read between the lines, Soi Lek, and what you said that time said a lot about the coalition your party is part of.

Do you think it is capable of responding to your calls for change? Right now, looking just at the Cabinet line-up, we can see what a far cry it is from the days of Tunku Abdul Rahman. Will we ever see an inclusive government that has non-Malay ministers for the portfolios of Finance, Trade and Industry, or Defence? That no longer looks at skin colour but at ability, integrity and character?

I think you might better serve the people by taking the first step that leads away from race-based politics. If you choose to do that, you will be blazing a trail. And that could bring honour not only to you but your party as well. Unless, of course, you're a politician first and a public servant last. Then all I've been saying here would be worth doodley-squat.

Sincerely,
Chye

NO DIFFERENCE
WITH OR WITHOUT

MalaysianDigest.com, May 3, 2011

Prime Minister Najib Razak has changed his tack in relating to the Chinese electorate. He seems to have discarded his role of the charmer who spun 1Malaysia hogwash to win Chinese hearts and minds. He is now threatening them instead.

He's telling them that if they don't support Barisan Nasional at the next general election, they will not have representation in the Government. This is because Chua Soi Lek, the MCA president, has declared that his party will not accept government positions if they don't get Chinese support.

Najib's switch to a threatening mode shows that he's desperate. He clearly must be after what has happened in the recent Sarawak state elections, when the Chinese dumped the Sarawak United People's Party (SUPP) in favour of the Opposition. Despite Najib's 10-day campaign in the state, the Chinese there did not show him any face. They are simply fed-up with the corrupt BN Government and they want reform. But for BN, the loss of Chinese support, especially in Sarawak, with the possible spread to Sabah, could be crucial at the next general election.

Chua has since come forward to say that Najib was not issuing a threat but only making a "statement of fact" in response to the MCA's proposed stand. But knowing the kind of *pakat-pakat* (conniving) politics practised by BN, one is more likely to believe that Najib and Chua had both cooked up this ploy together right from the start — to supposedly strike fear in the hearts of the Chinese.

But should the Chinese be cowed? Should they worry if they had no representation in government — to be specific, the BN Government? Why should they? What has MCA (and Gerakan) representation in the Government done for them? Hasn't Chua woken up to the fact that it is because the Chinese feel the MCA has been useless in BN that they dumped the party in 2008?

And as if to reaffirm the hopeless situation that both the MCA and Gerakan are in, the same day Najib issued his threat, Perkasa president Ibrahim Ali issued his own — warning the two parties to stop bringing up sensitive issues or risk having their candidates undermined at the next general election. By this, Ibrahim meant Perkasa would urge Malays not to vote for the MCA and Gerakan. He even insisted that both parties must defend the Malays and Islam before they should get Malay votes.

Of course, we can dismiss Perkasa as a minnow that appears bigger than it really is because its president has a loud mouth and exaggerates his own importance. But it is no less humiliating for the MCA and Gerakan to be publicly chided in this fashion. What's more, big brother Umno has made no move to chide Perkasa back, which merely underscores the weakness of the lesser parties.

Should the Chinese support such weak parties? If the MCA and Gerakan were to remain in the BN Government after the next general election — and that's assuming BN wins — they would merely be playing the same old second fiddle. Supporting them would probably just give them a chance to continue to get a share of the loot, like the MCA did in the PKFZ scandal. Why elect them for that purpose?

In any case, if the MCA wants to turn down government positions, that's its own business. It has no right to put the onus on the Chinese or attempt to blackmail them.

Threats won't work. Chua should know that. So should Najib. Former prime minister Abdullah Badawi issued the same threat on the eve of the 2008 general election; it was on the front page of mainstream newspapers. The Chinese didn't give a damn; in fact, they were pissed off even more. Taib Mahmud did the same in the run-up to the Sarawak state elections. The Chinese told his coalition to go fly a kite.

If Najib wants to win back the Chinese, he has to take positive, radical measures. He has to assure them that the Government would be squeaky clean, that there would be no more rent-seeking, that the country's institutions will be respected, that the Government will strictly follow the rule of law, that the Chinese would have a place under the Malaysian sun as is guaranteed by the Federal Constitution.

It will not be enough for him to merely say that he will attend to these things; he has to be seen to be doing it because talk is cheap. The reason the Chinese don't buy his 1Malaysia drivel is that it's precisely nothing but drivel. In reality, nothing has been done to make things better for them. And meanwhile, the corruption and the rent-seeking continue. The Chinese realise more and more that the taxes they pay are going to the wrong causes. But what are they getting in return? Has there even been an improvement in the quality of Malaysian life?

The MCA and Gerakan have failed them. They are as culpable in the corruption that has set this country back. Their leaders get shouted down each time they make a squeak about any issue that displeases Umno. They get insulted by Umno seniors like Nazri Aziz and Hishammuddin Hussein.

Why should the Chinese want any party to represent them that has no cojones?

In fact, the MCA is a reminder to them of what a disgrace it is to Chinese dignity. As for Gerakan, whenever a politically aware Chinese person says something about its president, Koh Tsu Koon, they would accompany it with spittle. And they don't even have to be from Penang.

The greatest irony about Najib's threat is that for one who espouses 1Malaysia, he should even have entertained the thought. A truly 1Malaysia government would not look at race in its appointment of ministers. It would serve all races, whether or not there are Chinese representatives among its Cabinet. And if indeed the MCA did pull out of government positions and Najib still craved to see Chinese faces at Cabinet meetings, he could still do what he has done before — appoint non-politicians, like he did Idris Jala. Or appoint Chinese from other BN parties. If they haven't been duly elected, he could simply make them senators first. He's not new at that game either.

So, whatever it is, the Chinese have nothing to worry about. With or without representation in government, there is no difference — they will still be as they are. Chua and his MCA can do what they like; it won't matter anyhow. The Chinese will vote according to their conscience. After all, they have a saying: "It is better to die a hero than to survive in disgrace". Perhaps the MCA should take note of that before the next general election.

DO THE HONOURABLE THING

theSun, October 19, 2009

Ong Tee Keat should stop saying he is a politician who upholds principles. He has not done the honourable thing of resigning as MCA President although he promised he would. And yet last Thursday, he was not embarrassed to write in his blog, "People who know me well know that I uphold my principles ... It has never been my practice to renege on my words (*sic*) ... ."

This posting was made right after the MCA's Central Committee meeting to discuss the implications of the October 10 EGM. Much as one would like to believe him, one is also reminded that he has still not done the thing he said he would do. Besides, why say this in a blog? Why did he avoid facing a press conference and questions from the public?

The message from the EGM is clear — a vote of no-confidence in Ong's leadership was carried with a simple majority of 14. Although his supporters are arguing that a two-thirds majority is required to unseat the president, the fact remains that Ong himself has said in an interview with *The Star* on September 19 that "a simple majority [on the no-confidence vote] once carried, I will be left with no choice but to bow out and step down".

He even underscored that by saying, "Anyone who argues that I do not need to do so, that only a two-thirds majority is required to boot me out, I think that is a great lie."

Yes, we heard that loud and clear. And there seemed to be a ring of cocksure certainty in that statement. So, why is he stalling now? He should not live that lie. He should simply keep his word.

And yet last Thursday, he came up with a counter-proposal that could indicate that he wants to stay on. He overruled the Central Committee and used his presidential powers to call for another EGM — to decide if fresh party elections should be held or to reaffirm confidence in the present leadership. Is he buying time so he can do whatever he's planning? Is he hoping to seek a fresh mandate for himself?

One would hope not. If he wants to stay on as a caretaker till a smooth transition of power has been effected through the proposed elections, that should be fine. But he still needs to reassure everyone that he will not throw his hat into the ring, that he will leave when the issue has been settled. That is, if his word can still be trusted.

No doubt, Ong's supporters will clamour for him to stay on as president. And perhaps, too, those who have been saying that he is such a breath of fresh air for Malaysian politics because he has been daring enough to expose the Port Klang Free Zone (PKFZ) scandal.

I, for one, think that he has not exposed everything about that scandal. It looks like there's more, and there may be a limit to how far he can or dares to go. But even if the second lot does have a case, and even if Ong is indeed exemplary in being unwavering in his quest for the truth, we still have to expect him to do what he promised. Simply because if he breaks this promise to resign, what faith can we have in him in the future? How can we trust him again?

What are we Malaysians becoming? Should we lower our expectations of the integrity of our politicians? Isn't it enough that we have been so forgiving of them that even someone like Isa Samad, who was found guilty of money politics — a euphemism for corruption — could be named the Barisan Nasional candidate for the Bagan Pinang by-election and actually win it by a landslide?

Is it any wonder then that our country is in the state it's in? We tolerate corruption in high places. We let off politicians who make promises at election time but later forget to fulfil them. We stand by while state governments are destroyed because of dishonourable politicians who ignore the people that voted them in. We even let politicians get away with murder.

All this is happening because we don't hold our politicians accountable to their word. We don't take these maxims seriously: *Kata itu kota. Berani cakap, berani tanggung.* A man's word is his bond. Especially a man who is in high office. The rot sets in because we don't insist on that.

On this score then, there are no two ways about Ong Tee Keat's case. If he doesn't step down, he will be compared unfavourably to Chua who at least resigned from his ministerial and party posts when his sex scandal broke out in January 2008. And he won plaudits for it from the public.

If Ong takes the opposite course, there will be those among the public who will heap scorn on him. I, for one, would. And I have no personal stake whatsoever in this entire business of the MCA. Neither Ong nor Chua means anything to me. Nor, for that matter, any political party that is based on race.

What means more to me is a man's word and his integrity. That's what separates the men from the boys.

NO CHEERS FOR
FARCE OF THE YEAR

theSun, October 27, 2009

Sure, "politics is the art of the possible" — especially if it involves politicians who can change their tune overnight. That's why it has been possible for Ong Tee Keat and Chua Soi Lek to suddenly become friends again after a year of fierce animosity between them.

The art of the possible also works with politicians who can forget about scruples and put on a show. Nothing exhibits this more clearly than the outwardly awkward reconciliation between these enemies last Thursday. For added value, the would-be usurper of the presidency, Liow Tiong Lai, was also dragged into the act, a seemingly reluctant performer at that. So, too, was Kong Cho Ha, who had until now kept a dignified low profile.

It was a show that could easily have given the Goons of that famous British TV comedy a run for their asininity. I laughed so much, I had to call it the Most Laughable Farce of the Year, and nominate Ong, Chua and the supporting players for Best Comic Ensemble.

Who in their right mind would give much credence to this quick-glue patch-up that is aimed at reunifying the MCA? From reports, Ong had to leave the press conference room for 10 minutes to bring Liow and Kong in. Scriptwriters would have their imagination fired up by what transpired in those 10 minutes. They would be wondering, too, about what might be simmering behind those counterfeit smiles flashed for the media cameras. The tears of a clown? The resentment of facing a checkmate?

Scriptwriters would also be wondering if there was an unseen hand behind this sudden *volte-face* on the part of Ong and Chua since both have said that Prime Minister Najib Razak gave them his blessing to get back together. Was this an example of *deus ex machina*, a la Artistotle? Who is the *deus* ("god" in Latin)? Are these four men in actuality *wayang kulit* characters putting on a show at the command of their puppet master?

Sorry, I got carried away with the dramatic possibilities. I actually meant to ask: Where is the concern for integrity in this latest episode of the MCA saga? At what level is the moral quotient of these men who purport to lead the MCA? How is the MCA going to be credible in the eyes of the Chinese community — let's not even consider the wider Malaysian public — when what its leaders have done must force us to suspend our disbelief? Besides, how workable is this hasty marriage of inconvenience between Ong and Chua likely to be?

Chua was the duly elected deputy president. Then he got sacked from the party because Ong looked hell-bent on getting him out. That riled Chua up and he fought back with a vengeance. At the October 10 EGM, the delegates sent both a message — they registered a vote of no-confidence against Ong as president, and reinstated Chua as an ordinary member but not as deputy president. In short, both should bow out.

Ong had promised to step down if the no-confidence motion was carried by only one vote, but he broke his promise. After the EGM, 20 Central Committee members urged him to resign. Ong said he felt betrayed by his friends and so, he turned the tables on them. A deal was struck between him and his former foe. And now they're back, shaking hands. How does one perceive all that? Can one view these two men as being other than desperadoes who want to cling on to their positions?

Chua now seems to question the outcome of the EGM. Although the delegates voted against his reinstatement as deputy president, he has applied to the Registrar of Societies (ROS) to clarify whether he should be reinstated in spite of that — since his sacking from the party has been overturned. This doesn't show good faith. It shows that he is willing to respect only the resolution that is in his favour and to dispute the one that is not. Surely, this will infuriate some of the delegates. How then can his new pact with Ong help to reunify the party?

There is still a chance that the ROS — or Home Minister Hishammuddin Hussein — will decide to have Chua restored to his number two post in the party. If that should happen, what would become of Liow, who has meanwhile been elected deputy president, after the EGM, by the Central Committee? Is he going to be eventually played out and left in the cold? What then might be the consequences?

Chua has said rather glibly, "Then I become deputy president *lah*." That's easy to say, but there may be other ramifications. Right after the EGM, Liow was not thinking of only becoming number two; he had ambitions of becoming the chief. Is he likely to quietly go back to being vice-president and be a model MCA man?

On the other hand, what if Chua does not get reinstated? Would his followers be happy that Liow remain in what was Chua's domain since the latter was the duly elected one whereas Liow was merely elected by the CC? Is everyone going to take it lying down for the sake of reconciliation and unity? Are warring factions likely to become peaceniks overnight?

Ong says the leaders can now "re-focus on strengthening the party to regain the confidence and trust of the Chinese community and Malaysians in general". Of course he would say that. What else is there? It's a platitude he needs to hang on to since he didn't do the honourable thing of stepping down like he said he would. Who can believe what he says now?

Chua, too, has his own platitude. In justifying the reconciliation, he said, "In politics, they say it is an art to make the impossible possible *and the possible impossible* (my italics)." He might have thought he was adding a new twist with the second clause of that statement, but it could even turn out to be a prophecy. What might have been possible for the MCA — the chance of renewal with the departure of the two "tigers" Ong and Chua — could eventually become impossible.

MCA'S THREE-RING CIRCUS ROLLS AROUND

Free Malaysia Today, March 16, 2010

Ong Tee Keat doesn't know when to quit, does he? Despite all that bravado he exhibited in promising to step down before the mess hit the fan at the MCA EGM last Oct 10, he is still adamant that he will be an asset to the beleaguered party that he caused to split apart through his high-handedness as president. He has declared — the first candidate to do so — that he will defend his position at the upcoming fresh party elections on March 28.

This is the very man who promised to quit as president if the no-confidence vote against him at the EGM was passed by just one vote. It was actually passed by a margin of 14, with 1,155 delegates voting for it and 1,141 against. He should have kept his word, done the honourable thing, but instead, he chose to stay on.

That more than 600 members attended the party's AGM on March 7 indicates that he enjoys their support, but that is only a quarter of the 2,379 delegates who will be voting in the fresh elections. Besides, some of those 600 could have attended the AGM just to hedge their bets, and there may be opportunists among them who will join another faction if the latter looks the surer winner. Furthermore, the political complexion has just changed, now that former president Ong Ka Ting has announced his candidacy.

This is another pathetic twist to the MCA soap opera. In 2008, Ka Ting was the one who led the party to its worst general election defeat ever when it lost more than half of the seats it had held prior to that. During his tenure as president, he was also noted for having no gumption to stand up to Umno when it was trampling over Chinese concerns. He also didn't stand up for Tee Keat when the latter was reprimanded in 2006 by then deputy prime minister Najib Razak for urging the Education Ministry to act on corruption in Chinese schools.

It would be a desperate day indeed for the MCA to vote back a leader like that.

What will Chua Soi Lek and Liow Tiong Lai, who have been touted as likely candidates, do now?

Chua had been considered the front-runner because, according to pundits, he could rely on the support of at least 900 delegates. How will his chances be affected with Ka Ting's entry? As for Liow, since a large chunk of his supporters are also those of Ka Ting's, will he settle for the number two position?

What about Ka Ting's brother, Ka Chuan? Surely, there would be something in all this for him? But Ka Chuan's track record is not impressive. He was trounced in the 2004 general election in Batu Gajah and managed to win in 2008 in the safe seat of Tanjung Malim. And in the MCA party elections of 2008, he lost to Chua in the contest for the deputy presidency. Why would the delegates want him this time?

The MCA is in for intriguing times. There will be a lot of horse trading right up till the elections as the factions scramble to make up the required figures. Liow was an ally of Tee Keat's till he apparently betrayed the latter after the October 10 EGM. Are we likely to see further betrayals by any of the players involved? Will Chua the "magician" be wily enough to pull off "the art of making the impossible possible, and the possible impossible"?

It looks like we're back to the same circus. You can hear the orchestra strike up the opening strains of *Send in the Clowns*. The sad part is, the delegates may be faced with only these options: a man who broke his promise, a man who betrayed his friend, a man who cheated on his wife, and a man who lacked courage when he was president. And then after the March 28 elections, with the factions already so split, will the party be reunified? In the past, there was only a Team A vs Team B scenario; now there are Teams X, Y and Z.

Even if Ka Ting becomes president again, there will be animosity. If Tee Keat wins, it will be back to square one. All the grief and disgrace the party has had to experience since before the EGM will have been much ado about nothing. And he was the one who started the whole mess by behaving the way he did when he first stepped into the presidency, and showing his contempt for his then deputy, Chua. So, where's the solution? One doubts whether the team leaders know the answer.

Whatever it is, the whole MCA dramedy has shown up the reality about the party — that it is no longer a force in Malaysian politics. The Malaysian Chinese world didn't end while the in-fighting was going on. Life in the Chinese community still went on, debunking whatever claim may be made that the MCA still matters to the Chinese. Its days are nearly over. Why fight over a dying cause?

Time to move on. Time to heed the words of Lim Keng Yaik who has suddenly wised up now he's been out of the Gerakan leadership for a couple of years: "After March 8, politics is going towards an ideological base that is multi-racial in approach." Perhaps it's time for the MCA to implode and start all over again.

FORMATION OF CHINESE PERKASA: A DANGEROUS WAY TO WIN GENERAL ELECTION

MalaysianDigest.com, July 11, 2010

The call for the setting-up of a Chinese Perkasa to counter the Malay right-wing group's racial attacks is one of the most outrageous things I've ever heard. Yet this is a call that comes from none other than Deputy Finance Minister Donald Lim Siang Chai, who is also an MCA vice-president.

How can a deputy minister suggest such a thing? Is he speaking as an individual or does he have the endorsement of the MCA or, worse still, the Government?

That he is part of the ruling administration makes the call suspicious. It seems to corroborate what many have come to suspect — that Perkasa (Pertubuhan Pribumi Perkasa Malaysia) is linked in an informal way to Barisan Nasional, that the NGO is actually doing the dirty work that BN cannot be seen to be doing, i.e. championing Malay rights and taking a hardline stance against perceived adversaries.

Chauvinism has been outsourced to Perkasa, observers say. In light of Lim's statement, one might be persuaded to see a connection.

What is objectionable about Lim's call is that it will reinforce what Umno itself has been drumming into the minds of the Malays — that the non-Malays, particularly the Chinese, are a threat to them, that the non-Malays want to take over the country.

This has been the crux of Umno propaganda since the day after the 2008 general election, with even people like former prime minister Mahathir Mohamad going around the country spinning the myth that

"Malay land has fallen into non-Malay hands". Most days when you open *Utusan Malaysia* or *Berita Harian* or switch on to TV3, you'll get reminders of this insidious message.

It is unlikely that Lim and the MCA are not aware that the call for a Chinese Perkasa will reinforce the fear of the Malays about a takeover by the non-Malays. They would also be aware that although it's an imagined fear with no basis whatsoever in reality, if you tell it often enough, it can become real. Even more effective is when the telling turns into showing. And that is what will happen if a Chinese Perkasa comes into being. When it starts yelling at the Malay Perkasa and proceeds to quarrel with it, it will automatically reveal its own aggressiveness. That will certainly make the Malays feel even more fearful of the Chinese.

That will turn Umno's propaganda into palpable proof of Chinese ambitions. That will then ensure that the Malays vote for Umno at the next general election. And that will also translate into victory for BN.

Lim may be thinking that his suggestion could help the MCA win back Chinese votes because to the less enlightened Chinese, this could show that the MCA is finally standing up for their race. But this is a dangerous way of going about it.

The formation of a Chinese Perkasa will merely cause deeper resentment between the races. As it is, the country has become more divided than it has ever been; Lim's suggestion can only make race relations worse. What happens when relations become so bad that they reach a point of no return? What good will it do for either the Malays or the Chinese? What good will it do for the nation?

Didn't Lim think of this before he opened his mouth? Such irresponsible talk coming from a deputy minister must be censured. If his party does not do it, Prime Minister Najib Razak should. It is one thing to think of winning votes for your party and another to cause greater strife in society. Because the call comes from what will be perceived as an authorised source, it may just turn out that some fanatical Chinese individuals or groups will respond to it. If that happens, we may all be in for tumultuous times.

Lim has hinted that the Kuala Lumpur and Selangor Chinese Assembly Hall (KLSCAH) would be the proper body to play the Chinese Perkasa role. This is utterly misguided. The KLSCAH has been at the forefront of pushing for civil rights and social progress. It is by no stretch of the imagination a chauvinist body. It presents annual Civil Society Awards to individuals and organisations that promote multi-culturalism and multi-ethnicism.

I have attended several forums held on its premises that propagated the idea of working towards a better Malaysia for all Malaysians. Many of these activities are not organised by the KLSCAH itself but they reflect its broad-based leanings.

How could Lim even think of calling on the KLSCAH to perform a detestable role? Is it his ulterior motive to discredit the KLSCAH, whose orientation is antithetical to the MCA's ethnocentricism?

For saying what he said, Donald Lim is not only prescribing trouble but also revealing how warped his thinking is. The MCA has been castigating Perkasa for its rightist, racist stance. How can he then propose the formation of something that is similarly rightist and racist? This is a clear-cut case of double standards and hypocrisy.

Is it any wonder, then, that if the MCA has leaders like Lim, Malaysians should have even more reason to reject the party?

TWEEDLEDUM MIC

THE MALAYSIAN INDIAN CONGRESS (MIC) WAS SEVERELY HIT AT THE 2008 GENERAL ELECTION. INDIANS AWAKENED BY THE HINDRAF MOVEMENT FORSOOK THE PARTY THAT HAD CLAIMED TO REPRESENT THEM FOR THE LAST 50-ODD YEARS AND SWUNG TO THE OPPOSITION. HINDRAF MADE THEM REALISE THAT AFTER ALL THESE DECADES, THE MIC HAD DONE LITTLE TO IMPROVE THE INDIAN LOT. LIKE THE MCA, THE PARTY HAD BEEN TOO TIMID TO ANNOY BIG BROTHER UMNO AND HAD GONE ALONG WITH WHATEVER THE LATTER DECIDED.

TO WIN BACK THE SUPPORT OF THE INDIANS, NAJIB STARTED THROWING MONEY AND PROMISES AT THEIR FEET. SO DESPERATE WAS HE IN THIS ENTERPRISE THAT AFTER SAMY VELLU, WHO HAD BEEN PRESIDENT OF THE PARTY FOR FAR TOO LONG, WAS PERSUADED TO STEP DOWN TO LESSEN THE PARTY'S LIABILITIES, NAJIB GAVE HIM A JOB WITH MINISTERIAL STATUS. THEN HE MADE SAMY'S SUCCESSOR, G. PALANIVEL, A FULL MINISTER DESPITE THE MIC'S POOR REPRESENTATION IN PARLIAMENT, DESPITE THE FACT THAT PALANIVEL HIMSELF HAD BEEN DEFEATED IN THE 2008 GENERAL ELECTION.

SAM AND PAL
GET SLAPPED

Free Malaysia Today, April 17, 2010

You could feel the ferocious impact of the slap hitting Samy Vellu's cheek. In a manner of speaking. He had allowed Big Brother Umno to bully him and the MIC yet again. He had allowed Umno to nominate a candidate for the Hulu Selangor by-election other than the one he originally wanted.

Once more, MIC clearly showed its impotence in the shadow of Umno. The image of the party that emerged from this episode was of a mongrel wagging its tail at its master after having been manhandled by the latter.

It was pathetic to hear Samy voice his support for the candidate announced by Umno Deputy President Muhyiddin Yassin — a relative unknown named Kamalanathan, a "compromise" choice, because Umno wanted V. Mugilan and Samy was all for G. Palanivel, his deputy.

It was pathetic to hear Samy say, as if in subservience and surrender, "I have promised (Muhyiddin) that he will say everything. Today, we are listeners and will stay behind and listen to his commands and directives to ensure absolute victory."

It was pathetic to hear Samy give the assurance that Hulu Selangor MIC branches would not close their operations centres when only the day before, nearly half of the 72 branch leaders had threatened to do so should Palanivel not be chosen. "MIC has not learned the art of sabotage yet," he quipped, but it sounded like a lame joke. One wonders if he still has the power to stop any sabotage.

It would be interesting to see how Palanivel's supporters and those of Mugilan react on April 25, the day of voting. Some have threatened to cast protest votes to teach Umno leaders a lesson for their haughty attitude. That might well be what the latter deserve. Such an act would at least show them that the MIC will not take condescension lying down, unlike what its president has done. Perhaps it's about time the MIC grassroots hit back. Time to tell Umno that the latter alone is not the be-all and end-all of Barisan.

When and where else could the MIC do so? Certainly not in the Cabinet where its lone minister is hopelessly outnumbered. Nor at a Barisan Nasional convention where someone like Noh Omar, who is merely the Selangor Umno deputy chief, can tell non-Malays that they should be grateful for being granted citizenship. Nor at a 1Malaysia seminar where someone like Nasir Safar, at the time no less than the special officer to the prime minister, can say the Indians came to this country as beggars. Perhaps, in light of the present circumstances, he was not off the mark.

The time for reckoning is here. How often can the MIC turn the other cheek and continue to be pushed around by Big Brother? Does it have any shred of dignity left? Much as Samy Vellu tried to reclaim some of it through his stoic declaration of support for what is essentially Umno's eventual choice of candidate for Hulu Selangor, he still appeared a defeated man.

What could also undermine him is the fact that he, together with the MIC Central Working Committee, threatened to sack Mugilan if he was chosen to stand in Hulu Selangor because that would go against the leadership's insistence on having Palanivel or bust. At first glance, that was already an ill-advised move. Its immediate effect would be alienating Mugilan and his supporters. On closer examination, although Mugilan was eventually shut out, the selection of Kamalanathan further underscores the weakness of the MIC in not having its way despite its earlier insistence. What, we may well ask, happened to the original argument that anyone other than Palanivel standing for that seat would be detrimental to the party?

As for Palanivel, his rejection as candidate is also a slap on his face, not least because prior to 2008, he had served four terms as MP for Hulu Selangor. Casting him aside shows that Umno has little respect for him either, even though he is the MIC's number two.

There's talk that he might be made a senator and given a deputy minister position to make up for this. Samy's revelation that Palanivel will be meeting Najib soon "to resolve some matters" reinforces that. But if Palanivel takes up the offer, he would lose more respect. In the eyes of the public, he would have accepted something that was offered only as consolation, not something he truly deserved. He would have got in through the back door, like Gerakan's Koh Tsu Koon, who is certainly not well respected.

When all is said and done, however, the real loser in this entire debacle is Samy. It's quite clear that the writing is already on the wall. Najib obviously disregarded his effectiveness as a leader of the Indians by directly endorsing the Makkal Sakthi Party and also by addressing a rally at Batu Caves last year without Samy being present. Logically, too, an old-politics straggler who seems to have been around too long and outlived his political shelf-life cannot be an asset to a prime minister who is trying to redefine the Barisan agenda in the new political landscape. Choosing Kamalanathan and saying that a new face was needed could well be a pointed message to Samy.

If Samy cannot command Najib's respect, it's unlikely he can command many others' respect. And yet he wants to cling on to the presidency till 2012, when his term of office ends. He may have won the last party elections and got most of the candidates he endorsed elected as well, but he needs to redeem himself.

The one thing that might do that for him is to pull the MIC out of Barisan Nasional. After all, it has been proven time and time again that the MIC is a poorly regarded partner in Barisan, that it cannot really stand up for the community it represents.

In leaving the coalition, what would the party lose? On the other hand, what might it gain? Self-respect and dignity, surely. And perhaps the acknowledgement that it had the guts to do what it should have done. And for Samy Vellu, that might well be the saving moment in the twilight of his political career.

WHEN YOU GOTTA GO ...

MalaysianDigest.com, July 8, 2010

This weekend, at the MIC's annual general assembly, will Samy Vellu give in to the mounting pressure for him to quit as party president immediately or will he carry on regardless? Can we expect fireworks that might climax in an earth-shaking announcement from him or will it be business as usual?

Chances are Samy will not budge from his position. He has declared that he will not see through the rest of his term as president, which ends in May 2012, and will instead step down in September 2011. But the voices calling for him to depart earlier are getting louder, especially after he used his powers to expel four party leaders for ostensibly urging him to quit. Even S. Murugessan was removed as secretary-general for speaking out against the expulsion.

It is Samy's intolerance of dissent that has made him less than endearing even to some of his own party members. His other major downside is that he has been president for far too long — 31 years is practically half the time the 64-year-old party has been in existence.

Significant events over the last three years have shown up his declining worth as a national leader and as that of a party claiming to represent his ethnic community. First, the Hindraf rally in 2007 dealt a severe blow to the relevance of the MIC to the Indians, for which Samy must shoulder the bulk of the responsibility. Then at the March 8, 2008, general election, he lost his self-proclaimed "fortress", the parliamentary seat of Sungai Siput, conquered by the humble Michael Jeyakumar.

Last April, for the Hulu Selangor by-election, his choice of candidate was rejected by the Barisan Nasional leadership. He wanted his deputy, G. Palanivel, to stand, but Prime Minister and BN Chairman Najib Razak and his Umno colleagues had other ideas. The word going round then was that they preferred MIC Deputy Youth Chief V. Mugilan whom Samy opposed. In the end, a compromise was made and P. Kamalanathan got the job.

Nonetheless, Samy lost face. How could he henceforth stand up for his party within the coalition and effectively represent his community?

And then, before he could recover from it, his detractors let out GAS. Mugilan, one of the four expelled by Samy "for working against the MIC and BN", organised a campaign called Gerakan Anti-Samy (GAS) to pressure him to quit. If nothing else, it has caused untold embarrassment to Samy.

On top of that, they are demanding that he step down on July 10, the first day of the general assembly. They have threatened that if he fails to do so, they would expose the details of scandals that have been plaguing the party and the wrongs that Samy has allegedly committed.

No other prominent national leader has had to suffer such ignominy. Samy should have left while the going was still good. Like Mahathir Mohamad, whom he avowedly reveres despite the former PM's exhortation to him to step down earlier. Like Ling Liong Sik of the MCA. Like Lim Keng Yaik of Gerakan. They, too, might have also been pressured to go, but the good thing for them is, they did.

Now it might be too late for Samy to make an honourable exit. He won't be able to salvage any pride. The response to it among detractors and even neutrals would be one of relief, certainly not sympathy or respect. And in future, history would still record that he long overstayed his tenure.

It should be interesting to see what Najib, who is opening the MIC general assembly on July 10, will say in his address to the MIC delegates, and how telling his body language will be when he relates to Samy. Najib has been long enough in the business to know that politicians have their sell-by date and he can recognise one that's gone way beyond that. Going by his expression of admiration a few days ago for the German team in the World Cup tournament, a team that invested faith in young people with talent and team spirit, one could infer that he would prefer a new, perhaps even younger, MIC president. Perhaps someone like S. Subramaniam, who made a meteoric rise to become Human Resource Minister when his party seniors lost their seats on March 8, 2008.

Interestingly, those who have been pushing for Samy to go have not talked about what should happen afterwards, like who would succeed him and what plans the successor would have for re-energising the party to win back voter support.

Although Samy has recently announced that Palanivel will be the one to succeed him, it may not turn out to be as clear-cut as that. With talk already rife that Mugilan is being sponsored by outside forces, which Samy's son, Vell Paari, has publicly identified as Umno, who's to say that Najib and Umno might not want to get into the act again and influence the succession outcome? Why would they not intervene when this may be crucial to BN's performance at the next general election?

July 10 will be an interesting day, indeed. Political pundits watching for signs may indeed spot a few. Mugilan can still hope to bring Samy down if one of the delegates calls for an EGM to vote on a motion of no-confidence against Samy. But who will be brave enough to bell the cat? Who will risk being sacked from the party if the subsequent vote favours Samy?

At the end of the day, if no one makes a move, Samy will remain as he is. And the bravado he displayed when he said this last Sunday will continue to pique his antagonists: "No one can do anything to me or the party. And if anyone tries to destroy the party, fate will ensure that they themselves are destroyed."

Some might call that chutzpah; others call it hubris.

DOES SAMY DESERVE
A DIGNIFIED EXIT?

Free Malaysia Today, December 4, 2010

Samy Vellu should have no cause to rejoice when he steps down as MIC president on December 6 and takes on his new job as a special envoy for Malaysia. In fact, if he were a man who has the slightest bit of self-pride, he might even feel ashamed. Because from the look of it, he has been bought out. He has been told to step down even earlier than he had planned to.

If he had had his way, he would have opted to quit in September 2011, which was what he had announced earlier in the year. Then at the July MIC general assembly, as pressure mounted within his own party calling for his departure, he hinted it could be in January.

But in politics, a month is apparently too long, so he now has to go in early December. Apparently, too, Najib Razak, prime minister and Barisan Nasional chief, knows he cannot afford to have Samy stay on longer if the general election is going to be called next year. Some pundits say it could be as early as March.

So the deal was made. Samy leaves and in return, he gets the post of Malaysia's special envoy for infrastructure to South Asian countries — a position with ministerial status. It is also apparently to give him face, provide him a dignified exit.

But why should the MIC get another ministerial position after its poor performance at the last general election? Where is the regard for values if rewards are given when they are not deserved?

More important, why create a new position which would incur cost to the taxpayer? Samy's salary, perks, claims and whatever else in the new position he's taking will amount to a substantial amount. Why does the *rakyat* have to pay for it?

And if indeed it is to get him to step down as MIC president earlier, why does the *rakyat* have to pay for a strategic move made by Najib to safeguard his coalition's position at the next general election?

This is not the only sweetening deal Najib has made in recent times with the MIC. Only some months ago, he made G. Palanivel, Samy's proclaimed successor, a deputy minister apparently for having left him out as candidate for the Hulu Selangor by-election. That was not right either. It was another case of misplaced values. It was sending out the wrong message to Malaysians, cultivating the wrong kind of culture.

Obviously, Najib wants to win Indian hearts to make them swing back to BN at the next general election, but the means he employs can only reflect poorly on him.

What happens next, when deputy minister Palanivel assumes the MIC leadership with a designated second-in-command, S. Subramaniam, who is already a full minister? Will the new party boss be happy with being of lower rank in the Cabinet to his subordinate in the party? Would another deal be made to set things 'right'? But why should yet another ministerial position be granted to the MIC just to give Palanivel face?

The *rakyat* should be incensed by all this wheeling and dealing.

Does Samy deserve the position he's been given? He was one of the most unpopular members of the Cabinet prior to 2008, and when he lost his Sungai Siput constituency in the last general election, there was jubilation all round. It marked the most famous defeat of March 8.

By then, he had served as a minister for 29 years, and the public had been grumbling for years that he had stayed too long. So, why must they still put up with his presence and pay him a salary? After all, as a minister, was he outstanding in terms of performance?

Many of us are more likely to remember him for his habit of side-stepping responsibility and talking big. When cracks appeared on

Kuala Lumpur's Middle Ring Road II, he blamed the weather. "There's some problem with the design but it's the weather in this country that contributed mainly to the structural problem," he said.

Then, when serious cracks appeared on beams supporting the Ampang-KL Elevated Highway, he got defensive and told the press off, and challenged them to check all the flyovers in the country and write about how bad they were.

When the landslide occurred in 2004 on the North-South Expressway near Gua Tempurung, he conveniently said it was an "act of God". Critics pointed out that as Works Minister, Samy distinguished himself more in covering up construction incompetencies and thereby protecting the real culprits.

Always the bravura showman who spoke before thinking, he once invited the public to call his mobile phone if they had any complaints to make. "Don't go to the TV stations," he said. "Is the TV station doing the repairs and maintenance work?" No more than a couple of days later, he announced that he was unable to sleep at night because he was getting too many calls and SMSes, so he told the public to stop complaining to him.

As a politician, he said things that brought him ridicule and embarrassment. Prior to the Lunas by-election of 2000, he boasted that the MIC would win it, and that if it didn't, he would stay on in Kulim and not return to KL. The MIC did lose, but he was back in KL in no time, probably suffering from amnesia.

Just before the last general election, he said, "An army can come but I know how to fight it out ... The people in Sungai Siput are with me." On March 8, the army of voters did come and they swept him off his seat. It was probably the umpteenth time he had had to eat his own words.

After December 6, the question he will have to ultimately answer, at least to himself, is whether his lording over the MIC for three decades has brought improvement to the ethnic community it claims to represent. If it has, would there have been the Hindraf demonstration of 2008?

As one commentor on *Malaysiakini* once put it eloquently: "The job that Samy Vellu should have done over so many years as president of the Indian community was done by Hindraf in single day only (*sic*)." Nothing could be more telling of the MIC's ineffectuality as a partner in BN.

Samy promised poor Indians a dream by getting them to invest in Maika Holdings Berhad, but it was mismanaged and made huge losses. He kept promising them that they would get back their money, saying, "Samy Vellu is their guarantee". In 2006, he said a buy-back scheme would pay investors back RM130 for every RM100 they put in. But it didn't happen.

The following year, he said, "For those who want their money back, I have made arrangements to give their money back to them." As it turned out, no one quite believed him. Investors had not even been paid dividends since 1995.

He finally managed to get G. Gnanalingam to buy over Maika Holdings on the eve of the Hulu Selangor by-election voting, aptly timed to win Indian votes. Even then, the poor Indians who had invested their money would get back only what they had put in and nothing more, and some had been investing for more than two decades. They had hoped the money would grow, but Samy Vellu let them down.

Will it therefore be a dignified exit for Samy on December 6, despite the Government's bid to help him out? This, of course, is a rhetorical question. Samy, no doubt, will provide his own big answer. But perhaps it would be best that he kept it to himself.

DOES MIC DESERVE THREE MINISTERS?

MalaysianDigest.com, August 4, 2011

Prime Minister Najib Razak is being cavalier with taxpayers' money in making MIC president G. Palanivel a full minister. His promotion from deputy minister will incur increases in Palanivel's salary, perks, claims and pension — and the *rakyat* will be paying for them. Is it justifiable?

The MIC has only four Members of Parliament, but it now has a line-up of three ministers and two deputy ministers. How is that proportionate? If T. Murugiah had not lost his senatorship last April and thereby his deputy minister position, there would be three MIC deputy ministers now.

It's surprising Ibrahim Ali and Perkasa have not uttered a squeak about this — which reinforces the general perception that Perkasa fights shy of criticising the ruling party and may actually be linked to it, despite claims to the contrary.

Why do I say the MIC now has three ministers?, you ask. Well, let's not forget Samy Vellu. Less than eight months ago, he was appointed — also by Najib — to be Malaysia's special envoy to India and South Asia *with ministerial status* (my italics). That was apparently his reward for stepping down as MIC president. It was to give him face through a dignified exit. But why was that necessary?

I raised questions about it then. I asked why the MIC should get another ministerial position after its poor performance at the last general election (GE). Where is the regard for values if rewards are given when they are not deserved?

Now Najib has further displayed this lack of values by giving a third ministerial position to a party that has performed miserably. So, to answer my own question about whether it's right to make Palanivel a minister, I say unequivocally, "No."

What purpose is served by promoting Palanivel?

According to Najib: "I want to return to the era of Abdul Razak where there were two Indian ministers in the Cabinet." Is that all? Just because he wants it? Where's the good reason? It sounds almost as whimsical and flippant as saying Abdul Razak was his father and therefore, he must emulate the latter.

He also says the decision proves that the Government is committed to the Indian community and intends to work closely with them; and giving them another minister is giving them the opportunity to play an even more effective role.

What, pray tell, is that "role"?

If you suspect it is to support Barisan Nasional (BN) at the next GE, you would probably be right. Najib is clearly trying to win Indian votes with this move. But if public funds have to be incurred for him to do that, it cannot be proper. Why should taxpayers' money be used to keep BN in power? BN is only the government of the day; it cannot use public resources to improve its chances of getting re-elected.

Najib may also feel that Palanivel should hold the same rank as MIC's deputy president, S. Subramaniam, who is already Human Resources Minister. But it is not Najib's duty to give Palanivel face by putting him on ministerial par with his deputy. Palanivel must, first of all, deserve the position.

The question is, does he?

He was not duly elected at the 2008 general election. He, in fact, lost his Hulu Selangor parliamentary seat. And when it came time for a by-election for that same seat in 2010 — because the PKR candidate who had defeated him died while in office — he was not chosen to be the candidate. Instead, a much junior MIC member, P. Kamalanathan, was selected. What did that signify?

It seems at the time, Najib himself did not favour Palanivel, and for a good reason: Palanivel was not liked by his constituents when he was the MP there; they said he was seldom seen in the vicinity.

Nonetheless, when the by-election was over, Najib made Palanivel a deputy minister in the Plantation Industries and Commodities Ministry. This was apparently both consolation for his being bypassed as Hulu Selangor candidate and preparation for his takeover as MIC chief.

Najib accomplished this by using the back-door method of making him a senator first. This was the same method he employed to make ministers out of other politicians openly rejected by the *rakyat* in 2008, like Koh Tsu Koon and Shahrizat Abdul Jalil; and also to make deputy ministers out of Awang Adek Hussein and Chew Mei Fun.

Bringing back election losers in this unsatisfactory manner has made Najib's practice questionable. The same goes for his appointment of Palanivel as Minister in the Prime Minister's Department.

Besides, why do we need yet another Minister in the Prime Minister's Department when there are already five — Koh, Nazri Aziz, Nor Mohamad Yakcop, Jamil Khir Baharom and Idris Jala? Is there so much work to go round for six?

What positive effect will his appointment have on the public interest? How will he better serve the *rakyat* when he was a disappointment to his Hulu Selangor constituents?

Such considerations, however, don't seem to matter to Najib. What matters most is the Indian vote. He probably sensed that he had lost some Indian support after the unpopular month-long detention of the six Parti Sosialis Malaysia (PSM) members under the Emergency Ordinance (EO). Making the offer to Palanivel is his attempt to salvage the loss.

The timing tells it all.

First, Subramaniam (on July 27) and then Palanivel (on July 28) publicly called for the PSM 6's release. "I spoke to the Prime Minister several days ago and asked him to release them," Palanivel said, as if to declare that the PM would listen to him. Then on July 29, the PSM 6 were actually released.

This made it look like the MIC could take credit for the release of the PSM 6, which would go down well not only with Indians but other Malaysians who had expressed outrage at the detention. But knowing how our *wayang* politics works, we may not be wrong in thinking that the release decision had already been made before the MIC's appeals.

After all, why did Subramaniam and Palanivel choose to speak up only a month after the six were detained? Why did they not speak up when the arrest was first made of the six and 24 others on June 26 on suspicion of "waging war against the King" and "resurrecting Communism"? Why did they not come out then to say that such a suspicion was ridiculous? They kept quiet; their silence was an endorsement. They were complicit to the arrests as partners of the ruling regime.

Be that as it may, on July 30, at the MIC's general assembly, Najib announced making Palanivel a minister. That being the day after the PSM 6's release, it was obviously calculated to add to the feel-good momentum. As a result, Najib's ratings might well go up, and those of the MIC's as well.

But before Indians exult and decide to swing back to BN, what they might need to ask is how they will benefit from this. As minister, will Palanivel dare to speak up for them when at his own party's general assembly last weekend, delegates were directed not to discuss the *Interlok* issue? When it comes to the big issues, will he be able to stand up to big brother Umno or just be a "running dog" doing its bidding?

And as for the PSM 6, the story is not yet over. Five days after their release, they were charged for being in possession of subversive documents, and will be tried together with the other 24.

Perhaps Palanivel's first test as minister should be talking to the Prime Minister and asking him to drop the charges. Let's see how far he can get with that. If he succeeds, then we can truly say that he deserves being made a minister. And that taxpayers' money is being well and wisely spent.

HOW CAN GERAKAN RECAPTURE PENANG?

MalaysianDigest.com, September 20, 2010

Is Gerakan still relevant, especially since it has lost Penang, which was its base for nearly four decades? Can it lead the Penang Barisan Nasional (BN) to win back the state at the next general election (GE)? Will it even win any seats there?

These are pressing questions that Gerakan must be asking itself. Yet, when its vice-president Mah Siew Keong said last week that BN still has a good chance to recapture Penang, and that Gerakan was still the best party to lead the coalition at the next GE, it sounded like either wishful thinking or self-delusion.

Even Mah's colleague, Teng Hock Nan, doesn't believe BN can do it. And he's the man on the ground, he's the Penang Gerakan chief.

At present, of the 40 seats in the State Assembly, BN has only 11, and they were all won in the last GE by Umno. The MCA lost all its nine seats, the MIC lost the two it had, and Gerakan was totally crushed — it had 13 seats but lost every single one of them, including that of Penang's then chief minister, Koh Tsu Koon.

Earlier this month on 'Say Sorry Day' (September 6), Koh, who is still Gerakan president, said he wished he could have done more for Penang when he was head of its government.

He held that position for four terms, spanning almost 18 years, and in his final term, he lost the whole island to Pakatan Rakyat, which won by more than a two-thirds majority. Like his party, he went from head honcho to zero.

To lose so decisively after not one or two terms but four says a lot about how effective a chief minister he was. It was therefore amusing to hear Koh say, "if I've not done enough, I should say sorry". "Not enough" is an understatement after four terms of governance. How many more terms would he have needed to get it right?

And now Mah Siew Keong still harbours hope of BN retaking Penang?

Why would the people of Penang, who have in no uncertain terms rejected Gerakan, want to vote it back? What has it done since losing power? How has it proven to be an effective partner in the BN coalition? What waves has it created within BN itself? What strategies can it come up with to promise Penangites a better future under Gerakan?

It has made a bit of noise here and there over some things done or said by Umno that it thought deviated from the spirit of multi-racialism, but each time it does that, it comes out sounding like a cat in a cage whining at the bulldog glaring at it through the bars.

Gerakan is in the same situation as the MCA and the MIC – all three are stunted standing next to Umno. And what's crucial is that the electorate know it. But while the MCA and the MIC can raise Chinese and Indian issues that appeal to some in their communities, Gerakan is out of place within an essentially race-based coalition. It is an avowedly multi-racial party, but one that voters with a multi-racial outlook have forsaken. Furthermore, its appeal to the Chinese of Penang has all but disappeared. What can it bank on now to make itself worthy?

Its desperation is highlighted by its occasional strikes against the DAP for consorting with PAS and pointing out the incongruity of their relationship, but the arrows it shoots make no dent on their targets. This is simply because many who might have been sympathetic to Gerakan before have come to accept the DAP–PAS partnership. They don't perceive it as being "unholy" any more.

What will be of concern now to Gerakan is whether it still has a legitimate case for holding on to the BN chairmanship in Penang.

Umno has been lobbying for it. It will likely push for more seats in Penang at the next general election concomitant with its long-held aim of getting a Malay into the chief minister's office. It might argue – and quite rightly, too – that BN cannot depend on Gerakan and the MCA to deliver the goods. And as it stands, Umno is the one with the seats, so why should it not be the party that takes the chairmanship?

This will not be something the BN leadership can ignore. How it decides will indicate how much it appreciates Gerakan. Taking away this last vestige of self-respect from Gerakan would be akin to kicking the party when it's already down and almost out, which is something you don't do after a partnership of nearly four decades. But if the people out there who will be casting votes do not appreciate Gerakan much or feel it is still relevant, the BN leadership may be compelled to take a pragmatic approach. If it comes to that, Gerakan will have to reassess its position within BN.

But what can it do?

Last February, its former president, Lim Keng Yaik, expressed lack of confidence in Koh Tsu Koon's ability to take the party out if its decline, and told Gerakan to stop thinking of taking back Penang. He advised the party to return instead to its ideological base of multi-racialism, and play "a more prominent part as the influencing partner in future politics" to move towards that ideological path.

Would it be able to do this within BN? Does it have the clout? Or should it pull out and be on its own? But then, how will it survive? While the MCA as an independent party can still pander to Chinese voters in some constituencies, what kind of voters would an independent Gerakan attract?

Should it join Pakatan Rakyat, which exhibits some semblance of multi-racialism? Or, as Lim hinted, link up with the multi-racial parties in Sabah and Sarawak?

However one looks at it, the future for Gerakan looks uncertain. Even now, time doesn't seem to be on its side. With talk being rife that the next GE might be called next year, the party will have to get its act together soon and decide which way it's going.

The question is, does it have the gumption to forget about its past achievements and set a new course? Does it have visionaries with a broader view and a game plan? Or does it merely have self-deluding and effete leaders who can only say sorry when the *nasi* has already become *bubur*?

A CHANGE IS GOING TO COME

I was asked by my old friend Marion D'Cruz to write a poem she could choreograph a dance to for Aliran's 'People First, Democracy Now!' dinner that was eventually held on June 26, 2010, at the Petaling Jaya Civic Centre. She gave me the theme and the title. I set about writing it and here's the result. Marion read the poem at the event while Elaine Pedley and Judimar Hernandez danced to it.

sing my beloved country
a change is going to come
when the hornbill flies from the white-haired rajah
and the dog's head comes to its senses
from Kinabalu to the Kinta Valley
the monsoon flood will cleanse the dirt
listen, Gilgamesh, to the words of Utnapishtun
restore the order of Hammurabi
the tainted and the greedy will be swept away
and the earth will swallow the rent collectors

arise my beloved country
a change is going to come
when the ghosts of the murdered are finally appeased
and we dance on the graves of unjust judges
embrace the Kingdom of Heavenly Peace

where no one calls himself a lord
go forth, Yuanzhang, make bright the light
that shines for Umar on his nightly rounds
as he seeks out the hungry and cares for the weak
while the city sleeps in the lap of justice

rejoice my beloved country
a change is going to come
when the immigrant sheds the skin of the lion
and becomes his genuine self again
the scales that are faulty will no more serve
to weigh out favours in unequal parts
give us instead Ashoka's wheel,
his welcome to all faiths, his love for all children
Martin will see the promised land
and the *imam* will sit down with the priest

a change is going to come, my beloved country,
so sing, arise, rejoice

THE OTHER SIDE

PAKATAN RAKYAT (PR) — COMPRISING MAINLY PKR, THE DAP, PAS — GAVE A STRONG SHOWING AT THE 2008 GENERAL ELECTION BY MANAGING TO BREAK BN'S HOLD ON A TWO-THIRDS MAJORITY IN PARLIAMENT AND TO WIN FIVE STATES. ONE OF THE STATES, PERAK, WAS EVENTUALLY LOST THROUGH BN'S MANIPULATION, WHICH LURED SOME PR STATE ASSEMBLYMEN TO DEFECT. AFTER THAT, PR SUFFERED MORE DEFECTIONS THAT SEVERELY DAMAGED ITS IMAGE. THEN PKR'S PARTY ELECTIONS WERE BOGGED DOWN BY ACCUSATIONS OF POLLS RIGGING; INTERNAL STRIFE WAS REPORTED WITHIN PR'S COMPONENT PARTIES; AND APPARENT DISAGREEMENTS OVER CERTAIN ISSUES AMONG THE PARTIES APPEARED UNRESOLVED, PARTICULARLY THE IMPLEMENTATION OF HUDUD LAW. ON TOP OF THAT, PR'S DE FACTO LEADER, ANWAR IBRAHIM, FACED A CHARGE OF COMMITTING SODOMY, AND A VIDEO WAS LATER RELEASED SHOWING A MAN WHO RESEMBLED HIM PERFORMING A SEXUAL ACT WITH A PROSTITUTE. THE SEX VIDEO INCIDENT WAS OBVIOUSLY POLITICALLY MOTIVATED AND BACKFIRED, BUT IT NONETHELESS PLANTED QUESTIONS IN PEOPLE'S MINDS. IN SPITE OF ALL THE NEGATIVE PERCEPTIONS ABOUT PR, IT STILL HAS TO BE ACKNOWLEDGED THAT THE PRESENCE OF A STRONG OPPOSITION IS ESSENTIAL IN MAKING THE RULING PARTY MORE MINDFUL OF THE PUBLIC AND MORE CIRCUMSPECT IN ITS FORMULATION OF POLICIES. THIS IS SOMETHING MALAYSIANS NEED TO APPRECIATE.

WHY BE AFRAID OF PAS?

MalaysianDigest.com, August 10, 2010

Should non-Muslim Malaysians be afraid of PAS?

That is a question that will be extremely pertinent when the next general election comes around. With a large percentage of the non-Muslim population being currently disillusioned with Barisan Nasional (BN), how would they vote if they were faced at the next general election with choosing between a candidate from BN and one from PAS?

The people who are most suspicious of and averse towards PAS are the Christians. Not all are like that, however; for instance, I know Christians who voted for PAS in the 2008 general election, including a pastor in Kedah. A Catholic friend in Penang says she and her church members fully support PAS. And many among the flock of the Church of the Divine Mercy in Shah Alam, who gave PAS MP Khalid Samad a standing ovation when he visited it in 2008, must have voted for him.

But on the other hand, I have also come across Christians who are educated, middle-class and very sensible, but who are so scared of PAS that their fear seems irrational.

The religious aspect is, of course, of utmost concern to them. They are scared that if PAS came into power, it might establish an Islamic state, and that would seriously affect Christian worship. Considering that the Christians have become a beleaguered lot over the last 20 years because of increasing restrictions being placed on them by the Government, their worry about facing worse circumstances may be understandable.

For example, getting a permit to build a church, which is probably the most basic of their concerns, now takes an inordinate amount of time. The Catholics of Shah Alam had to wait 14 years before the then BN Selangor State Government allowed them to build their church. Christian groups wanting to circumvent this problem have resorted to registering themselves as non-religious organisations.

New churches are now expected not to look like churches. Some of them look like factories, especially the St Ignatius Church in Petaling Jaya, which reportedly was prohibited from putting a cross on top of its building. Furthermore, many churches are now located in shophouses because getting religious land for the building of churches is next to impossible.

On top of that, from time to time, some BN MP would kick up a fuss in Parliament or elsewhere about crosses existing on the facades of missionary schools and agitate to have them all removed.

Would all this get worse if PAS came to rule the country?

First of all, it is unlikely that PAS can do that on its own. It now has 23 seats in Parliament. It must win 112 of the total 222 seats to gain a simple majority and become the ruling party. That would amount to a huge quantum leap.

But even if that near-impossible event did become a reality, and PAS wanted to turn Malaysia into an Islamic state, it would still need to get enough support to amend the Federal Constitution for that purpose. It would need a two-thirds majority to pass the Bill, i.e. 148 votes. Where would it get the extra 36 to add to its 112?

It may then be argued that if Pakatan Rakyat (PR) got elected to form the government, PAS would be part of it. That is true. But if it still insisted on going ahead with its Islamic state agenda, it would need the support of its coalition partners to vote for the Bill. Given that its partners are PKR and the DAP, how many votes is it likely to garner from them? Enough to make two-thirds?

I reckon that even if BN, which would then be in the Opposition, relinquished the whip in the voting on the Bill, thereby allowing its

MPs to vote according to their conscience rather than follow the party line, it would still be very unlikely that the two-thirds will be obtained.

Mathematically, then, the fearful Christians need not fear that PAS can impose an Islamic state. But for the sake of argument, even if it could and did, how much different would it be from what we're in now? After all, Najib Razak has already declared Malaysia an Islamic state, which he did in July 2007. Since becoming Prime Minster, he hasn't retracted that declaration.

Let's have a look at PAS' idea of an Islamic state. In its document on the establishment of such a state, it makes clear that Syariah law will hold sway but only Muslims will be subjected to it. Non-Muslims can choose to be subjected to it or to the current penal code of the land. In other words, there is no change for them.

It also guarantees "the rights and freedom of the individuals and the citizens of the state", and among the rights protected are freedom of religion and right to cultural expressions; freedom of speech, political association and assembly; freedom to private ownership; freedom of education; freedom to engage in business; and so on.

It pledges to uphold parliamentary democracy as PAS has accepted democracy "as the best methodology" for realising its political struggle, and to take full cognisance of the reality and sensitivities of Malaysia's multi-ethnic, multi-religious and multi-cultural make-up.

From the look of it, there is not much difference in principle from the current state. The one major difference in PAS' idea of an Islamic state, however, is that Islam will be the basis of socio-political life and it will be implemented as a comprehensive way of life.

This may be the difference that the Christians would recoil from. Even if they stopped to consider that Islamic principles are rather similar to those of Christian ones, especially in relation to the concepts of justice, equality, humanity, and that these principles are, in fact, consistent with the guarantee of religious freedom, they would not be comfortable with the setting-up of an Islamic state.

I am not a Christian myself but I do not want an Islamic state either. Neither do I want a Christian state or a Buddhist state or whatever-religion state. And that's simply because I am strongly in favour of Malaysia being a secular state.

MCA president Chua Soi Lek recently came out to say that if PR wins the next general election, the prime minister might be from PAS. He was, of course, capitalising on the non-Muslims' fear and distrust of PAS. But even if what he said does materialise, the PAS prime minister would most likely behave accordingly. The PAS politicians are not new to the game, and they are pragmatists too. They will rise to the occasion. And that occasion is recognising the realpolitik.

Malaysia is a diverse society and its major interest groups have to be pacified. The PAS prime minister would not be so naïve as to jeopardise his position by alienating them. The lessons of March 8, 2008, have been properly learnt.

Furthermore, can a PAS prime minister be that awful an option? Not if he is the likes of Nik Aziz or Nizar Jamaluddin. Both are held in high regard even by non-Muslims. Nizar even came to be adored by non-Muslim Perakians in just the short time he was their *menteri besar*. It is true that when he was named MB, there was initial apprehension among non-Muslims, but when they saw his subsequent performance, they became full of admiration for him.

Of course, it may be argued that neither of them will become PM, anyway, and in all likelihood the position would fall to Abdul Hadi Awang. He, too, is an old hand. He would know that as PM, he would not be able to behave as he would as PAS president. His constituency would be radically different, and he would have to juggle the needs of a whole spectrum of groups — ethnic, religious, cultural, etc. — and keep them satisfied. He would have to sustain their support for him. Otherwise, the outcome at the following general election would be disastrous not only for him but also for his party and coalition.

There would be things he could not do. Just as an example, it would be foolhardy (no pun intended) to ban alcohol. Not only would this anger non-Muslims who drink (and even some Muslims who do); the international community would leave in droves. Then how would Malaysia obtain foreign direct investment? Malaysia would be seen as a repressive and regressive state. How would it be competitive in this globalised world?

The rules of the political game are different now from those of the past. If Hadi were to take a hardline Muslim stance in his policies as PM, his partners in PKR and the DAP would not let him, not to mention those in Sabah and Sarawak.

Christians and non-Muslims who fear PAS need to, therefore, reassess their feelings. This is not a country that is homogeneous. There is a large non-Muslim population that cannot be ignored. They might also consider that PAS' stand on the "Allah" issue has been consistent and in support of Christian usage of the word. Pit that against a BN government that is deadset on banning it by appealing against the High Court ruling that allowed it.

Personally, I believe that a religion-based party is anathema to the harmonious development of our diverse society because politicisation of religion can be divisive. But PAS is a political reality that cannot be wished away, and it has the potential, in partnership with PKR and the DAP, of unseating the incumbent government, which needs to be removed for the sake of real and positive change.

As such, when the time of reckoning comes at the next general election, some of us when faced with the option of having to vote for PAS or BN would have to exercise the option without the baggage of irrational fear. If we don't set aside these fears, we might end up making the wrong choice.

DO WE WANT TO BE 'GREATER MALAYSIANS'?

MalaysianDigest.com, August 23, 2010

Last May, PKR supremo Anwar Ibrahim came out with a new catchphrase which was rather compelling.

While addressing a PKR-organised dinner at Gelang Patah in Johor, he told his mainly non-Malay audience, "To those who say this country is for the Malays and that they are under threat in their own country, I say you are a greater Malaysian when you fight against the plunder of your country's wealth by a few."

The "greater Malaysian" refrain was the centrepiece that resounded through his speech and found connection with those who shared his sentiment.

"You are a greater Malaysian when you are concerned about the rights and welfare of the poor among the Malays, Chinese, Indians, Dayaks and Kadazans in the whole country," Anwar asserted.

"You are a greater Malaysian when you decide not only to be good at Bahasa Melayu but also at English and then go on to learn Mandarin because that would help your country economically in a highly competitive world.

"You are a greater Malaysian when you are not only roused to indignation by the shooting death of an Aminulrasyid Amzah but also over the deaths of Teoh Beng Hock and A. Kugan while they were under investigation.

"You are a greater Malaysian when you say, 'Enough is enough, this country is mine as much as it is yours', and you decide to use your vote for a new future for your country at the next general election."

Anwar should use this catchphrase repeatedly from now on, especially in tandem with the examples he cited to illustrate what it means to be "a greater Malaysian". If he uses it to great effect, he could change some minds.

After all, what he proposes in that speech should, to any level-headed person, sound sensible. Isn't it "Malaysian" to care for the poor, the downtrodden and the victimised regardless of their race? Isn't it "Malaysian" to care about what is happening to our country — the plunder of its wealth "by a few", the ever widening of the racial rift?

That same night in May, after leaving the dinner event, Anwar proceeded to Plentong, also in Johor, and spoke to a largely Malay audience. He reportedly told them that he felt more authentically Malay and Muslim when he fought for the rights of all Malaysians, regardless of their race or religion.

"Am I not a greater Malay for doing so?" he asked them.

"Greater Malay" and "greater Malaysian" are indeed potent catchphrases. They may seem to pander to different ethnic groups but in terms of the larger idea of forging a Malaysian consciousness, they are at least consistent with each other. And they could capture the imagination of Malaysians who respect democracy, justice, fairness, and who believe in the paramouncy of the human race.

In any case, while spouting either, Anwar cannot be accused of speaking in forked tongues, saying one thing to the Malays and saying the total opposite to the non-Malays, as has been the practice of most of our politicians, particularly those of Barisan Nasional over the decades. Both "greater Malay" and "greater Malaysian" are aimed at the same goal.

Anwar should perhaps have been in Johor last week and speaking these words, in light of the controversy over the school principal who is alleged to have exhibited traits directly opposed to those of a "greater Malaysian". She had reportedly told the non-Malay pupils in her school that they were merely "*penumpang*" (passengers or tenants), and that the Chinese could go back to China. She apparently also insulted the Indian religion by likening the Indians to dogs for wearing prayer strings around their neck and wrist.

A task force has been established by the Ministry of Education to investigate this matter even though 50 police reports have been made against the principal by students of the school and parents. The authorities seem to be taking a serious view of the matter.

But then, what Deputy Prime Minister Muhyiddin Yassin has said in a statement last week is ominously telling. "There are contradictory claims to what [the principal] said," he declared, somewhat diminishing the testimonies of the 50 police reports. Already, too, the Education Director-General, Alimuddin Mohd Dom, has said that it was all a "misunderstanding" and that the matter has been resolved.

The parents, however, are adamant that it was not a misunderstanding and want disciplinary action to be taken against the principal. But there is always the likelihood that at the end of the investigations, it may still be concluded that the students and parents who complained, had misinterpreted what the principal meant.

Actually, Muhyiddin is in an unenviable position. He has to be seen to be doing the right thing as Education Minister but Johor is also his home state and he has to protect his turf. What might he risk if it were true that the principal made those racist remarks, and action were to be taken against her?

Well, let's see how it goes. All this is just speculation. It might well turn out that the ministry will do the right thing. And the "fair" thing too, as Muhyiddin has instructed. Even though "fair" is also open to interpretation.

We still remember when the reporter Tan Hoon Cheng was detained under the ISA for merely reporting that Penang Umno leader Ahmad Ismail called the non-Malays "*pendatang*". The messenger was the one who got shot; the one who originated the message escaped the ISA. Was that fair?

Coming back to Anwar, it looks more and more obvious that a future Malaysia less afflicted with racial conflict is more likely to be realised under a Pakatan Rakyat government, if Anwar's catchphrase is not just rhetoric.

He hasn't said anything yet, however, about the Johor school principal's alleged action. Perhaps he considers it something best left to other PR partners, particularly the DAP, but he should know quite well that a comment from him condemning the action would have significant import and reinforce his "greater Malaysian" call.

His point about caring for the Aminulrasyids, Teoh Beng Hocks and Kugans is interesting. I know non-Malays who showed concern about Aminulrasyid. There were NGOs comprising non-Malay members that took up the cause. Surely, Malays share the same concern for Teoh and Kugan? Surely, they can see the injustice in the system with regard to these cases?

The shenanigans that have been exposed in the Teoh case, the sudden appearance of a suicide note, the MACC's attempt to stop the Thai forensic expert Pornthip Rojanasunand from testifying, the ludicrous antics of the MACC lawyer — wouldn't these have moved the Malays as much as they have moved the non-Malays? I would not believe that the Malays by and large do not share the feeling. I know Malays who care. There must be more of them, and I don't mean only those from PAS.

Perhaps the Merdeka Centre should conduct a survey to ascertain how the races respond to the three cases. I think Malaysians are by and large decent people and if left on their own to decide between right and wrong, they will not disappoint. It is the influence and conditioning of the political leaders that have poisoned the minds of those who are not able to think for themselves. For their own advantage, these leaders would make lesser Malaysians of these people. Thus, the issue of race has been politicised for nefarious aims.

Anwar is asking all of us to be "greater Malaysians" in order to reject the racial politics that have long divided us. Surely, that is something worthy of our consideration.

In any case, I would prefer to be a "greater Malaysian". How about you?

ZAID IBRAHIM
IS BAD NEWS

MalaysianDigest.com, November 15, 2010

Zaid Ibrahim is bad news. He has proven he is not a party man and, worse, not a team player. Now he's thinking of forming his own party — a move that could hurt the Opposition.

That he's not a team player is borne out by his recent behaviour. If you join a political party, you don't go around criticising it left, right and centre in public. That hurts the party's image. And no matter how big your grouses are about the party for whatever reasons, you bring them up through the proper channels within the party, not by going to the media. If the party ignores you, then you resign honourably. After that, you can choose to keep your mouth shut or spill the beans about the party.

Zaid has been in politics a long time — more than 20 years in Umno — and he's even been a minister before; he should have known that very well. But hurting the party's image is exactly what he has been doing, especially since the PKR party elections started.

This has made him come across as someone who throws tantrums. In addition to that, he told his rival for the PKR deputy presidency, Azmin Ali, to step down from the leadership. Then he went even further and asked the party's supremo, Anwar Ibrahim, to do the same.

He said both of them were the source of the party's problems and that they should stand aside so that the party could progress. He even offered himself as the alternative leader. This was prima donna behaviour. Some might even say, it was egotism personified.

What did he achieve by doing all these opprobrious things? He had Barisan Nasional leaders and members laughing their hearts out at the farce and feeling ecstatic that PKR was breaking apart without BN having to do a single thing against it. They are still revelling in the spectacle of the Opposition being served up to the people looking misshapen and in tatters, complete with warts and bruises.

More than ever, and especially in the wake of the two BN victories in the Batu Sapi and Galas by-elections, BN has come to feel confident that the next general election would probably be a breeze for them.

Is Zaid aware of the extent of the damage he has caused? Will he take partial responsibility at least for PKR's — and, by extension, Pakatan Rakyat's — drop in image and standing? Is he even aware that he has done much damage and is continuing to do it, or is his spoilt-child ego preventing him from seeing this fact?

From his interviews in the *New Sunday Times* and *Mingguan Malaysia* both published on November 14, it would seem the answer is no. And perhaps it's because he doesn't care because he now says he may set up his own party.

He concedes on one hand that it may be just a small party, but on the other hand, he hopes that the party will encourage BN and PR to reform and transform. How could a small party perform such a major task?

He says he would be happy if his party won only one or two seats in Parliament. With that low a representation, how effective can it be? It would more likely be snuffed out by the giant coalitions. Even his declaration of wanting to be "seen as a reformist who tried to help bring maturity to the process of democracy in this country" is, in light of his recent antics, ironic.

Obviously, all of that has to do with Zaid Ibrahim the person, including what he has just expressed in his interview with the *New Sunday Times* — that he would like to return to Parliament in 2012. But Malaysian politics is not all about Zaid Ibrahim, and this he has disappointingly failed to see. Given his intellectual capacity, one would have thought he was sharper than that.

Only a month and a half ago, when he gave a dinner-lecture organised by Saya Anak Bangsa Malaysia (SABM), he said the next general election would be very tough, and one of the reasons for it was that the incumbent government coalition would not give up its power without doing whatever it would take to retain it. He said in view of that, not only the Opposition but the awakened public as well should be vigilant.

He said the Opposition would have to be united and work many times harder because the next general election would be many times harder to win than in 2008.

He suggested to Haris Ibrahim, prime mover of a third force comprising hand-picked individuals of impeccable integrity to contest in the next general election, to instead offer the third-force candidates to PR. From standing with PR, said Zaid, they could achieve the goal of bringing about reform more effectively.

This is a tune quite different from the one Zaid is singing now. In fact, if he were to set up his own party, he would force three-cornered fights in constituencies where his party also chooses to stand, and this could draw votes away from the Opposition. As a result, it could help BN win those constituencies.

If BN wins big at the next general election, Zaid knows the process of reform could be further delayed. But instead of helping the Opposition cause, his setting up of a new party would subvert it. And it would contradict all that he said at the SABM dinner-lecture.

So which is the real Zaid? Which of the things he had been saying since he joined the Opposition until just before the PKR elections represent his true beliefs? How much credence do we give him now?

Is he truly the man of principle and idealism he prides himself to be? Many Malaysians really wanted to believe he was. Some still do. But the way he is going, is he, instead, just another politician like so many of them, and perhaps not even a mature one?

On November 9, when he called on Anwar to step down as leader of PKR and offered himself as successor, he said, "I'll be a good leader." Coming from someone who sounded like a loser even before the PKR elections started, one finds that hard to imagine.

BN ONLY TALKS, BUT PAS TRANSFORMS

MalaysianDigest.com, June 6, 2011

PAS has never been so appealing to non-Malays as it is right now. Its just concluded *muktamar* (general assembly) has seen the rise of the progressives, and PAS president Hadi Awang has redefined the party's goal of setting up an Islamic state to that of a welfare state. In essence, they mean almost the same thing, and Hadi himself has acknowledged that the difference is merely semantic, but "welfare state" has a friendlier ring to it to non-Muslims, and even some Muslims. It also connotes concern with earthly matters, which in these days of rising prices and inflation are more pressingly relevant to most Malaysians, especially those whose income is low.

This change of emphasis bodes well for PAS as it shows the party's sensitivity to the times. Its delegates exhibited awareness of political realities by voting in more of the progressives and diluting the influence of the conservative *ulamas*. It should cheer non-Malays to see the return of Husam Musa as vice-president and also to see among the Central Committee names like Khalid Samad, who has gained the respect of many non-Malays for his intelligent and inclusive stance, Mohd Hatta Ramli, Kamaruddin Jaffar, Mujahid Yusof Rawa and Dzulkefly Ahmad. I know of a Chinese person who can listen to Dzulkefly discourse on religion for hours!

PAS' biggest step towards change is probably the election of Mohamad Sabu as its new deputy president, making this the first time a non-*ulama* has taken that position since the party adopted the *Kepimpinan Ulama* (Leadership by the *Ulama*) policy in 1985. Mat Sabu is well-regarded by the non-Malays; he is a powerful orator, and he is expected to be an effective counter to Umno's attempts at brainwashing the Malays with irresponsible propagandising. His inclusion in PAS' top leadership will be an asset to Pakatan Rakyat (PR) as the coalition braces for the next general election.

To be sure, the general election could have been a factor influencing the *muktamar* voting outcome as PAS would need to consolidate itself as a party that can gain support. Party members know that if it is to present itself as an alternative to Umno, it will need votes not only from the Malays but also the non-Malays. But such an agenda does not detract from affirming the party's other attributes and the course it has set for itself.

Hadi has announced that PAS will remain with PR, which is a boost to the coalition and a blow to Barisan Nasional (BN), particularly Umno. Despite the recent overtures that have been made by Umno to PAS to join BN and form a "unity government", PAS has rejected them outright. Its spiritual adviser Nik Aziz Nik Mat disclosed last month that Umno offered PAS three ministerial posts to cross over. At the *muktamar*, Hadi said in no uncertain terms that a merger with Umno would lead to narrow communalism, whereas Islam recognises the existence of plural societies.

On the whole, he spoke out strongly against Umno, excoriating it for practising "corruption, money politics, slander, racism, lying and every other filthy act that pollutes young minds". He accused Umno of having "created a flock of Malays and Muslims who are blind as a result of money politics and excessive entertainment that has made them weak and consigned them to a state of stupor".

Apart from all that, PAS' rejection of the offer achieves a dual purpose — it proves itself to be morally superior to Umno, and it shows that it stands by its partners. This confirms the perception the public already has of PAS — that it is a party with integrity, a party whose faith is unshakable and whose commitment is solid. Even if you don't like it or agree with it, you have to respect it.

That its party elections were free of money politics already speaks well for it and its members; that the party has now clearly told Umno off gives a feel-good twist to current politics. This is something truly welcome when so much that has transpired in recent weeks has been so ugly, sordid and plain dirty.

What automatically springs to mind in this regard is the sex video antic pulled by the Datuk T trio to implicate PR leader Anwar Ibrahim in a compromising position. Although the underhanded attempt by the trio has actually turned against Umno — now publicly perceived, rightly or wrongly, to have been involved in one way or another — it has nonetheless tainted Malaysian politics and given the country a negative image.

To its credit, the PAS Ulama Council has now come out to call the use of sex videos for political slander "a sin". It also berated the BN government for allowing the sex video to be aired on television and excerpts to be published in the print media. "We condemn the silent stance taken by the official government *ulama*," it declared. This move has further put Umno on the defensive.

Apart from providing the feel-good factor, PAS also shows it is rising to the need for better governance, social justice and national healing. Its welfare state idea has been around for some years already, but now seems the right time to promote it.

As Husam spells it out, the welfare state is about following the rule of law, establishing a fair system, sustaining strong finance and providing equality to all the races in the country. "One of the components of a welfare state is saving the country's revenue, which can only be achieved with good governance. The country's extra revenue can then be returned to the people," he explains.

Hadi reinforces this by referring to the current Government practice of going into business through government-linked companies (GLCs) and dividing the profits among its cronies while burdening the losses on the people by way of taxes. "PAS must remove the culture of obtaining revenue by way of burdening the people, which is the hallmark of the Umno–BN government," he advocates.

Of course, PAS needs to explain in greater detail to the people its vision of the welfare state. And it needs to do so before the next general election rolls around. But for now, it seems a better deal than what the BN Government is dishing out — rising prices of essential goods due to higher costs of fuel and electricity, and the prospect of a goods and services tax (GST).

It's ironic that for all the Government's talk about transformation, including political transformation, it is PAS that has transformed, while Umno and its BN partners remain dinosaurs, plugging outdated racial politics. They continue to play on Malay insecurity and to threaten the Chinese with no representation in government if they don't support the MCA. They are still dominated by warlords, and their members continue to hanker after projects.

In view of all this, when the reckoning comes at the next general election, which side should the voters stake their future on?

excerpt

FROM THE PLAY
*WE COULD **** YOU, MR BIRCH*

*We Could **** You, Mr Birch* was written and staged twice in 1994. It is an irreverent and cheeky satire that, among other things, points out that history can be manipulated and that historical truth depends on who is telling the story. I have included this excerpt because it recalls an episode in recent Malaysian history that is pertinent to the Datuk T trio sex video scandal, and also to affirm that Mohamad Sabu of PAS is right in saying that the history most Malaysians know is the history Umno wants us to know. Besides that, the question at the end of this scene is one we could all stop to think about. The actor playing Sultan Abdullah then was my dear friend Mano Maniam, so he is referred to by name in the text. The incomparable Ahmad Yatim played Datuk Sagor and S. Subramony gave Maharaja Lela a powerful presence.

(*ACTOR PLAYING SULTAN ABDULLAH enters with a newspaper.*)

ACTOR/S (*reads*): Speaking of power, not so long ago a politician in very high office was alleged to have had illicit sex with an underaged girl. If this was proven true, he would have been guilty of committing statutory rape. Fortunately, the most powerful man in the land intervened and saved the politician from embarrassment. Surely, the politician must have been an honourable man. He even resigned from all his official posts. Would a man who was guilty resign? Besides, how could a man of such high standing be guilty of such a lowly act? He must be the victim of a plot to topple him. Sure enough, the case was eventually closed. The highest law authority in the country pronounced that there was not enough evidence to prosecute the politician. But, the authority added, "there were strong suspicions". He said the evidence was purely circumstantial. He was right, of course; just because other cases had been brought to court based on circumstantial evidence, it didn't mean this one had to follow suit. He also said the case would be stronger if there had been witnesses. He was right again; if nobody actually saw the politician and the girl having sex, they couldn't have done it. Right? Even though the girl *did* allege that she *did* have sex with the politician, her statement cannot be considered to have credibility. Well, she's only a nobody who doesn't know better. The politician was clearly relieved that he would not be charged. In a public statement, he declared, "I am not guilty of the allegations." He affirmed his belief in "the rule of law" for its having given him "due protection". As a parting shot, he added, "The truth has finally prevailed." Meanwhile, the country's highest law authority diverted attention away from the politician and onto the girl. He revealed that she was eight weeks pregnant. But, he was quick to add, the pregnancy had no connection with the politician "based on the date of the alleged sex act between him and the girl". The law authority also revealed that the girl had alleged that she had been to bed with 14 *other* men. *Other* than whom, I wonder? Eight of the 14 had admitted to having sex with her, and this prompted a morally upright minister to declare that they should be duly prosecuted. Well, they should be – for admitting they did it. They should have said they were "not guilty of the allegations". The minister said the girl must also be prosecuted even though she was a minor. He proclaimed, rightly and righteously, that "the sanctity of the law must be upheld".

(*Enter ACTOR PLAYING DATUK SAGOR.*)

ACTOR/DS:	What is that all about, Mano?
ACTOR/S:	History.
ACTOR/DS:	According to whom?
ACTOR/S:	The newspapers.
ACTOR/DS:	Do you believe everything you read in the newspapers?
ACTOR/S:	Don't you?

(*Enter ACTOR PLAYING MAHARAJA LELA with newspaper.*)

ACTOR/S: More history.

(*ACTOR PLAYING SULTAN ABDULLAH goes.*)

ACTOR/L (*reads*):   A minister once said, quote: "The media must be given freedom to express opinion freely, even the right to be wrong. But if it abuses its right, then the authorities have a duty to intervene." Unquote. In 1987, three newspapers had their publishing permits withdrawn.

ACTOR/DS: I'm glad I'm not a journalist.

ACTOR/L: The same minister said, quote: "The judiciary must be free to discharge its duties but it cannot have 100 per cent freedom or it will lose its sense of responsibility and do something wrong." Unquote. In 1988, the Head of All Judges and three very senior judges were sacked.

ACTOR/DS: I'm glad I'm not a judge.

ACTOR/L: The minister also said, quote: "Everyone must realise they cannot abuse their power. No government should be allowed to have the freedom to do exactly as it pleases." Unquote.

ACTOR/DS: Who ensures that?

ACTOR/L (*indicating the audience*): Ask them.

(ACTOR/DS *goes to some members of the audience and asks them the question,* "*Who ensures that the government of a country does not do exactly as it pleases?*")

SEX, LIES AND VIDEOTAPE

....

· ·

POLITICS IN MALAYSIA CAN BE UNSPEAKABLY DIRTY. THE LOWEST FORM OF GUTTER POLITICS IS PROBABLY THE SORT THAT CENTRES AROUND ILLICIT SEX. IN A COUNTRY THAT HAS ISLAM AS ITS MAIN RELIGION, THIS SEEMS IRONIC. IT'S IRONIC, TOO, THAT FEW PEOPLE SEEM TO QUESTION WHICH PARTY IS THE MORE IMMORAL —— THE ONE THAT PERFORMED THE ILLICIT SEX OR THE ONE THAT EXPOSES IT FOR AN ULTERIOR PURPOSE.

WHO IS THE MORE IMMORAL?

MalaysianDigest.com, March 22, 2011

Oh no! Not again! They're gunning for Anwar Ibrahim over another alleged sex scandal. The video revealed by the mysterious Datuk T showing a man resembling an Opposition party leader having sex with a woman, said to be a prostitute, is obviously targeted at him.

But the timing of its revelation to the media on March 21 suspiciously coincides with the dissolution of the Sarawak State Assembly, paving the way for state elections. Not to mention the part in Mahathir Mohamad's recently launched memoir, *A Doctor in the House*, that claims Anwar arranged to have sex with four girls when he was deputy prime minister in 1998.

What has Malaysia turned into? The sordid sex opera capital of the world? What are we showing the world? That we are a nation of sex maniacs? Or, worse, that our politics is so dirty that we turn to sex to discredit our enemies?

We have done it to Chua Soi Lek, and now we are doing it to Anwar — for the third time. Who will be next in the near future?

On the other hand, the case in which a minister was alleged to have raped his Indonesian maid seems to have been adeptly swept aside.

Rape is certainly serious because it causes harm to another person. But if a politician visits a prostitute, what's the beef? Isn't it his private matter?

When Soi Lek had sex with the woman with whom he was caught on video, that was also his private matter. But what is more despicable in that case — and the current one — is that the videotaping was arranged.

If we want to accuse Soi Lek (and now, apparently, Anwar) of being immoral, what about the morals of the person or persons who masterminded the videotaping? Aren't such individuals more devious — and therefore, more worthy of our contempt — for conniving to destroy another human being? Aren't such people cowardly for resorting to such covert acts?

Isn't Datuk T cowardly for not revealing his identity? He claims he was not the one who set up the videotaping, that he actually discovered it, so why is he afraid to come forward and show who he is?

He says he was shocked when he discovered the four cameras and a recorder in the hotel room where the sexual tryst took place, and decided to take the recorder with him. As someone who was presumably close to and trusted by the politician concerned, why did he not show the video to the latter? Why was he keeping it to himself? Did he there and then plan to use it at some point in the future for his own benefit?

If he wasn't the one behind the videotaping, who was? Why did he not investigate it further? Especially since he was at the time an "insider" in the politician's camp? Why is he now allowing himself to be a pawn of some other person or persons without finding out who they are and why they did it? How can he simply take over the product of someone else's handiwork and use it for his own purpose?

Why is he now turning against the politician who had trusted him? Why does he now call on the politician — and even the latter's wife — to quit politics? What has she got to do with this?

Is he even sure about the authenticity of the video? If he is, why does he write in the statement given to the press: "*If it is true* ... [the couple] must step down from politics" (my italics)? He says if they did not accede to his demand, he would call on several NGOs to set up an independent panel to investigate and study the authenticity of the video. Does that connote that he's not sure?

It's interesting that the set-up of the press conference to reveal the video smacks of an organised and sophisticated backing. The security checks on the journalists attending it were reportedly done with metal scanners, and the journalists were provided with jackets to wear to prevent them from touching their pockets. The event was held in the luxurious Carcosa Seri Negara. Who sponsored all that?

Datuk T's motive, expressed in the statement given out to the press, sounds like politicalese: "Why am I doing this? There is a limit to lies — 'Enough is Enough' and it is high time the public know … THE TRUTH." Does that reflect the sentiment of an "insider"?

As for the video itself, it is reported to have been recorded with high quality equipment which rendered clear and sharp images. It's "professionally done", Datuk T reportedly commented. This again smacks of organised and sophisticated backing. Why aren't we asking who was behind it? Why did Home Minister Hishammuddin Hussein initially dismiss it as something that could not be investigated because no one had yet lodged a police report? Now that Anwar has made such a report, let's see what proceeds from there.

This could be a case not only of invasion of privacy but, more seriously, one of conspiracy. It is also possible that the entire sexual liaison was staged, with a look-alike being employed to pass off for the politician — as is done in movies.

Why was the woman not brought along to vouch for the video's authenticity? Datuk T says when he went back to the hotel room to look for the politician's Omega watch and found it not there, he confronted her about it and she gave it back to him. This indicates that he knows how to contact her directly. So, wouldn't he be able to produce her if her testimony is required?

A lot of intriguing questions have arisen from this drama, raising a lot of suspicion. In light of that, the quintessential detective might well say, "I smell a rat."

Ironically, this episode could turn out in Anwar's favour as people begin to be disgusted by how low his enemies will go to try and destroy him. Many would no doubt have already been put off by the front page of *The Star* of March 22 carrying a huge picture of him next to the headline 'Sex video shocker'.

The newspaper's intended message is clear — in the picture, both his index fingers are pointing at himself as if to say, "I'm the one". Considering that no one, not even Datuk T, has been reported to name the politician in the video, it is distasteful to run a picture of Anwar on the front page in relation to the story, and especially in such a pose.

The Sarawak state elections may be coming up and the stakes may be high for Barisan Nasional to score a big victory, but this is a blatant spin that speaks poorly of a national newspaper.

All these underhanded tactics must cease. Politics may be a dirty game, but let's not make it more dirty than it already is. The general consensus among the public is that there are national problems that need to be urgently solved. Energy should be concentrated on these priorities, instead of spent on distracting us from them.

WHY HAVE THE SEX VIDEO TRIO NOT BEEN CHARGED?

MalaysianDigest.com, March 24, 2011

So, those who surmised that the sex video revealed by Datuk T was a political ploy have been proven right. The people behind it — three of them — have confessed to it. They were forced to reveal themselves because PKR's MP Johari Abdul had earlier spilled the beans on them. It all unravelled like a cheap soap opera.

Former Melaka chief minister Rahim Thamby Chik, businessman Shazryl Eskay Abdullah and Shuib Lazim, treasurer-general of Perkasa, have come out to say they are Datuk T. And they have the cheek to call for a Royal Commission of Inquiry into the sex video.

In the first place, they have transgressed Section 292 of the Penal Code for possessing and distributing pornographic material. Regardless of who the person in the video is, the trio are culpable. Exposing a politician's sexual activity does not protect them from the law.

After their intended target, Opposition leader Anwar Ibrahim, had lodged a police report, the Inspector-General of Police, Ismail Omar, announced that the case would be investigated under Section 292.

That being so, the police should now logically arrest all three for possession and distribution of pornographic material and have them charged in court. They should have moved in right after the trio gave their press conference to reveal themselves.

If the trio were the authors of the statement given out to the media calling on the politician (said to be in the video) and his wife to quit politics, they should also be charged for blackmail.

So, what's holding the police back? Are they awaiting further instructions from Home Minister Hishammuddin Hussein? If so, Hishammuddin should observe the rule of law. He should not protect these people because they are Umno members or pro-Umno. This is where the public can judge how sincere the Government really is. If the trio go scot-free, it will be a sure sign that the Government practises double standards.

The trio's call for a Royal Commission of Inquiry (RCI) into the sex video is unwarrantable. Why should there be one? In the case of V.K. Lingam in 2007, there was ample cause for an RCI — the issue of the fixing of judges was of immense public concern as it affected one of our country's institutions. Where is the public concern for a case involving a man, even though he may be a public figure, visiting a prostitute as a private matter? How does that affect the public? It's his own private concern, and the public is no worse for it.

In calling for an RCI, the trio appear to be trying to distract us from the offence they have actually committed. In fact, if they were also the ones who masterminded the videotaping, it would mean they are far more immoral than anyone who merely visits a prostitute. They would have no moral right to cast stones at others. Their action would have to be seen to be nothing less than repulsive, even inhuman. For what kind of human being would do something as despicable as this to destroy another human being?

But for now, they have not said they were behind the videotaping. They maintain that Shazryl discovered the four cameras and recorder in the hotel room where the sexual liaison took place when he was asked by the politician to go back there and retrieve his Omega watch. If that is so, who set up the cameras and recorder? Who wanted to catch the politician in the act? And why? There might be a larger force at work here. Finding out who or what it is would be finding the key to the mystery that surrounds the whole drama.

Another key question is why, after discovering the video, Shazryl hooked up with Rahim and Shuib to expose the politician. Why did Shazryl not ascertain the source of the videotaping before deciding to go public with the video?

He admits he was also in the tape but refuses to say why he was at the hotel where the sexual liaison took place. Does this mean he was caught on tape unknowingly or was he in on the taping as well? From his saying that he had felt "used by Anwar for far too long", could it imply that he wanted to get back at the man by setting the whole thing up?

The association with Rahim is most intriguing. He was the Melaka chief minister who had to resign in 1994 over allegations of his sexual relations with an underaged girl. At the press conference, he indicates he has a score to settle with Anwar by accusing the latter of lying to him. He urges Anwar to take responsibility for his actions by stepping down, like he himself did in 1994. Did Shazryl go to Rahim after discovering the video, or was Rahim also in it from the beginning?

Is all this part of a plot to exact revenge? Is it also one that is aimed at luring PKR MPs to defect? As PKR's Johari Abdul has revealed to the media, he was invited to privately view the sex video on Monday by the trio, after which they made him offers of financial incentives, suggesting that he defect.

He says they also offered to take him to meet Prime Minister and Umno President Najib Razak, and asked him to bring more Pakatan Rakyat MPs to see the video. He inferred that the trio wanted to also turn them against Anwar. If all this is true, we are seeing yet another instance of gutter politics being practised — the sort that is as dirty as that perpetrated in the Perak coup of 2008.

The soap opera, however, has apparently not unfolded as it was scripted, and as it has turned out, this whole ugly and sordid drama could actually hurt Umno and Barisan Nasional. Even if Rahim and gang were acting on their own, we have now managed to see further evidence of what Umno (and Perkasa) people can resort to. Besides, we still don't know who actually masterminded the videotaping. There could be deeper and more sinister implications. There could even be a larger conspiracy. This is a mystery the police must solve.

But first, the police must also do what's right. Already, the public has lost much faith in them. If they don't act against the trio in accordance with the law now, they will be seen to be mere puppets of the Government.

THE SEX VIDEO COMEDY AND THE MALAYSIAN MALADY

Free Malaysia Today, May 5, 2011

The sex video saga is really turning out to be a farce. It's so funny you can't help but laugh.

First, the Datuk T trio, who brought public attention to the video, have been made the butt of countless jokes. Second, the police seem to be hesitant in revealing their findings even as the video has been leaked out and posted on Youtube and Umno-friendly blogs although the only copy is supposed to be in police custody. And now one of the trio has taken the *sumpah laknat*. Last week, Shazryl Eskay Abdullah swore on the Quran to make us believe he is telling the truth in saying that the man in the video is Opposition leader Anwar Ibrahim. What's going to happen next?

This act of swearing on the Quran is getting to be a trend. In 2008, Saiful Bukhari Azlan did it to attest he was sodomised by Anwar. That same year, no less than Prime Minister Najib Razak himself also did it to have us believe he was never involved with Altantuya. Despite their gestures, many people are still sceptical.

In the case of Eskay, the act is hugely ironic. He would have to be a good follower of the faith to take such an oath and be believed, but has he not been tainted by his own admission that he is one of the people caught on the video? As it is, he has not come clean on why he was there. His narratives are often cloudy and enigmatic.

It's just as well that his collaborator Rahim Thamby Chik did not swear on the Quran too. His record of allegedly having had sex with an underaged girl, an act amounting to statutory rape, would have wrecked his credibility. In fact, it's another laughable point that Rahim is part of this trio — he, of all people, accusing another man of immorality!

Besides, what the trio have done in regard to the sex video is already immoral. And that's not even saying they were behind the videotaping itself, which is still a mystery. Simply using it to destroy the reputation and career of another human being is already without doubt an immoral act. How, then, are we to believe that by swearing on the Quran, Eskay exhibits religious conviction? Does it not more likely appear as some kind of stunt?

Does it not also appear as an attempt to win public sympathy? Or a desperate measure? After all, the day before he took the *sumpah laknat*, Eskay intimated to the media that he and his collaborators would soon be charged in court; although what the charge would be, he wouldn't say.

That was actually quite a revelation, because up till that time, no one had known if the police were ever going to take any action against the trio for possessing and exhibiting pornography. The Inspector-General of Police (IGP) had said from the outset that the case would be investigated under Section 292 of the Penal Code, which covers that offence, but along the way no action seemed to have been taken.

The Star did report on March 25 that according to Deputy Commissioner Ghazali Md Amin, three unnamed individuals had been arrested in connection with the sex video, but when the Datuk T trio were asked if they were the ones, they said they were not. Rahim even told the media that when the police questioned them on March 24, they did not sign any document stating they were arrested and released on bail.

Thereafter, nobody gave a straight answer when asked about the truth. Not even the cops. In fact, on March 25, when the IGP himself was asked why Rahim and Eskay were not arrested when they went to the police headquarters for questioning, the country's top cop actually said, "What offence (did they commit), you tell me." But then on the eve of his *sumpah laknat*, Eskay told *Malaysiakini* he was arrested "that day" (without specifying which) and "was bailed out with RM10,000". Intriguing! More so when you consider that the IGP seemed ignorant of the offence when earlier he had mentioned Section 292. Did he have a lapse of memory?

Going by the events, the public perception so far is that the police are biased in their handling of the case — and that's cause for another hoot. There was reportedly even a police escort for the Datuk T trio when they arrived at the mosque for the *sumpah laknat* ceremony. This reeks of VIP treatment. At least one of them, Eskay, wore a bulletproof vest, which he, however, claims belongs to him. Nonetheless, do these three, who should instead be charged in court under Section 292, deserve police escort?

To reinforce the public perception of the police bias, the next day Parti Keadilan Rakyat (PKR) alleged that a police officer with the rank of senior assistant commissioner had been giving talks to school principals and teachers in Kelantan in which he told them Anwar was the man in the sex video and a threat to national security. Whatever the truth of PKR's allegation, it's hard to bet now on police impartiality.

Moreover, the police still haven't told us how the sex video in their custody managed to get into cyberspace. More important, the central and most pressing question has not yet been answered although they have reportedly been investigating the case intensively. That question is: Who was actually behind the videotaping? Is it so difficult to find out who the culprits are? Who was the prostitute in the video? Have the police got to her? What has she revealed?

Are we going to get any answers at all? Or will this, like the many intriguing mysteries that have arisen in this wonderful land of ours, such as the murder of Altantuya, be swept under the carpet?

Could it be that the police are waiting for instructions from their political masters? Are these political masters calculating when the right time would be to take action, how the case should be spun, who should be arrested, what should be done so that they can make political capital out of it?

It seems there is no going by the truth any more in Malaysia, and this sex video saga illustrates it clearly. It is now all about twisting the truth to one's advantage, hiding the truth, turning the truth into falsehood. And, worse, making falsehood the truth.

This, fellow citizens, is the Malaysian Malady. And the people who are suffering for it are the innocent *rakyat*.

Stricken with it, we have to laugh or face despair, and no amount of crying will bring us relief. On that note, perhaps the best laugh stems from Najib Razak's response when he was asked by the media if he had watched the sex video when it was uploaded on the Internet. "*Apa punya soalan ini* (What kind of question is this)?" he said, dismissing it.

Don't you think it's a fair and legitimate question? But why is the PM evading it? Well, that, fellow Malaysians, is the crux of the Malaysian Malady.

BERSIH 2.0 AND ALL THAT DIRT

BERSIH 2.0, A COALITION OF NGOS, HAD BEEN CALLING FOR FREE AND FAIR ELECTIONS. IT HAD ENGAGED WITH THE ELECTION COMMISSION TO PRESENT ITS CASE A FEW TIMES BUT NOTHING CAME OUT OF THE MEETINGS. THEN THE SARAWAK STATE ELECTIONS WERE HELD IN APRIL 2011, AND BERSIH 2.0 FOUND NUMEROUS INSTANCES OF FRAUD AND DIRTY POLITICS. IT WAS COMPELLED TO CALL FOR A RALLY TO CREATE PUBLIC AWARENESS OF THE URGENT NEED FOR ELECTORAL REFORM. THE DATE IT SET WAS JULY 9. PERKASA AND UMNO YOUTH, FOR NO REAL OR GOOD REASONS, COMPLICATED THE MATTER BY ANNOUNCING THEY WOULD STAGE COUNTER-RALLIES. WHAT? TO DEFEND DIRTY ELECTIONS? THE GOVERNMENT REACTED IN REPRESSIVE FASHION. ABETTED BY THE POLICE, IT PERFORMED THE SILLIEST AND MOST VICIOUS ACTS. IT ARRESTED A MOTLEY CREW OF SEEMINGLY HARMLESS ACTIVISTS AND BRANDED THEM TERRORISTS, ALLEGED THEY WERE "WAGING WAR AGAINST THE YANG DI-PERTUAN AGONG". SIX OF THEM WERE THEN DETAINED UNDER THE EMERGENCY ORDINANCE, WHICH WAS ALMOST LIKE BEING HELD UNDER THE ISA. NAJIB AND HIS PEOPLE ASSASSINATED THE CHARACTER OF AMBIGA SREENEVASAN, THE CHAIRMAN OF THE BERSIH 2.0 STEERING COMMITTEE, TO THE EXTENT OF CALLING HER AN ENEMY OF ISLAM (BUT WHY WAS ISLAM RELEVANT?). WARNINGS WERE ISSUED AGAINST ANYONE TAKING PART IN THE RALLY. NAMES OF PERSONS PROHIBITED FROM ENTERING THE CITY CENTRE WERE ISSUED BY THE POLICE. EVEN PEOPLE WERE ARRESTED FOR WEARING YELLOW BECAUSE THAT

WAS THE BERSIH 2.0 COLOUR. DESPITE ALL THE THREATS, MANY BRAVE CITIZENS TURNED UP ON JULY 9 TO SHOW THEIR DEFIANCE. SOME REPORTS PUT THE NUMBERS AT 15,000, SOME AT 50,000. THE POLICE WERE WAY OFF IN THEIR ESTIMATE OF 6,000. I WAS THERE, AND I COULD SEE THAT THE CROWD I WAS WITH EXCEEDED THE POLICE ESTIMATE — AND THAT WAS ONLY ONE GROUP. THE PEOPLE WHO SHOWED UP STAGED A PEACEFUL PROTEST, BUT THE POLICE RESPONDED TO THEM WITH VIOLENCE. THEY SHOT TEAR GAS AND WATER CANNONS AT THE CROWD. THEY KICKED AND BEAT UP SOME OF THE PROTESTORS. THEY STORMED INTO TUNG SHIN HOSPITAL. THEY ATTACKED AMBIGA AND OPPOSITION POLITICANS WITH TEAR GAS IN A TUNNEL AND ARRESTED SOME OF THEM. ON THE WHOLE, THE POLICE ARRESTED NEARLY 1,700 PEOPLE ON THAT DAY OF SHAME. (IF 1,700 WERE ARRESTED, IS IT LIKELY THE TURNOUT WAS ONLY 6,000?) THE HANDLING OF THE ENTIRE EPISODE BY NAJIB WAS DISGRACEFUL. HE ACTED TOUGH AFTERWARDS BY ROUNDING UP ABOUT 6,000 UMNO MEMBERS AND MALAY NGOS AT PUTRA WORLD TRADE CENTRE IN A SHOW OF FORCE. HE SAID THE MOST UNBECOMING AND SHAMEFUL THINGS THAT A PM COULD SAY, LIKE "WHAT IS BERSIH? ALL WE HAVE TO DO IS GET ONE MILLION UMNO MEMBERS TOGETHER AND WE CAN CONQUER KUALA LUMPUR!" AND "LET THE MALAYS UNITE AND SHOW THEM WHOSE COUNTRY THIS IS!" AND HE CALLS HIMSELF PM OF 1MALAYSIA? LATER, WHEN HE REALISED THAT THE PUBLIC LARGELY DISAPPROVED OF HIS HANDLING OF THE BERSIH 2.0 RALLY, HE TRIED TO MAKE AMENDS FOR IT. OR SO IT SEEMED.

WHY IS PERKASA
AGAINST BERSIH 2.0?

MalaysianDigest.com, June 14, 2011

Many people have come to regard Ibrahim Ali as a clown, including Minister in the Prime Minister's Department Nazri Aziz. On that score, one hopes Ibrahim was just talking like a clown when he recently announced that his organisation, Perkasa, would oppose the planned Bersih 2.0 rally on July 9 by staging a counter-demonstration. "That means," as he himself says, "on that day, there will be confrontation."

This is militant talk. This is a threat to cause violence. And to add fuel to it, Ibrahim has pledged that in the event of a clash, "I will fight to the end."

But why would Perkasa want to oppose the Bersih 2.0 rally? The rally has nothing to do with race — it is not demonstrating against Malay supremacy, which Perkasa was set up to defend. The rally is calling for electoral and institutional reform. It is calling for the electoral roll to be cleaned up, postal voting to be reformed, indelible ink to be used at elections, all political parties to be given free and fair access to the media, automatic voter registration, a minimum of 21 days for the campaign period, the strengthening of public institutions, a stop to corruption, and a stop to dirty politics.

Is Perkasa against free and fair elections? Is it against calling for a stop to corruption?

Ibrahim explains: "A big demonstration like the Bersih rally, which expects to draw about 100,000 protestors, will cause chaos. It could be like the protests in the Middle East."

Ibrahim thinks people will throw stones, burn cars, and injuries will result like in Tunisia. History has shown that this was not the case during the last Bersih rally in 2007. About 40,000 people were estimated to have taken part then, but it was an entirely peaceful rally, except when the police fired water cannons and hurled tear gas at the protestors. No one was out to throw stones or burn cars.

This time around, the rally is expected to be peaceful as well, aimed at creating awareness among Malaysians of the need for electoral reform. If no one intervenes, including the police, if the permit is granted and the police keep vigil merely to pre-empt untoward incidents, there should be no harm done.

So, what Ibrahim has predicted is unfounded. Besides, his reference to Tunisia is ironic. The protests there actually brought down an unpopular and repressive regime. Is such a positive cause, like Bersih 2.0's, to be spoken of in negative terms?

In fact, what will cause chaos is the clash that could result if Perkasa and the other NGOs he proposes to co-opt take to the streets at the same time to oppose the Bersih 2.0 rally. What he is proposing to do is the real danger. But Ibrahim knows he can get away with expressing it because he has always been untouched in the past. Many have been the times when he said things that could have caused him to be charged with sedition, but never has he been called to account for them. Last month, he said he would launch a *jihad* against Malaysian Christians if they tried to usurp the position of Islam, and before that, he had said other things that incited hatred against non-Malays.

It may be that the Government takes no action against him because it considers him a clown, or even a paper tiger. Or it may be that he is actually helping the Government by opposing the Bersih 2.0 rally because the ruling party seemingly does not endorse the idea of free and fair elections. After all, the 2007 rally was partly instrumental in its loss of its two-thirds majority. The ruling party would no doubt be worried that another such rally could dim its prospects at the next general election.

Whatever the reason or reasons, in the context of Ibrahim's current pronouncement, it looks bad for the Government. Speculation has already been rife that Perkasa is actually affiliated to Umno, that it is the organisation to which Umno has outsourced the job of defending *Ketuanan Melayu* so that Umno is not seen to be racist; now, with Perkasa going outside of its prescribed agenda and *raison d'etre* as an organisation to oppose Bersih 2.0, it appears to be another Government stooge.

In politics, perception often takes ascendancy over reality, so even if it were not true that Perkasa is affiliated to Umno, the perception that it is has now been confirmed.

Ibrahim says he is stopping the Bersih 2.0 rally in the name of democracy. This is based on his reasoning that "there are people who do not agree with this rally". Well, fine. The people who do not agree have a right to express it publicly, too. But by the same token, Bersih 2.0 has a right to stage its rally, so stopping it is actually anti-democratic.

He reportedly goes on to say that he is not worried by the expected Bersih 2.0 turnout of 100,000 people because most Malaysians will not accept the movement's demands. If he's not worried, then why bother to oppose it? He reasons that since Malaysia has a population of 27 million people, even if Bersih 2.0 were to bring 300,000 to the rally, there would still be 26 million plus who would not agree with it. His mathematics is okay, but his reasoning is clearly faulty and hopelessly warped.

Nazri may be right after all in calling Ibrahim Ali a clown. But even so, if there is a movement going on to campaign for reform, clowns should not be allowed to spoil the party. Especially if they are clowns who might start an unwanted fire.

WHAT IS THIS COUNTRY COMING TO?

MalaysianDigest.com, July 1, 2011

What is this country coming to? Many Malaysians are asking this question in view of the numerous actions taken by the police over the past week.

First, they arrested 30 Parti Sosialis Malaysia (PSM) members, including MP for Sungai Siput Michael Jeyakumar Devaraj, and are now investigating them for resurrecting Communism and waging war against the Yang di-Pertuan Agong. While on their way to a Bersih roadshow in Penang, they were arrested in Kepala Batas and found to have in their possession T-shirts bearing faces of Chin Peng and Rashid Maidin. They have been remanded for seven days.

Communism? That's an old story. The Communist Party of Malaya is long dead and gone. Chin Peng is a geriatric and Rashid Maidin is dead. The party disbanded in 1989 after signing a peace treaty with the Malaysian Government, and its members were allowed to reside in Malaysia if they chose to do so. After 22 years of its being defunct and virtually forgotten, why is Communism still a threat today?

And if it were — by some stretch of the imagination — are we to believe that this threat is manifest in these 30 PSM members among whom 14 are women, the oldest aged 64?

A friend of mine who was at the court in Penang when the 30 were brought in told me they were just "a motley crew" of people who didn't look like they would carry a stick to fight, much less wage war against the Agong. "When I saw that, my faith in the system hit rock-bottom," he said.

"And to see Jeyakumar in handcuffs was too much," he added. "He alone is worth many of our people in power put together. Top scorer in exams, a doctor, a man who has dedicated his life to helping poor people — he doesn't deserve this."

Like my friend, I, too, knew Jeyakumar while at school. He was one year my junior at the Penang Free School, and I remember him well as a thoughtful, gentle person. He was soft-spoken, cerebral and humble despite his well-to-do background.

I find it hard to believe that someone like him would wage war against the Agong. Only someone stupid or deranged would consider doing that. He might be a socialist, but that's a far cry from being a Communist. Don't the police and the Government know the difference? To all intents and purposes, he is probably someone who transcends labels and merely cares for the poor.

And why remand him and the others for a week? The High Court has since upheld this decision and said it is correct. Justice Zamani A. Rahim said the case was serious. "It involves the security of the country, of everyone — you and me and our children." These 30 people are so dangerous that they are a threat to us and our children?

Case number two. Sasterawan Negara (National Laureate) A. Samad Said was called in by the police and told he was being investigated for sedition because he had read part of a poem at the Bersih launch on June 19. When has reading a poem been seditious? In any case, did it provoke an uprising afterwards?

Look at the poem. Can it threaten national security?

Unggun-bersih

Semakin lara kita didera bara —
kita laungkan juga pesan merdeka:
Demokrasi sebenderang mentari
sehasrat hajat semurni harga diri.

Lama resah kita – demokrasi luka;
lama duka kita – demokrasi lara.
Demokrasi yang angkuh, kita cemuhi;
suara bebas yang utuh, kita idami!

Dua abad lalu Sam Adams berseru
(di Boston dijirus teh ke laut biru):
Tak diperlu gempita sorak yang gebu,
diperlu hanya unggun api yang syahdu.

Kini menyalalah unggun sakti itu;
kini merebaklah nyala unggun itu.

Cleansing Fire
(translation)

Even as we are lashed by the sickening fire,
we still shout out the message of Merdeka:
Democracy as brilliant as the sun,
united in purpose as pure as self-worth.

Long have we been restless – democracy is wounded;
Long have we been sad – democracy is ill.
Democracy that is arrogant disgusts us;
We dream of a free voice that is full and strong!

Two centuries ago Sam Adams declared
(in Boston while tea was being poured into the blue sea):
No need for noisy, trivial cheering,
all that's needed is a serene bonfire.

Light now that magic fire;
illuminate to others the flame of that fire.

Samad Said was prompted to say to the media afterwards that instead of intimidating writers, the action the police had taken against him could spur fellow writers to use the power of literature to state their views openly.

Indeed, it is time for Malaysian writers to come forward and defend what is right. All those who have been conferred the Sasterawan Negara award, like Shahnon Ahmad, Abdullah Hussain, Muhammad Haji Salleh, Noordin Hassan, Anwar Ridhwan and the newly installed Kemala should use their pen to "*menyala unggun sakti*" and "*merebak nyalanya*".

Case number three. More than a hundred people have been arrested for wearing Bersih T-shirts. Eight of them were among 14 people giving out the national flag at a wet market in Sungai Siput. All 14 were arrested.

But what is the offence? Which part of the law says it is an offence to wear Bersih T-shirts in public?

Home Minister Hishammuddin Hussein has come up with the justification. "If the Bersih T-shirt is related to an illegal activity, then wearing it is illegal," he said.

Is that logical? What "illegal activity"? The Bersih rally hasn't happened yet. Until the rally is carried out, no illegal activity has been performed yet. So how could he declare it illegal? On that score, why should it be illegal to wear a Bersih T-shirt?

As an analogy, if I were to express an intent to do something illegal, like smoking marijuana openly in public, but I haven't done it yet, would it make sense for the police to arrest me? If they should do so, the case would be thrown out of court straight away. Doesn't Hishammuddin, who is a lawyer himself, know that?

Case number four. The police raided the Bersih secretariat and detained its staff members. According to Bersih, the cops did not produce a search warrant. They confiscated Bersih T-shirts, leaflets and other paraphernalia.

Why raid only the Bersih secretariat? Why not raid those of Perkasa and Umno Youth as well since they will also be holding rallies? And why did the cops not produce a search warrant but, instead, threaten to break open the gates?

Later that day, the announcement came from the Inspector-General of Police, Ismail Omar, that the police would not only arrest those wearing Bersih T-shirts but also those using any medium to promote the Bersih rally. "Not just T-shirts but shoes, cars, buses. If these are the tools used to encourage people to gather (illegally), this amounts to sedition," he said.

Shoes too? Sedition? For dressing as one likes? Aren't Malaysians allowed the freedom to dress as they like? Are there new laws that have come into place without our knowing?

Gopeng MP Lee Boon Chye was arrested for wearing a yellow T-shirt the next day. It did not even have "Bersih" printed on it, it was just a plain yellow collared T-shirt. The police told him he was arrested for illegal assembly as he was with three other people at a wet market. Two of them wore Bersih T-shirts and the third, a white shirt.

Ipoh OCPD Asst Comm Azisman Alias said, "The shirts are evidence that they are trying to get people to take part in the illegal rally." Is that all it takes?

What is happening to our beloved country? Is it all turning into a farce? Do we laugh or cry?

My friend in Penang was full of admiration for the 30 PSM members arrested in Kepala Batas. He said when they were marched out to face the music, they were not cowed by it. "I tell you, I never thought I would live to see this. Despite the situation they were in, they were shouting, 'Hidup rakyat! Hidup rakyat!'," he said. "I'll never be able to forget that."

Now the question is, will the rakyat be able to survive the power of the police? And also that of the State?

MOVE FOR A HEALTHY DEMOCRACY

Malaysiakini, July 5, 2011

The King has issued a statement on the developments surrounding the proposed Bersih 2.0 rally for free and fair elections. What do we make of it?

It is quite clear that he is not in favour of the rally proceeding on July 9, although he does say that the original intentions of street demonstrations can be good. This, read together with his acknowledgement of "the political fervour of a section of the people to bring about a healthy democracy (*menyuburkan demokrasi*) in our country", indicates he is not condemning Bersih 2.0. He is aware that the people are involved (even though it constitutes "a section"), and what they desire is something positive, i.e. *menyuburkan demokrasi*.

He is, however, concerned that "street demonstrations bring more bad than good" and he wants it ensured that the people's democratic demand "does not bring destruction to the country".

He advocates that whenever a problem arises, "we, as a civilised society, should (*hendaklah*) resolve it through consultations".

What has been the effect of the King's statement on the parties involved?

Prime Minister Najib Razak's first reaction is to offer Bersih 2.0 the opportunity to protest in a stadium. This is the most accommodating posture he has struck since the controversy began. In doing so, he has now come to 'legitimise' Bersih 2.0 without openly saying so, although only a few days ago, his Home Minister, Hishammuddin Hussein, had declared Bersih 2.0 an illegal organisation effective July 1.

Najib's offer indicates he has lost the battle of wills against the movement for electoral reform and is now scrambling to save face by making this offer. But it's not good enough. He has done too much damage; he has used an atom bomb to annihilate ants through his unreasonable, even maniacal arrests of people in the past week. The worst is alleging that the 30 Parti Sosialis Malaysia (PSM) members arrested in Kepala Batas were waging war against the King, and subjecting six of them to detention under the Emergency Ordinance.

The King has not, figuratively speaking, slapped Najib's face but he has tapped him on the shoulder by saying in his statement, "I also urge the Government to carry out everything that is entrusted to it by the people in a just and wise (*bijaksana*) manner". The words "just and wise" can be read as a reminder to the Government that it has been using unfair and sometimes inane tactics over the past week. The most inane would be either alleging that the PSM 30 were resurrecting Communism or declaring Bersih 2.0 illegal.

Najib is like the head prefect who has been caught out by the headmaster and is now being told to carry out his duties within the school rules.

It is noteworthy that the King uses the line, "entrusted to it by the people". It issues a very important reminder to a government that has become arrogant and unmindful of the rule of law, which is evident in its arbitrary arrests of people over the past week, in one case for simply wearing a yellow T-shirt.

It is further significant that the King says he does "not want to see animosity develop between the communities in our plural society or a section of the people being enemies with the Government, on whatever grounds". This could be alluding generally to the racial drumming of Perkasa, *Utusan Malaysia* and even Mahathir Mohamad that has contributed to racial tension of late, and specifically to Perkasa's role in inflaming the Bersih 2.0 rally by wanting to counter it and issuing veiled threats of violence.

The reaction on the part of Bersih 2.0 is to seek an audience with the King. Opposition political parties have indicated that they want to be included, but on no account must Bersih 2.0 allow this. It has, all this while, maintained that it is a movement that is led and initiated by civil society; it should remain so. If the King grants the audience, what Bersih 2.0 might request is for him to advise the Prime Minister to initiate negotiations with it and the Election Commission on carrying out electoral reform. If this is not forthcoming, Bersih 2.0 should still have the option of holding its rally on July 9.

But what if the King does not grant Bersih 2.0 an audience soon enough? This would then pose a quandary for the NGO. Should it then proceed with the rally on July 9? When it comes to that, Bersih 2.0 would have to answer the ultimate question: Does it listen to the King or to the *rakyat*?

Ours is a constitutional monarchy; on political matters, the King can offer advice but it is up to the listener to accept it or not. However, many Malaysians are still infected with a feudal mentality and to them, going against the King's advice is tantamount to *derhaka*. It is this that Bersih 2.0 will have to guard against, because if it were to be branded *penderhaka*, a fair part of the sympathy it has been getting so far through the Government crackdown will be obliterated.

On the other hand, it could be comforted by the thought that Perkasa and Umno Youth have said that if Bersih 2.0 goes ahead with its rally, they would also go ahead with theirs. This would expose them to accusations of *menderhaka* as well, so Bersih 2.0 would not be alone.

The best course for everyone, however, might well be negotiation, at which a timetable should be set for the electoral reform process to take place, before the next general election is held. But before going to the negotiating table, Bersih 2.0 should be given due recognition, which means Hishammuddin must revoke his order of illegalising it. This is a prerequisite; otherwise it will make the Government look silly negotiating with an "illegal" organisation. But even if Hishammuddin refuses to admit his high-handed mistake, Bersih 2.0 may have already been legitimised by the King's call for "consultations", and of course, by Najib's offer of holding the rally in a stadium.

Furthermore, the six PSM detainees should be released immediately, and the charges against the other 23 PSM members dropped. As it is, charging them with associating with an illegal society does not seem right. Bersih 2.0 was declared illegal several days after they were arrested; how could they have looked into the future to predict it would become illegal?

The next few days will be interesting to watch. The clash of wills between Bersih 2.0 and the Government (with Perkasa and Umno Youth as secondary players) may now be raised to a higher level. Najib may not want to give in for fear of appearing weak, and Bersih 2.0 may feel it has right and the *rakyat* on its side. It would take an impartial referee who has the country's best interests at heart to arbitrate the matter and bring about a satisfying solution.

NAJIB AND GANG SAY THE DARNEDEST THINGS

Free Malaysia Today, July 7, 2011

The Bersih 2.0 episode has taught us a few important things about the officials who are supposed to serve us, the *rakyat*.

First, it has taught us that our prime minister, Najib Razak, is a coward, a passer-of-the-buck, and a man with a slippery tongue.

Although he has now offered the Coalition for Clean and Fair Elections (Bersih 2.0) a stadium to hold its rally on July 9, he refuses to say if the Government no longer considers it an illegal organisation.

"This is a point whereby we consider them illegal, they don't consider themselves as illegal but what's important is public interest, I'm concerned with public interest," he says. What kind of waffle is that?

Because he is wishy-washy about this matter, he appears utterly contradictory in allowing an illegal organisation to hold a public rally in a stadium that his government will provide.

Related to this, when asked by the media whether the police would continue to clamp down on Bersih 2.0 supporters nationwide, he said, "You have to ask the police."

Asked if supporters would be arrested for wearing Bersih T-shirts at the rally at the stadium, he again said, "That is up to the police to decide."

He doesn't know? He doesn't have a say? Who is the boss? The prime minister, who is the chief executive of the country, or the police?

He dared not even answer the media's question about whether he was called to see the King on the morning of July 5 before the latter

was to meet with Bersih 2.0. His lame and characteristically evasive reply
was: "When I meet the King is my right, and as the prime minister, I am
the chief adviser to the King." He wasn't man enough to be honest and
transparent.

Now let's look at Deputy Prime Minister Muhyiddin Yassin. A few days
ago, on the Bersih 2.0 rally, he warned that it could lead to chaos and
invite "interference from major powers". Where did he pull this out from?

"Based on the experience in the Middle East, we know that foreign
powers are all too eager to send their troops on the pretext of helping to
solve the crisis," he said. What a hoot!

How ridiculous it is to draw from the Middle East experience (is the
United Nations about to authorise the bombing of Malaysia?), and how
convenient to blame it on some phantom foreign powers. It's the same
old trick the Government used on Hindraf in 2007, linking it to the
Tamil Tigers of Sri Lanka. In the end, not a shred of evidence was ever
produced. Once bitten, twice shy.

Sure enough, what Muhyiddin said was to provide justification for
six Parti Sosialis Rakyat (PSM) members, who were pro-Bersih 2.0, to be
detained under the Emergency Ordinance (EO), on suspicion of being
involved with "foreign elements" and having "subversive tendencies".

One of them is Michael Jeyakumar Devaraj. If you knew him for the
soft-spoken, humble and dedicated helper of the poor that he is, you
would laugh in Muhyiddin's face. Jeyakumar would not be so stupid as
to align himself with foreign elements to subvert the State. He toppled
Samy Vellu in Sungai Siput not by resorting to subversive measures but
by working hard steadily for the poor people there.

Let's turn now to Information, Communication and Culture
Minister Rais Yatim, who disparaged "desperate parties" for making use
of Communism to drum up support for the Bersih 2.0 rally.

"They see this as an opportunity to stir up dissent and seize power,"
he said. "Spreading Communism is against the law. It is evil and illegal."

What wild words would these ministers not use against a rally that
was aimed at nothing more sinister than asking for electoral reform,

for the good of democracy? Do they not realise we can gauge from their words the level of their intellect? How did Rais get his PhD?

Melaka Chief Minister Ali Rustam called on the Government to strip Bersih 2.0 chairperson Ambiga Sreenevasen of her citizenship. "If she thinks that we should have democracy by going on demonstrations like the way other countries do, then let her be the citizen of another country," he said.

He also said she was against the tenets of Islam for previously defending Lina Joy in her apostasy case.

Alamak! What has the Lina Joy case got to do with the Bersih 2.0 rally? But then, that's the Umno–BN dirty tactic, isn't it? Turn a non-religious issue into a religious one. Never mind if it's irrelevant. Never mind if it's divisive.

Najib was worse in making a similar personal attack: "We know who this Ambiga is. She is the one who threatened the position of Islam." He must have known it was totally uncalled-for and outrageously irresponsible, but his audience was in Kelantan, comprising mostly Muslims; reportedly about 20,000 of them there.

When Ali Rustam said that sort of thing, it was inexcusable. But when Najib, the advocate of so-called 1Malaysia, said it, it was unforgivable.

More than that, he warned, "Ambiga should not think herself so strong. We will not bow down to her at all, we will fight for the truth. We will *simpan kuku kita*." This is menacing; the threat is in *simpan kuku kita*, implying Najib and his supporters will hide their claws for now and use them when the time comes.

This is undignified talk unbecoming of a prime minister. He sounds like a street brawler.

Let's save the best for last. And who else might that be but the Home Minister, Hishammuddin Hussein, already famous for the numerous bloopers he has made in the past?

When the police started arresting people for wearing the Bersih T-shirts, without any apparent law to back them up, Hishammuddin justified it thus: "If the Bersih T-shirt is related to an illegal activity, then whatever they are wearing is illegal."

But the rally has not happened yet, so how could it be an illegal activity? By the same logic, how then could the Bersih T-shirts be related to an illegal activity?

Caught in a corner, Hishammuddin then resorted to declaring Bersih 2.0 illegal. One of the reasons cited was that Bersih 2.0 had been spreading propaganda with the aim of toppling the Government. What propaganda? Its eight demands for electoral reform constitute Government-toppling material? Which school did this minister go to?

And now that the King has met with Bersih 2.0 and the coalition has agreed to hold its rally in a stadium provided by the Government, Hishammuddin is still clamouring: "They are banned. They are still banned ... just because Tuanku met them doesn't mean they are no longer illegal."

One would have thought that the King, in showing respect to Bersih 2.0 in granting it an audience, would have legitimised the coalition, but Hishammuddin seems to have a different view. He must have felt the egg all over his face when the King granted the audience.

His reaction is, therefore, understandably defensive. He has screwed up big-time, but he won't admit his mistakes. If he has been doing his job like he should have, he would not be vilifying Bersih 2.0; he would be going after Perkasa instead.

No matter how you look at it, there's no denying that the real trouble-maker is Perkasa. It never had a real cause to rally for on July 9 except to disrupt Bersih 2.0's serious purpose. And now it wants to create further trouble by applying for the same stadium that Bersih 2.0 is applying for and hold its own rally there. And the reason for it? Merely to show that "there are others who feel differently".

Perkasa is obviously envious that the King acknowledged Bersih 2.0 by granting it an audience, so it, too, is applying for an audience with His Majesty. Perkasa is nothing but an envious bulldog that won't let go until it gets to spite Bersih 2.0. And all for what? Do its members even know?

If there were one organisation Hishammuddin should act on, it would have to be Perkasa. And yet, for all its antics and for all the veiled threats of violence its president, Ibrahim Ali, has been issuing since the whole episode started, the minister has said or done nothing.

Hishammuddin is plainly inept in his handling of the entire mess. And for that, he should resign or be kicked out of the Cabinet by his cousin, Najib.

In fact, both of them have clearly shown in the past two weeks that the Government has two laws for Malaysians — one for itself and those it favours, and one for the rest of the people. You can guess for yourself which side is the worse off for it.

But not to worry. What we the *rakyat* have learned, we can use to good effect. Taking the wisdom from Najib, we can *simpan* our *kuku* for now and reveal them when the time is right.

GOOD THINGS THAT CAME OUT OF BERSIH 2.0 RALLY

MalaysianDigest.com, July 11, 2011

What the Bersih 2.0 rally of July 9 has shown is that Malaysians of all races are willing to risk arrest to speak up for their rights; that Perkasa president Ibrahim Ali is nothing but hot air and the media should no longer give him any attention; that Umno Youth is just a directionless bunch of brats; and, above all, that the Government is the biggest loser for mishandling the entire issue.

As it was, the rally turned out to be peaceful, as the organisers had pledged it would be. The only acts of violence were those committed by the police, when they attacked the protestors with tear gas and water cannons although the latter did not provoke them. In retrospect, if the Government had allowed the rally to go on without fuss from the start — and it must be said that Bersih 2.0 (Coalition for Clean and Fair Elections) asked modestly for only two hours, from 2 p.m. to 4 p.m. — it would have just gone on without fuss, and everything would have been all right.

The Government would have been seen to be accommodating and benevolent, and not afraid of a call for fair elections. Instead, by choosing to clamp down on the rally even weeks before its scheduled date — in ways as brutal as detaining six people under the Emergency Ordinance and as absurd as arresting more than 200 people, some for merely wearing yellow T-shirts — it has lost immense favour and, some analysts say, the middle ground. It is also seen to be insecure and irrational in its overreacting to the rally, surely not a trait of good governance.

Be that as it may, two positive things emerged from July 9.

One, the culture of fear that was forged during the time of Mahathir Mohamad is forever gone. If Malaysians were daring enough to defy the strong, repeated calls by the police and the Government to stay away from the Kuala Lumpur city centre on July 9, they will not be intimidated any more by future threats as long as they know what they are doing is right and the Government is wrong.

Sure, pro-Government critics will argue that the Bersih 2.0 supporters did not comprise *all* Malaysians, but what is significant is that it comprised the *knowing* ones. In the history of revolutions, these are the ones who agitate for change and cause it to happen, not the ones who have been brainwashed by official propaganda.

Two, the most heartening feature about the rally is the composition of the protestors. They came from all races, young and old. They came from all over the country, including Sabah and Sarawak. Even a one-legged man walked (on crutches) for fair and free elections.

Many were the Chinese on the streets shouting, "*Hidup Bersih!*" and "*Hidup rakyat!*", giving the lie to Ibrahim Ali's prediction that the Chinese would stay home. As it turned out, he was the one who stayed home!

After the event, the *New Straits Times* interviewed a Universiti Sains Malaysia lecturer about his observations of the rally. When he said he did not see any Chinese there, he told a blatant lie. I was there and I saw a few thousand Chinese, if not more. Many were women, many were elderly. One of them said to me, "We are walking for our rights." To see how wrong he is, this lecturer should go to Youtube and type in "Bersih 2.0 at Petaling Street" and watch the video.

My friend, the writer-filmmaker Amir Muhammad, said it very well in response to the lecturer's observation: "Maybe he meant that there were no Chinese because everyone there was MALAYSIAN."

Indeed. Everyone there must have been a Malaysian who cared enough for the country to dare to defy the odds against them, in order to ask for their country to be set right again.

Many of them actually booked rooms in KL hotels the night before so that they would not be locked out of the city on the historic day. Many came from other states one or two days ahead to elude the authorities' restriction on travel. Many from the outskirts found ways to get into the city centre despite the police road blocks and checks, causing massive traffic jams.

Many feared arrest as they made their way to gathering points. I walked with trepidation, with my friends, from KL Sentral to Stadium Merdeka. We passed by policemen stationed along the way. When we got to the stadium vicinity, we found the road to it barricaded so we hung out for a while in Petaling Street. Throughout our wait for the rally to start, we felt a sense of unease; at any time, the FRU could rush us and catch us unawares.

When the march started, many faced the dreaded power of the police as the latter shot water cannons and tear gas at the crowd. But whenever the crowd was thus scattered, they regrouped a short while later to carry on the march. Some protestors were chased and beaten up, but spirits were not broken. In the end, nearly 1,700 people were arrested, including the leaders of Bersih 2.0 and those of Opposition parties that had responded to Bersih 2.0's call to all (including the ruling Barisan Nasional) to join its cause.

Ten thousand is an underestimation of the total crowd size at the rally, although that's what an online news website puts it at. The police's estimate of 6,000, on the other hand, is far too few. That puts the 1,700 arrested as being a quarter of their total, which doesn't seem plausible. The crowd I marched with to Puduraya, at the base of Menara Maybank, was already about 10,000. This did not include the other groups elsewhere at the time.

If there had been no road blocks, no court order barring the leaders from entering certain parts of the city, no restriction on travel from other states to KL, no shutdown of public transport, no fear-mongering, no warnings from sultans to subjects to stay away, many, many more people would have come.

Even so, in spite of all these formidable stumbling blocks, the turnout was fantastic. The people's belief in the cause overwhelmed their fading belief in the Executive, the Police and, even to a certain extent, the Royalty. And when a people come to lose faith in their country's institutions, that is when change is inevitable.

The July 9 rally marked a moral victory for Bersih 2.0. And it was a well-deserved one. It proved more than ever to Prime Minister Najib Razak that the people wanted electoral reform — and, more than that, a better government. He and his government would have been spared all this drama if they had read the writing on the wall from the very start.

Last week, when it seemed he had relented by agreeing to let the rally be held in a stadium, he could have still achieved some damage control, but instead his ratings dropped further when his team came up with a Catch-22 that made it impossible for Bersih 2.0 to get the stadium.

Now it seems he's still rejecting the writing on the wall. He's still talking tough and trying to put on a brave, even aggressive, front by hastily arranging an unusual gathering called Majlis Penerangan Perdana, attended by reportedly 6,000 Umno members and Malay NGOs, at which he ridiculed the Bersih 2.0 rally and boasted, "Umno has three million members. If we gather one million members, it is more than enough. We can conquer Kuala Lumpur."

This is pathetically childish behaviour for a prime minister. It is as if he is playing the game of 'Anything You Can Do, I Can Do Better'. His need to stage this show of force clearly shows his insecurity. One wonders which adviser of his suggested this move, but the effect of it is more laughable than impressive.

Deep down, Najib is afraid. That explains the paranoia he exuded over the Bersih 2.0 rally before July 9. Now, in its aftermath, neither he nor anyone can stop the reform movement. The wheels of change are already rolling. Even if BN wins the next general election, it will not rest easy.

The knowing Malaysians are already sensitised to BN's dirty rule and want to have a clean government. They will continue to press for change and reform. If BN tries to stop them by applying repression, it will not frighten or deter them any more. If one group is put down, another one will rise and take its place.

To BN, Bob Dylan sings:

> Then you better start swimmin'
> Or you'll sink like a stone
> For the times they are a-changin'

If BN doesn't hear that, it will surely sink.

ELECTORAL REFORM A MUST BEFORE NEXT GENERAL ELECTION

MalaysianDigest.com, August 17, 2011

Prime Minister Najib Razak is suddenly so generous in calling for electoral reform. He has even called for the establishment of a parliamentary select committee (PSC) to look into this. While it is still premature to say whether this will ensure effective participation by the Opposition in the process, it is nonetheless a radical change from his previous stubborn position against Bersih 2.0's demands for free and fair elections.

As with much of Malaysian politics, there is probably more to all this than what appears on the surface. Najib must have been comforted by some assurance of electoral victory — and possibly a landslide one — before he would allow himself to accede to an initiative begun by Bersih 2.0. Otherwise, he would be seen to be weak by his own party, Umno, which no doubt would have players in the wings with knives behind their backs.

One hopes this assurance of certain victory does not involve giving illegal immigrants the right to vote. In light of Wanita PKR's revelation that it has evidence of illegal immigrants taking an oath to vote for BN, this is disturbing.

That's putting it mildly. For nothing could be so heinous on the part of our government, indeed any government, than to sell the country to foreigners just for the purpose of staying on in power. Such a move of granting citizenships to immigrants overnight would also be extremely unfair to the many who have lived in this country for decades and continue to hold red ICs. But above all, it is the sinister motive that makes it inexcusable.

Talk has indeed been rife for the past few months that a project of this sinister nature is already in the works. More suspicions were raised when the Election Commission (EC) announced it would use the biometric system to identify voters as this is the system also being used by the Government in its 6P amnesty programme to register foreign workers as well as illegal immigrants. Opposition politicians are especially worried that those not qualified to vote could, in the process, get registered as voters. The illegal immigrants that Wanita PKR says were made to swear an oath of allegiance to Umno/BN are allegedly from the 6P amnesty programme.

This sort of tactic, together with the granting of citizenships to new immigrants, has supposedly been used in Project M (also known as Project IC) in Sabah when Mahathir Mohamad was prime minister, so that the demographic and voting patterns would favour BN and entrench it as the ruling regime there. If this is being repeated now, it would reaffirm BN's ruthless tendency to stoop to underhand tactics to serve its own cause, without any regard for the people.

There is also the possibility that Najib's call for the setting-up of a PSC is merely a public relations ploy, in light of what Dewan Rakyat Deputy Speaker Datuk Wan Junaidi Tuanku Jaafar has said in response — that it would take a year before the committee can conclude discussions.

If Najib had prior knowledge of that before making his announcement, then his move counts for nothing. The next general election (GE) may very well be called soon, less than a year from now. Which means it may be held prior to the electoral reform. Which means it may be held with the shortcomings of the current system still intact. How can that be satisfactory?

If doing it via the PSC takes too long, even though Najib still has one and a half years left before calling for fresh polls, then another method must be sought.

For example, on the pressing and crucial issue of cleaning the electoral roll, which has been found to be full of dirt and discrepancies,

Bersih 2.0 chairperson Ambiga Sreenevasan has suggested this: "Set up a committee, give it three months and let's just clean it up." Why not take this suggestion up? The committee could be made up of the EC, BN and Pakatan Rakyat representatives, the Bar Council and Bersih 2.0.

A few other issues can also be addressed through stakeholder discussions that could take only a matter of a few months. One is the debate on Bersih 2.0's advocacy for the use of indelible ink versus the EC's proposal to use the biometric system.

Another is the debate over the length of the campaign period. Bersih 2.0 is asking for a minimum of 21 days but the EC has been giving excuses against it. In the 1959 and 1964 GEs, the campaign period was as long as 35 days, and for the one in 1969, it was 28 days. A reasonable length of time is needed to let voters acquaint themselves with the candidates and their promises, but Najib has scoffed at the idea that a short campaign period is a disadvantage to the Opposition, claiming that Pakatan Rakyat campaigns "every day ... with a *ceramah* here and a *ceramah* there". He, however, ignores the fact that his own ruling party gets to campaign day in day out on a much larger scale through the mass media it controls.

Even during the campaign period, the ruling party has almost total access to the print and broadcasting media. Prior to the 1999 GE, Opposition parties were given at least a bit of airtime on RTM's radio stations to broadcast their manifestoes. But in 1999, the Government announced that as RTM was Government-owned, preference would be given to government parties. Since then, no Opposition party has been heard on the air.

It is for this reason that one of Bersih 2.0's demands is the granting of free and fair access to the media to all political parties. As the ruling party becomes merely a caretaker government when a general election is in progress, it should not hog the media facilities but instead open them up to all political parties, including the Opposition. Resolving this issue through discussion should also not take long.

Neither should the issue of reforming postal voting.

Whatever the process adopted to ensure that electoral reform is achieved, it is imperative that it be completed before the 13th GE. If Najib is truly sincere about reform, if his statements that "we will only want to form a government if the *rakyat* truly chooses Barisan Nasional" and that "I do not want to be prime minister without the people's support" are to be believed, he should make a pledge not to call for the 13th GE until the reform has been effected.

And while all this is going on, let's not forget that Bersih 2.0 is still considered illegal, after Home Minister Hishammuddin Hussein declared it so last month. He should now admit that if it had not been for Bersih 2.0's insistence on electoral reform, embodied in its eight demands and publicly vented in its July 9 rally, we would not have arrived at this point.

Hishammuddin should admit that Bersih 2.0 has demonstrated the power that civil society can have to pressure the ruling party to re-examine its stand. He should also note that the Deputy Speaker has now actually said, that as electoral reform is a matter of great importance to the public interest, "It is best we discuss it in-depth and involve all stakeholders including Bersih, NGOs, the Bar Council and civil society."

If no less than the Deputy Speaker of Parliament has expressed recognition of Bersih 2.0 — and Najib as well, albeit implicitly — isn't it time that Hishammuddin revoked his order against the group?

excerpt

FROM THE PLAY
THE SWORDFISH,
THEN THE CONCUBINE

This part of the play compresses a variety of happenings and expresses them through a series of children's games. Tun Dara, Sultan Iskandar's wife, supposedly a virgin because he has never consummated their marriage, is the main focus ... until news comes that Majapahit is invading Singapura.

LET THE GAMES BEGIN

(A scream of terror. TUN DARA is the one who screamed. She starts to run round and round the stage.)

(ENSEMBLE emerges.)

ENSEMBLE:	Run, run, Tun Dara, run.
	Run, run, Tun Dara, run.
TUN DARA:	They're coming! ... They're coming ... after me!
ENSEMBLE:	Who? Who?

(TUN DARA's path is blocked by HANG NADIM. She tries to run past him a few times (as in the children's game 'kali toei', somewhat like the game called British Bulldog) and finally succeeds when he willingly gives up.)

ENSEMBLE:	Run, run, Tun Dara, run.
	Run, run, Tun Dara, run.

(TUN DARA runs past HANG NADIM into NURHALISA's path. She can't get through despite many attempts.)

ISKANDAR: The Bendahara has deserted me. Who will be my new Bendahara?

ENSEMBLE: Ask Tun Dara, she knows the game.

She knows people, she'll come up with a name.

TUN DARA: *(still trying to get past NURHALISA)*

Tuanku, Tun Perpatih Segalar is the most senior. He deserves to be made Bendahara.

ISKANDAR: He's the most corrupt.

TUN DARA: He's always willing to do what needs to be done.

(NURHALISA lets TUN DARA pass. She runs into RANJUNA, who has NURHALISA's dress slung across his outstretched arms.)

ENSEMBLE: Make Sang Ranjuna the Bendahara.

Sang Ranjuna's the best for Bendahara.

TUN DARA: No, no.

TOK GURU: He will clean up the moral dirt.

TUN DARA: No, no.

(RANJUNA lets TUN DARA pass. She runs, looking for SEGALAR.)

TUN DARA: Segalar ... Segalar ...

ISKANDAR: I won't make Ranjuna my Bendahara. He hates my guts.

PALACE OFFICIAL: Tuanku, I bring good news. Tun Dara is with child. Tuanku may have an heir.

ISKANDAR: What? Who's the father?

PALACE OFFICIAL: Tuanku?

ISKANDAR: Find out who the father is and bring him to me!

PALACE OFFICIAL: Yes, Tuanku.

(TUN DARA, still running, suddenly collapses and screams in pain.

A loud explosion goes off.)

PALACE OFFICIAL: Tuanku, I bring terrible ... uh ... I bring ...
                   I bring news. The baby was aborted. And it
                   was blown to completely nothing with a
                   powerful explosive. We have no DNA to find
                   out who the father is.
ISKANDAR: Get Tun Dara to tell you who he is.
PALACE OFFICIAL: Yes, Tuanku.

(TUN DARA throws a stone onto a hopscotch course. She hops onto it, then negotiates the squares on one leg. She loses her balance at the next hop and falls.

ISKANDAR stands over her.)

ISKANDAR: The game is up.

(TUN DARA gets up.)

TUN DARA: I was never pregnant. The information given to you
            was horribly wrong.
ISKANDAR: You screwed around!
TUN DARA: No. I would never do that. I've always loved you.
ISKANDAR: You have a sick way of showing your love.
TUN DARA: And what about you? Putting to death the only woman
            you have ever loved!

(ISKANDAR pushes her violently to the floor and moves off in a huff.)

ENSEMBLE: Tun Dara, Tun Dara, you're in deep trouble.
            It's your turn to catch us — on the double!

(TUN DARA gets up, hops on one leg and chases after the others to try and touch them.)

ENSEMBLE MEMBER: You're weak. You can't catch us now.
TUN DARA: Segalar ... Segalar ...

(She goes near SEGALAR but he hastens away. She falls, exhausted.)

TOK GURU: I have evidence that Tun Dara gave orders for her aborted baby to be blown up.
SEGALAR: Tok Guru, let's play a game of Hide and Seek. I'll count to five, you go and hide.
TOK GURU: I won't play your game. I'm going to make a statutory declaration of what I've discovered.
SEGALAR: Go ahead.

(TOK GURU disappears among the ENSEMBLE.

A few members of the ENSEMBLE form a corps of media personnel and swarm around SEGALAR.)

REPORTER 1:   Tun Perpatih Segalar, Tok Guru seems to have disappeared. Do you know where he is?
SEGALAR: No.
REPORTER 2:   Is he in a neighbouring country?
SEGALAR: I have no idea.
REPORTER 3:   Rumour has it that he disappeared because his life was in danger. Is it true?
SEGALAR: Don't listen to rumours.
REPORTER 4:   Is there any truth in his statutory declaration?
SEGALAR: Absolutely not. He will be charged with criminal defamation. All right, no more questions.

BENDAHARA: Tun Perpatih Segalar, I'm telling you this as a former colleague. People have been saying that a minister conspired with my daughter to bring down Nurhalisa — and that the minister was you.

SEGALAR: It's a malicious lie. I'm willing to swear that it's not true — on the Holy Book, in the name of Almighty God.

BENDAHARA: I can imagine why so many unfounded rumours are flying around. There has been much unrest among the people since the execution of Nurhalisa. Something must be done to reassure them.

SEGALAR: Yes! Let's have a top-spinning competition! An international one, with competitors from all over the world. The winner will get the Mongoose Cup ...

(Members of the ENSEMBLE take part in the competition, spinning tops.)

SEGALAR: ... and to preserve our culture, let's have a *joget* competition. We'll have the people choose the winners. It will give them the illusion of people power ...

(ENSEMBLE members break into dancing the joget.)

SEGALAR: ... and let's make the longest *dodol* in the world!

(In the midst of all that festivity, a frantic TUN DENDANG runs in.)

DENDANG: They're coming! ... They're coming ...!
ENSEMBLE: Who? Who?
DENDANG: Invaders! ... We are under attack! Singapura is under attack by Majapahit!
SEGALAR: What?

DENDANG: Majapahit has landed on our shore with a massive fleet! They took us by surprise. We haven't experienced war for so long, our warriors have become sluggish. We can't even tell how many ships are out there.

SEGALAR: Tell that to the Sultan!

DENDANG: Oh, that this too, too solid flesh would melt! I – I – feel dizzy.

ISKANDAR: How large is their force?

DENDANG: Huh? ... Oh! ... Uh – uh – we counted ... three hundred ships!

ISKANDAR: You senile jerk! Why did your men not spot them before they came close to the shore?

DENDANG: Uh – uh –

SEGALAR: The haze, Tuanku. There was a thick haze.

DENDANG: But we are not worried, Tuanku. We can vanquish them!

ISKANDAR: Then get our men on the shore and kick the bastards off our land!

DENDANG: Yes, Tuanku.

ISKANDAR: I hate war! You hear me? I hate war!

OTHER PRESSING MATTERS

· ·

MANY ARE THE ISSUES THAT NEED TO BE RESOLVED. MANY ARE THE REFORMS THAT NEED TO BE MADE. HERE ARE JUST SOME OF THEM.

TIME TO REPEAL
THE SEDITION ACT

MalaysianDigest.com, May 25, 2011

It's exhilarating these days to see so much open discussion in cyberspace on so-called "sensitive" issues. Never have we engaged in talking about race, religion and politics with such vigour and interest. For that, we have to thank the online news websites, blogs and social media like Facebook and Twitter.

The effect of this is that it has sparked more open discussion in other public spheres as well, even in the mainstream media, particularly those in the Malay and Chinese languages. Malaysians have become bolder and franker. They are rejecting the culture of fear.

It's also scary. We have seen the racist tone emerge from a lot of people, and the number is surprising. But then, that's to be expected because it's only now we are doing this. In the past, everything was swept under the carpet or suppressed. So now the shock of discovery is to be expected. A lot of people do think in racist terms.

The good thing is, it's now out in the open. And that's a whole lot healthier than keeping everything pent-up. It's also good that we can now engage in discussion and debate with people of other races that we could not do before. There's a lot to learn from such engagement.

We can disabuse people of the wrong knowledge they have about certain things, like what the Constitution really says about certain key aspects of Malaysian life.

Chief of these are Article 153, which clarifies the "special position" of the Malays; Article 3, which clearly states that Islam is "the religion of the federation"; Article 10, which grants every citizen the freedom of speech, the right to assemble peacefully and the right to form associations; and Article 11, which provides that every person has the right to profess and practise his own religion.

It's appalling that many Malaysians don't know at least the key articles of the Constitution. As such, they are not aware when the Government transgresses the provisions of the Constitution and abuses them for its own advantage, or when it fails to follow the rule of law.

Another revelation from the cyberspace debates is that a lot of people are in denial about what's happening in Malaysia today and why we need reform. They refuse to see reality, even when it's rationally explained to them, preferring to follow their tribal instincts, and when they run out of argument, they resort to name-calling. Like "traitor to the race" or "shit-stirrer" or worse. They cease to be logical. And that's the sad thing.

The tendency to be illogical stems from irrational fear. It is like that fear exhibited by the group of young people known as 1Malaysia Graduates Youth Club who made a police report last September against the distribution of MyConstitution Rakyat Guides, part of the Bar Council's laudable effort to make the Constitution understandable to Malaysians. Their objection to it smacks of classic illogicality. They feared that as more Malaysians were educated about their rights, it would encourage amendments to the Constitution. As such, they considered the Bar Council effort seditious!

Instead of acknowledging the positive aspect of making Malaysians aware of what the Constitution is all about, they saw ulterior motives that were non-existent. If they had been better-informed, they would have realised that Article 159 states that the Constitution can indeed be amended. And that since Independence, our Parliament has already made about 650 amendments to it.

Sedition! That's what has become a habitual invocation of late — by individuals and groups for good reason or for wanting to shut someone up for having said or done something they disapprove of.

Recent examples are Perkasa accusing MP Nurul Izzah Anwar of sedition for allegedly questioning the Constitution; National Union of Journalists (NUJ) president Hata Wahari calling for the Sedition Act to be used against Perkasa president Ibrahim Ali for inciting hatred among Malays towards others communities; International Islamic University law professor Abdul Aziz Bari saying Mahathir Mohamad can be charged with sedition for questioning the status of vernacular schools; and the DAP calling for *Utusan Malaysia* to be probed for sedition for alleging that a Christian plot was afoot to make Christianity the country's official religion.

This has transpired because the floodgates of open discussion have been opened. And as it would be unwise to close them now, because it has dispelled erstwhile fears that such discussion could lead to riots, we need instead to remove the impediments that still hold us back. One such is the Sedition Act.

De facto Law Minister Nazri Aziz has just come out to say it should be scrapped, and he deserves support for it. Both sides of the political divide would be helping the country to progress by following this up and campaigning for the Act's repeal.

Nazri is right in saying the Sedition Act has "no relevance in these modern times". It was enacted in 1948, when the British ruled Malaya. As one of its features was to pre-empt "disaffection" against the government, it served to protect British rule. In later years, judging by the cases that have been brought to court, the Act has been wielded for the same purpose, but this time protecting the Barisan Nasional government. Besides, the provisions of the Act are vague and, thus, vulnerable to the practice of double standards.

An excellent illustration of this is the case brought up by the DAP against the inflammatory rhetoric espoused by Umno delegates at their 2006 general assembly, when words as seditious as these were said:

"Umno is willing to risk lives and bathe in blood to defend the race and religion. Don't play with fire. If they (non-Malays) mess with our rights, we will mess with theirs." Although the DAP filed a police report on it, no action was taken.

On the other hand, over the years, Opposition politicians and non-BN-friendly bloggers have been the ones charged with sedition. The latest politician charged has been Selangor state assemblyman Shuhaimi Shafiei. And probably the most famous example is that of Lim Guan Eng, over the case of a chief minister alleged to have committed statutory rape on a schoolgirl.

Blogger Raja Petra Kamarudin was charged with sedition in 2008 for writing an article that allegedly implied that Najib Razak and his wife were involved in the killing of Altantuya. Why that was considered seditious is a question still being asked.

Meanwhile, people like Ibrahim Ali and his Perkasa comrades have not even been ticked off for the blatant remarks they make that could engender "feelings of ill-will and hostility between different races" (Sedition Act wording). The newspaper *Utusan Malaysia* does the same but is defended by Umno ministers. For its recent false report on the unbelievable Christian plot – seditious by the Act's provisions – it received a mere tap on the knuckles.

Clearly, the Sedition Act has been abused. And it's out of place in a time when the Malaysian mind is opening up and the electorate needs maturing to reach the next level. Cyberspace has shown the way by facilitating open discourse; it's now up to our elected representatives to push to open it wider. We need to speak freely if we want to grow up, and nothing should hold us back now.

FOOLS NO MORE,
THEY'RE BREAKING OUT

MalaysianDigest.com, March 4, 2011

Malaysian university students must surely realise that they have more power now than they have ever had in the last four decades. This accounts for their robust participation in politics in recent days, not only in university campuses, but also in the public sphere.

Suppressed for so long by the Universities and University Colleges Act (UUCA), introduced in 1971 because the ruling party feared the rise of student activism, today's students are breaking out.

The political landscape that emerged from the March 8 phenomenon has no doubt been an encouraging factor. Inspired by the aspiration of a more politically aware *rakyat* demanding greater democracy, students have been challenging university and government authorities by taking part in political activities they are banned from doing so by the draconian UUCA.

Their defiance has now been augmented by the revolutions spearheaded by youths in the Arab world. Like the Tunisians, Egyptians, Libyans and others, they want democracy, social and political justice. They want to reclaim their right as citizens to take part in the political process. And rightly so.

Indeed, it can be argued that the UUCA contravenes Article 10 of the Federal Constitution, which allows for freedom of speech and expression, and freedom of association. The Constitution does provide for the control of freedom of association but only on certain grounds, like the protection of national security, public order or morality. Political participation is not one of these grounds.

It doesn't make sense anyway that university students are being deprived of their right to be politically involved when other Malaysian youths enjoy that right. In fact, it's grossly unfair. Just the other day, a newspaper carried a story about a 20-year-old who had his barber design a Barisan Nasional symbol on his scalp. Any university student caught doing that could have been hauled up to face discipline. Or perhaps not if he sports a BN icon. Until the recent amendments to the Act, such a student could even have been dragged to court and faced the possibility of a jail sentence.

Last May, four Universiti Kebangsaan Malaysia (UKM) students were charged by their university under the UUCA for showing sympathy or support for Pakatan Rakyat when they were found in possession of the coalition's campaign materials during the Hulu Selangor by-election. It was, to say the least, pitiable.

Malaysian universities are what they are today because the UUCA not only prohibits students from expressing political opinion publicly and being members of political parties; it also bars them from joining *any* society outside of their university without the written consent of their Vice-Chancellor. This is too extensive a ban; and it is this that gives the Act a bad name.

Without allowing our students to participate freely in the larger community, how can we expect them to widen their horizons? How can they be expected to be thinking beings with an informed world-view? How then can we have world-class universities?

The Malaysian university students of the '60s and early '70s were so different. Progressive and aware of their social responsibilities, they engaged in the issues of the day. They rallied for the poor of Teluk Gong, Tasik Utara and Baling, and marched for other causes. They demonstrated against the invasion of Czechoslovakia by the Soviets and the oppression of Muslims in Pattani, and spoke up for the plight of the Palestinians. It was part of their own education.

But the student movement came to an end when amendments to the UUCA were bulldozed through Parliament in 1975. Mahathir Mohamad was then the Minister of Education. Students responded by holding mass demonstrations in 1976 at the MARA Institute of Technology to protest against the amendments. Guess who then threatened to revoke their scholarships and thereby managed to break them up?

After that, universities were reduced to 'glorified high schools'. More than shutting up the students, the UUCA curbed their intellectual freedom and sense of curiosity. What took root was a culture of obeisance and coconut-shell mediocrity and the prioritising of passing exams above all else. The academic staff were negatively affected as well. Lecturers who tried to promote independent thinking and free speech among their students found themselves to be a dwindling minority.

The most insidious outcome of all this was the cultivation of a breed of academics who, to find favour with the Establishment, perpetuated the closing of the Malaysian student mind once they got into influential positions. It epitomises the tragedy of Malaysian academia.

It could only have happened under a government that ruled with a strong mandate. And, of course, a government that preferred to keep university students mute and under its thumb.

But the times, they are a-changin', and the Government must now realise that it had better start swimmin' or it'll sink like a stone. The recent victories of the Pro-Mahasiswa group, said to be anti-Establishment, in a number of campus elections should cause the political rulers some concern.

Even more worrisome for them would be the indications that these students will no longer take unfair treatment without fighting back. The recent protests of the Pro-Mahasiswa group in Universiti Malaya (UM) and Universiti Putra Malaysia (UPM) that railed against alleged election meddling by university authorities showed a new spirit almost akin to that of the '60s and '70s firebrands.

What happened at UM and UPM generally reflects badly on the university authorities. Disqualifying Pro-Mahasiswa candidates who had won in the elections raised a fishy smell. To the students' credit, they demanded an explanation from their respective vice-chancellors and refused to budge unless they got one. When security guards were called, things got a tad tense, even violent. Although the mainstream media have been trying to blame the students for getting out of hand, the fact remains that they had right on their side. It was just too bad that the tough security guards were on the other side.

Fortunately, Deputy Higher Education Minister Saifuddin Abdullah played a role in defusing the tension at UPM by expressing regret over the annulment of the victories of the 11 candidates, 10 of whom were with Pro-Mahasiswa. When the victors were eventually reinstated, UPM declared that the candidates were not "disqualified" in the first place. The word used in the letters issued to the affected candidates was "*pembatalan*", which it said should mean "cancellation".

Pray tell, what's the difference? If a candidacy is "cancelled", doesn't that amount to disqualification? Are we hearing ivory-tower doublespeak?

Saifuddin seems to have read the situation well. He seems to understand the significance of student activism. The Arab uprisings would have provided a lesson, but more pressing is the prospect of the general election coming up at any time now. Suppression of student activism would be a huge mistake. Many of them would be going to the polling booths for the first time.

Already, some have even offered themselves as election candidates. At the Malaysian Civil Liberties Movement forum last December, it was startling but refreshing to see student leader Shazni Munir bin Mohd Ithnin openly and confidently declare that "the time for fear is over" and that his fellow students were offering themselves as candidates to pro-*rakyat* political parties to stand in the next general election.

This was open defiance of the UUCA, an act of courage. As more and more students show courage in the face of repression, many may be moved to join them. They have indeed come a long way since August 2008 when 100 of them staged a protest against the then proposed amendments to the UUCA at the entrance to Parliament, to the

December 2010 protest in Putrajaya against petrol, diesel and sugar price hikes for which three students were arrested, to the UM and UPM face-offs with the university authorities.

University students have found their voice again, as Ivy Kwek, a graduate from a Malaysian university, observed in an online site recently. They know they can make a difference and will strive to do so.

"When I was a student," she wrote, "among the first things first-year students were told in orientation week was that we should focus on our studies and not get embroiled in campus politics and illegal organisations ... I really believed what they said and thought that is what university is all about ...

"Later, I found out that under the Universities and University Colleges Act ... I cannot participate in a gathering of more than three people, as it is deemed illegal. I also found out that I, as a 21-year-old, can vote and even contest in national politics, but under the Act, am not allowed to be a member of any political party ...

"In retrospect, I feel that I've been treated like a fool."

Oh, well. The times, they are a-changin' ... and university students are fools no more. Oppressors, beware!

TIME TO RECLAIM
OUR TRUE HISTORY

Malaysiakini, September 16, 2011

We've never been colonised by the British! I've never heard anything so ludicrous. And it's coming from history professors. Not just one, but at least two. Yeah, professors touting hogwash.

Professor Zainal Kling first dropped the bombshell when he said several days ago that Malaya was never colonised. He said it was wrong to say that we were under colonial rule for 400 years, which would mean since 1511 when the Portuguese invaded Malacca. This would also mean that we were never colonised by the Portuguese, the Dutch and the British. No kidding?

He said under the British, the Malay states were merely protectorates because the Malay rulers retained their sovereignty. Only Singapore, Malacca and Penang, known as the Straits Settlements, were colonies.

He said Malaya was colonised by the British for only two years, during the Malayan Union period from early 1946 to the end of 1947, and by the Japanese during the Second World War. Wow!

And here's his punchline — it is, therefore, wrong to say that the police, political leaders and Malay officers before 1957 were subservient to the British.

Ah! That's the main point, isn't it? He brought all that up to discredit what PAS Deputy President Mohamad (Mat) Sabu had recently said about the attack on Bukit Kepong, didn't he?

Mat Sabu had said that the real heroes of that incident were not the police who defended the Bukit Kepong police station because they were serving the British, but that the credit should go to Mat Indera, the Communist who led the attack, because he was fighting against the colonialists.

Mat Sabu's remarks have created a storm since, and both sides of the political divide have been drawn into it. Their supporters have also entered the fray, either voluntarily or through being instigated to do so. Even ex-servicemen have joined in.

But supposing what Zainal has said is true, that we were never colonised. Why did he wait till now to point this out? Why did he keep it secret from the whole country and allow the Government to continue to celebrate Independence Day every year when there was really no liberation from colonialism to begin with? Why did he let Malaysians put up with this masquerade?

Something doesn't add up.

By withholding this crucial piece of information from the nation, is Zainal Kling being a true Malaysian? Why has he waited till this politically opportune time to drop the bomb?

The other professor who has come out to say the same is Professor Emeritus Khoo Kay Kim. He corroborated Zainal's viewpoint by saying that "the British never ruled the country". They had "merely taken over the administration of our country", he added.

Excuse me! Is there a difference between "ruling" and "administering"?

This whole thing sounds like a semantic quibble — the British merely administered, they did not rule; we were not colonised, we retained our sovereignty; we were a protectorate, not a colony.

Khoo said that from a legal point of view, Malaya was never colonised because the British made treaties with the Malay rulers before taking over the administration. That may be the form, but let's not forget the substance.

In being a part of this "conspiracy" of silence together with Zainal until this politically opportune time, Khoo's status as a true Malaysian must also be viewed with suspicion, mustn't it? Are there other professors involved in this "conspiracy"?

Suara Rakyat Malaysia (Suaram) President Kua Kia Soong hints that the professors' response to Mat Sabu's remarks is "sickeningly deferential". This seems to imply that they have been put up to it. And if so, their academic integrity would have to be questioned too, because aren't academics supposed to be independent rather than be politically partisan and therefore, subservient? The great sin for professors, especially History professors, would be revisioning history to serve political purposes; or to be deferential to the government of the day.

As it is, Malaysian history as presented to Malaysians has been little more than a construct designed to aggrandise the ruling party, especially Umno. The real history has not been fully told. And the reason for this is that the ruling party has been adept at manipulating historical facts, including omitting important ones, to present a story that glorifies the party itself and promotes *Ketuanan Melayu*.

To be sure, Umno was not the only party that engaged in the movement for independence. It was not even the first on the scene. Others came before it.

Watch the documentary *10 Tahun Sebelum Merdeka* by the film-maker Fahmi Reza and learn about the struggles of the multi-racial Putera–AMCJA for independence 10 years before 1957. Learn about the People's Constitution they drafted, the successful country-wide hartal they staged on October 20, 1947, to protest against the Federation of Malaya Constitutional Proposals made by the British. Guess who staged a counter-protest to the hartal in some rural areas like Senggaram and Bagan Datoh? Umno! (Doesn't it remind you of Umno Youth counter-protesting againt Bersih 2.0?)

Read about the struggles of Parti Kebangsaan Melayu Malaya (PKMM), which came into being seven months before Umno was formed. Its main goal was to attain full independence for Malaya. Read about Ahmad Boestamam, Shamsiah Fakeh, Ishak Haji Muhammad, Mokhtaruddin Lasso, Burhanuddin Helmi.

Read about the fight against colonialism by the Malayan Communist Party (MCP), founded in 1930. Yes, the Communists were freedom fighters. Anyone who says "those who regard the Communists as freedom fighters are traitors" (like retired lieutenant-general Ja'afar Onn) is talking rubbish. Who fought the Japanese when they invaded Malaya? And after the war, when the Communists went about killing people, whom were they targeting? Those who had collaborated with the Japanese.

In 1945, the MCP opted to work for national independence using legal means. But in time, the British began cracking down on what they considered radical factions opposing its rule. The MCP was declared illegal in 1948. Then the Emergency was declared as the MCP mounted an armed struggle against the British colonialists.

In 1955, the MCP made overtures to Tunku Abdul Rahman's government to negotiate peace. That led to the Baling Talks.

If you were to read the transcripts of that negotiation carefully, you would realise that Chin Peng, representing the Communists, was sincere in wanting to lay down arms and be part of the legitimate political movement towards independence because he acknowledged that the government was now an elected one and as such, he was no longer fighting the British.

It was the Tunku who made things difficult for the Communists by demanding total surrender and subjection to a period of detention for them to be investigated. This scuttled the talks.

These are not what have been taught in our schools. And so for generations, millions of Malaysian students have graduated not knowing the full story. Only the story that Umno wants them to know. And Umno has been revisioning history too, downplaying the contributions of the leftists and the non-Malay communities. Just visit the Independence Memorial in Melaka and see for yourself.

This is not unexpected. Our leaders have been twisting things to suit their political agenda for decades. And historical facts are not spared. But the spin against Mat Sabu has gone out of whack. His opposers have even extrapolated the meaning of his remarks to imply that he does not appreciate the sacrifices of the police and the armed forces. This is certainly not true. There is no such implication.

By saying that the Bukit Kepong police were serving the British, he did not say that the whole armed forces of this country from that era till now are worthless. No logical person would see such an implication in what he said — unless their agenda is to shoot him down regardless of logic.

All told, there has been a lot of vitriol thrown at Mat Sabu, and consternation expressed at the 'revelations' of Zainal Kling and Khoo Kay Kim, but there is also an upside to the whole episode.

It is opening up a new public debate that is much needed. And the theme of that debate is the reclaiming of our true history. Forums are being held, including one discussing the role of the leftists in the struggle for independence, featuring eyewitness Said Zahari himself.

More history experts should be joining in, as well as more chroniclers of those times. The Malaysian mental revolution starts now. And the reclaiming of our true history is its catalyst.

THE TRUTH ABOUT THE BALING TALKS?

Penang Economic Monthly, July 2011

We often think of the Baling Talks of 1955 as a serious attempt to negotiate peace between the Government and the Communists. But if we were to study the actual transcript of the talks, we might get a different impression.

While Chin Peng appears earnest about the Communists' willingness to lay down arms and rejoin society, Tunku Abdul Rahman and David Marshall, heads of the governments of the Federation of Malaya and Singapore respectively, appear to make it hard for them. While Chin Peng seems prepared to make concessions, the Tunku and Marshall seem uncompromising in their demands.

I have been involved in two public readings of the Baling Talks' original transcript, organised by the Five Arts Centre. This transcript, edited from eight hours to two-and-a-half, contains the actual words of the historic personages, as recorded during the four sessions they engaged in over two days. The first time I did it was in 2008 in Kuala Lumpur when I read the Tunku's part in one of the four sessions. Most recently, in May 2011, I read Chin Peng in the fourth session. This was as a presentation of the Singapore Arts Festival.

Both my readings have revealed to me that the Tunku and Marshall were not willing to even meet Chin Peng halfway. Right from the beginning, the Tunku makes it clear that "in my opinion, there is no way of bringing about peace other than to offer suitable terms for the surrender of the Communist Party." Surrender was what he was after and, as it turned out, little else. He sounds accommodating when he says that it is up to the Communists "to tell me what part of the terms you think unreasonable, or hard and strict, so that my partners and I will be able to consider them", but when Chin Peng subsequently points them out, the Tunku abandons his accommodating stance.

For example, in the second session, Chin Peng asks that the Malayan Communist Party (MCP) be recognised and allowed to take part in elections, but although the Tunku and MCA President Tan Cheng Lock expressly state that they have read the Communist manifesto and found it "quite good" and that on the basis of that manifesto, "there is no quarrel between the MCP and the people", they insist that the MCP must nonetheless be dissolved.

The Tunku brushes aside Chin Peng's point that all this while the MCP had been fighting against a government that is "not an elected" one, meaning the British, implying therefore that its goal was also independence. Ideology aside, this could brand the MCP patriots or freedom-fighters instead of terrorists.

The subtext here, when read together with later exchanges, shows that the Tunku could have feared a threat to his leadership from the MCP. So, even in this second session, although the Tunku openly says, "I have no doubt whatsoever that if [the MCP] were allowed to take part in free elections, the people would choose our system" and Chin Peng replies, "Yes, I know that too. I agree.", the Tunku would not allow it to be tested. Even though he declares that his Alliance government upholds the Five Freedoms.

He discourses, in the third session, about Indonesia and India recognising the Communist parties there, and even explains why the Indonesian Communists deserve to be recognised, but he will not budge on his government's refusal to recognise the MCP. "Do you mean it is because most of the members of the Communist Party in Malaya are Chinese?" Chin Peng asks. And the Tunku says, "Yes." This reply is very telling.

Ultimately, the outcome of the talks hinges on the issue of dignity. The Government wants the Communists to surrender and agree to be placed under detention for a period of time so that they may be investigated, to ensure they will not take up arms again and that their loyalty to Malaya is genuine. This is unacceptable to Chin Peng, who speaks about "the dignity of man". Both sides express different views of that concept. Marshall asks what dignity there is in the Communists making themselves "suffer indignities and miseries in the jungle with its diseases and its lack of the essentials of human life". Chin Peng clarifies it for him: "While we are in the jungle, we are free. Why should we come out to be detained?"

Even though Chin Peng is eventually willing to compromise by accepting the non-recognition of the MCP, his request for no detention after downing arms and coming out of the jungle is considered by Marshall as "unrealistic". The Tunku reinforces that by saying that "as far as restriction of movement is concerned, we must have it".

In the fourth session which takes place the next day, Chin Peng makes further concessions. He pledges that once Malaya attains self-determination in matters concerning internal security and national defence, the MCP will straight away lay down arms and disband its armed units. It is a clear indication that the MCP has no interest in fighting against a liberated Malayan government. What Chin Peng says in this regard is of great relevance: "Our armed forces are called 'National Liberation Army'. When we have attained our object, in other words, when this country is already liberated, then there is no point in continuing the existence of this army."

In return for disarmament, Chin Peng again makes a request for no detention. Such detention implies "that we come out to surrender", he explains. "If you demand our surrender, we would prefer to fight to the last man."

He proposes, instead, that the Communists be allowed to return to their respective homes, and from there if the Government carried out an investigation on them, that would be acceptable. "But if we were to be enclosed in one place and investigations are carried out, that amounts to surrender."

Looking back through the corridor of time, one might well think that such a request was not unreasonable. Chin Peng was merely being consistent with his plea for dignity. But how does the Tunku respond to that? "We would be powerless to control your movements if you were to come out of the jungle and put yourselves on the same level and the same status as we are. Therefore, if you do not come out to surrender, we would rather not accept you in our society."

He gives the example of China when it was divided into Chiang Kai Shek's Nationalist China and Mao Tse-tung's Communist China. "Chiang Kai Shek's Nationalist Government was driven out of the mainland," the Tunku said. "If I accept you on equal status, I have no doubt that I and my party will similarly be driven out of Malaya before long ... Therefore, you either give in to us ... or else this struggle will have to go on, much to my regret."

Interpret that how you will, consider its possible implications on the detention and investigation of the Communists if they had surrendered, and their subsequent status in society. Consider, too, that the Communists numbered only a mere 3,000. How potent could they have been? Was the Tunku driving too hard a bargain? Was the Baling Talks just a show?

Journalist Said Zahari has something revealing to say from his eyewitness coverage of the Baling Talks for *Utusan Melayu*. In a recent video interview that was screened at our reading in Singapore, he recounts that he managed to get a brief interview with the Tunku right after the talks concluded. As the Tunku was in a hurry to go off, he granted Said only one question. So, Said asked him whether he was disappointed that the talks were not successful. The Tunku's reply, according to Said, was: "No, no, not at all. I never wanted it to be a success."

Said, however, did not include that quote when he filed his news report because the Umno stalwart Syed Jaafar Albar, who was also present, told him it should not be made public. And so, it was not known to the world for decades.

Now that it's out in the open, it sounds plausible. Throughout the talks, the Tunku did not look like he was really willing to negotiate. He conceded nothing to Chin Peng's requests. He exaggerated the magnitude of the Communist threat and refused to acknowledge that their fight was also for liberation, for independence. He would have known that surrender would not have been acceptable to the Communists and yet, he demanded nothing less. He might have known this would ensure that the talks would fail.

POLITICS BE DAMNED, IT'S ENGLISH

theSun, June 12, 2009

You don't have to pass English to pass SPM. We have known that for a long time. A pass in English used to be compulsory when I sat my MCE (the precursor to SPM) in 1970, but that was stopped a few years later.

Lately, Education Minister Muhyiddin Yassin has raised the question of whether English should be made a compulsory pass. He said he was surprised to have discovered that it was not. "It was very revealing to me. I thought you must pass English, but was told that you don't have to," he said.

What's surprising to me about his statement is that he's only just found out that this is the case ... and he's supposed to be the Education Minister — and the Deputy Prime Minister, to boot! Where has he been all these years? Closeted in the Cabinet? What does this say of our government leaders? Have they lost touch with the Malaysian reality because they have been sending their children overseas for education instead?

Note that Muhyiddin has raised the matter of a compulsory pass merely as a question. These were his words: "I want to ask the public ...", "We want feedback ...", "I have not made any decision on it, I want to give a chance to the people to give their views." You don't have to be a CDA (critical discourse analysis) expert to understand the subtext of his discourse. He obviously doesn't want to upset the ultra-nationalist groups who view English as a threat to the national language despite the fact that enough discerning people have already said that one does not become less Malay, Chinese, Indian or whatever by learning English.

Nonetheless, it is a pertinent — nay, important — question. And my personal answer to that is: Of course, English should be made a compulsory pass at SPM! Otherwise, students will not take the language seriously. *Fail, fail lah, never mind. I still pass my SPM what.* That's the attitude that has partly caused the standard of our English to go to the dogs.

It all started with the wave of neo-nationalism that began after 1969 which, among other things, relegated English to an almost *non grata* status. I remember with some pain the years following that — when one felt somewhat unpatriotic for using English in public, especially in the presence of certain company. Even writers like Muhammad Haji Salleh and Syed Alwi renounced writing in English to reclaim their Malay *maruah*.

We overdid it, as usual. At the time, it was not foreseen by the legislators that one day, English would become the global language. And then globalisation sneaked up on us, and we suddenly realised we had lost that advantage we had three decades earlier, when we were among the top users of English in at least the Asian region.

So, what was our usual knee-jerk reaction to that? We scrambled for quick-fix solutions. But, as most wise people know, such measures don't work — at least, not effectively. We thought the answer lay partly in producing more English teachers, and to do that, the Government lowered the entry requirement at teachers' training colleges and some universities. Candidates with as low as a C5 in English at SPM were accepted.

If we were to conduct a survey of our teachers of English in national schools throughout the length and breadth of our nation today, we would encounter horror stories that would make most parents scream. Many would be the tales of how teachers who can't express themselves in English properly to save their own lives are ruining our young by imparting to them the wrong grammar, vocabulary, pronunciation and what-have-you.

I've heard students recounting how they had to correct their teachers' English repeatedly; and when I was editing an English page for a newspaper, I howled with laughter over a reader's account of his teacher's pronunciation. The teacher was reported to have on one occasion told her class, "Chindillela was very pooth thing." You might want to figure out what she really meant.

When the educators are not up to the mark, the vicious cycle perpetuates itself. I have read the writing of lecturers teaching TESL in universities, some of it even published in books and academic journals, and torn my hair out afterwards. Imagine the quality of the English of their charges, who will eventually graduate to teach English to your children and mine.

Then in 2003 came the farce of teaching Science and Maths in English — at a time when the teachers themselves were not equipped to do so or were indeed bad at English. The Government threw in the incentive of an extra allowance for teaching S&M (abbreviation pun intended), and in no time, even PE and Agama teachers were taking on the job without, firstly, having had foundation in the subjects and, secondly, proficiency in English. Soon enough, teachers were actually teaching S&M in Malay!

All this seems to smack of Malaysia Boleh! And Mahathir Mohamad, the man who is often credited with coining that risible slogan, should be held accountable. It was his regime that initiated the teaching of S&M in English. When he was prime minister, he touted the importance of English but didn't have enough guts and political will to push through a radical change. Teaching S&M in English was about the only compromise — and a feeble one, at that — he could strike. In 2002, he casually mooted the idea of bringing back English-medium schools, but he never followed it through.

Subsequent leaders have shown a similar lack of guts even when they know what the right course is. Pressured several months ago to make a stand on whether S&M would continue to be taught in English, the previous Education Minister Hishammuddin Hussein hummed and hawed, signifying nothing. His *keris* had apparently no thrust when it came to matters such as these.

It is clear that politics is at the base of policy decisions on the teaching of English. By floating the question, Muhyiddin is gingerly testing the waters. Any final decision will be made only when the factions that matter, including the ultra-nationalists, are in agreement with it.

Meanwhile, there will be discourse mired in rhetoric, such as that spouted by the Peninsular Malaysia Malay Students Front (GPSM): "There must be a comprehensive study on the available infrastructure for the teaching of English. The existing rural-urban dichotomy must be overcome as part of the 'democratisation of education'." There will also be half-past-six ideas thrown into the ring, like two types of SPM certificates being awarded — one for those who pass the English paper and the other for those who don't (courtesy of an online pollster).

Such sideshows merely complicate what is essentially a simple issue — English is important and we have to be proficient at it. Any plan that will help us in this regard should be supported. Politics be damned; it's a big world out there and we can't live under coconut shells. We need English to reach beyond our little land.

But this can only be attained if we work hard at it and do it with honesty and in the true spirit of excellence. We cannot have half-past-six teachers misguiding the students. We cannot be lowering the passing mark for English to allow students to get through their SPM as we have been doing for this and other subjects. This would be making a mockery of the whole plan and its purpose. It has to be impressed upon the students that doing well at English is a serious thing that they must take seriously, and if they don't, they will be failed, pure and simple. The issue of race should also not enter into this.

If this cannot be ensured and the Government doesn't have the political will to see it through to its logical conclusion, then there would be no point in discussing the issue further. In which case, we might as well shut up and stop wasting each other's time.

THE MALAYSIAN WAY TO BETTER ENGLISH

theSun, August 14, 2009

I was recently invited by the Ministry of Education to a discussion on "strengthening English" in schools, but from the way the proceedings went, it seemed like an exercise in futility.

The fact that it was being held in tandem with another discussion to "*memartabatkan*" (uphold) Bahasa Malaysia speaks volumes. As we all know, the standard statement that comes with any official announcement on the need to raise our standard of English must invariably contain the apologetic caveat: "but it must be carried out without threatening the position of the National Language". This occasion was evidently no different.

Both the English and Malay groups congregated at the outset in the same conference room where everyone was briefed on the purpose of the event and then parted ways to deliberate on their respective language concerns. During this initial common briefing, it was made unequivocally clear that even though there were plans to "*memperkukuh*" English, this should not be seen as a challenge to Bahasa Malaysia.

As to be expected then, the meeting on the English side was characterised by guardedness and underdog ambition. Issues raised were mainly those that had been raised before — again and again ("I'm hearing comments I used to hear 20, 30 years ago," said a veteran educationist). Many of the participants had been embroiled in many a discussion past and were now wary of whether their current proposals would amount to anything. You could tell by the conversations outside of the meeting room that most were pessimistic.

Nothing has changed. Certainly not the political will of the Government to truly revolutionise its attitude towards the teaching, learning and use of English in this country, which would call for a radical overturn of an official position that has been entrenched since 1970.

Who, in the current administration, would dare venture that way when their uppermost consideration is winning the next general election? Which explains why the vision on English has been always short-term. And what the recent reversal of the teaching of Science and Mathematics in English was motivated by.

No-one in power has dared to think of the long term, of the potential future of a Malaysia dragged down by its lack of proficiency in the global language, of the future of the rural populace who must continue to wallow in their lack of command of the language because they are not ardently advised otherwise. To get them out of their complacency with being monolinguistic would risk raising the ire of certain interest groups — and that could be disastrous for the ruling party.

Most of us at the meeting were too polite to bring this up, but an old hand in education did ask, "What is our language policy now? Monolingualism or bilingualism?" and ended up remarking that "trying to improve the rural situation is going to be very challenging".

So, by and large, we dutifully confined ourselves to discussing the areas of training, marketing and pedagogy. We gave suggestions on how to make the noble profession of teaching seem truly so to those going into it ("most students go into teaching English because they have no choice", observed a participant); on the need to take in only teacher-trainees who had an acceptable level of proficiency in English; on getting teachers to employ non-formal teaching methods that would be filled with fun for the learners and to organise out-of-class activities; on making more use of e-learning and ICT; on what to avoid if grammar were to be taught explicitly; on how to instil confidence in English teachers and give them the support they need when this is denied them by the school environment.

One of the best ideas — and possibly the only political one — was to urge the Government to commit to promoting "coordinate bilingualism" rather than "subordinate bilingualism", such that no language would be eclipsed or even dominated by another. That kind of commitment is essential, especially in a school environment where the *ustaz* can have a powerful influence on the headmaster's policy implementation.

At the meeting, no-one suggested bringing back the English-medium school or making a pass in English compulsory for passing SPM (Sijil Pelajaran Malaysia). Most of us thought this would be pointless, anyway.

After all, Mahathir Mohamad floated the English-medium school idea briefly when he was prime minister and then backed off. And only recently, Deputy Prime Minister and new Education Minister Muhyiddin Yassin sent up a test balloon regarding the compulsory pass but nothing has come out of it since.

To me, that meeting was a sad reflection of what we are — a people who are rich but are afraid to cultivate our wealth and let it blossom, and all because of our insecurities. We fear opening our minds so we deny our children access to our vaults.

Each time a new Minister of Education comes into office, there will be an attempt at some stock-taking and cursory spring-cleaning, but this is then followed by the same old, same old business as usual. We pay lip service, we opt for eyewashes.

Will this time be different? I much doubt it. So, as has been happening over the years, those who have the means will find ways to improve their English, mostly outside of the school system, and those who don't will lag behind. And when it comes time for university graduates to attend job interviews, that's when the difference will be telling. Still, at the end of the day, these will just amount to being mere statistics. It's the outcome at the elections that matters more.

It is, as we say, the Malaysian way.

THE TROUBLE WITH TITLED BEINGS

Free Malaysia Today, April 8, 2010

When Pakatan Rakyat took over a few state governments in 2008, one of the things I hoped the coalition would not do was to recommend its elected representatives for datukships.

At a gathering hosted by the newly elected Sivarasa Rasiah and Elizabeth Wong to celebrate their victories at the 2008 general election, I expressed this hope to the both of them. I also asked the same of Lim Guan Eng after he became Chief Minister. "We are not giving any titles," he assured me. "I will try if possible to remain what I am."

Well, it hasn't quite turned out that way. Guan Eng has stayed true to his word by not accepting any title but people under his watch, like Zahrain Mohd Hashim who has since become an Independent, were presented awards. Sivarasa and Elizabeth are still without titles, but the Selangor Menteri Besar, Khalid Ibrahim, already a Tan Sri, got a Datuk Seri last year. I was disappointed that not long after he became Menteri Besar of Perak, Nizar Jamaluddin became a Datuk Seri. Well, win some, lose some.

I can understand the desire to reward a person for his or her contribution to the advancement of society, but does this have to be in the form of a title that serves to set that person apart from the common folk? The French Revolution ignited the idea of equality for all citizens, and today, the idea of superior beings set apart from hoi polloi is, in many societies, unacceptable.

Britain, of all places, still sustains an order of knights and dames, although it is a democracy that sometimes exhibits socialist inclinations. The monarchy of course is a main reason for the continued practice, and certainly, too, the deeply entrenched class system that still operates in British society, with the ruling class continuing to be highly influenced by the aristocracy.

However, the good thing about the British is that they generally don't take their honorifics too seriously. Few, indeed, consider it a must to refer to the famous rocker Mick Jagger as Sir Michael or the actress Judi Dench as Dame Judi. In fact, Jagger's fans were disappointed that he accepted the title. The highly successful composer of musicals Andrew Lloyd Webber was made a peer by the Queen in 1997, but if he were to insist on being called Baron Lloyd-Webber, he would be laughed out of not only the theatre but anywhere in Britain. Except perhaps in the House of Lords.

While the knights and dames of Britain wear their titles lightly, the same does not seem to apply with their Malaysian counterparts (although "knight" seems a misplaced description for any of our Datuks or Tan Sris — how many have been convicted for corruption or criminal breach of trust?). A film credit for Jins Shamsuddin has to carry the honorific Tan Sri; the singer Siti Nurhaliza has to be acknowledged Datuk every time she is addressed or announced as a performer; and Lee Chong Wei has to be similarly addressed in news reports even though it sounds patently weird, especially when he's lost a badminton match. What? Our "knight" lost? Woe upon us!

Many Malaysian Datuks and Tan Sris take their honorifics so seriously that they will throw tantrums or threaten action if you ignore to acknowledge them as such in public. This appears unbecoming because it seems to place more emphasis on title than content of character or personal calibre. You may be an excellent engineer or judge, for instance, but if you have to depend on an honorific to define you, that's rather pathetic.

Besides, it is public knowledge that not all titles are awarded to those who are deserving. Sometimes, it all boils down to connections. That explains why a majority of public servants, including political leaders and civil service officials, seem to automatically get conferred them. Look at the list of candidates standing in the recent MCA elections. Of the 101 vying for positions, 38 have titles, including seven Datuk Seris and one Tan Sri. That's 37.6 per cent of the total number of candidates.

If that seems absurd, look at our Cabinet. Virtually everyone in it has a title. Just for comparison, imagine the British Government being run by a bunch of Sirs and Dames. And yet, as it is, even their prime minister is just plain Mr Gordon Brown.

I know someone who has been awarded multiple Datukships not because he is providing a creditable service to society but apparently because he knows how to suck up to the people in government and royal circles. To some of his professional colleagues, his vocational conduct is repugnant. I refrain from saying "professional conduct" because his conduct is actually unprofessional.

It is also public knowledge that in Malaysia, titles can be bought. In which case, what value does a Datukship have then? How does it sit on someone who had obtained it through actual creditable service and another who had paid tons of money to secure it? So, why should Malaysian society take these titles seriously?

In reality, most of us don't, but we refrain from expressing our personal feelings about the matter out of politeness or fear of reprisal. Behind the backs of incompetent Datuks, we snigger at their lack of calibre. Among ourselves, we privately pour scorn on Datins. "Ya *lah*! That woman so *aksi* and demanding, always saying she's so rich and powerful. Sure *lah*, she's a Datin what!"

This merely begets hypocrisy. Worse, it fosters an undertow of resentment against what is perceived to be an exclusive class of beings; and creates the apocryphal impression that Datuks and Datins are endowed with glamour. Have you taken a look at some of them? In those cases, the word "glamour" might wish it didn't exist.

One other point I have to make pertains to the tedious ritual of addressing the titled beings at public events. The master of ceremonies has to make sure he/she follows the right protocol; so, too, the people who have to subsequently make speeches. There's Yang Berhormat for those who are in public office and Yang Berbahagia for those who are not. Then, there's Tuan Yang Terutama and Yang Amat Berhormat and Yang Amat Berbahagia and Yang Berhormat Mulia, and if you should forget which to use, God help you! Everyone has to go through that rigmarole, naming one Yang Berbahagia or Yang Berhormat after another, spewing what amounts to a distasteful mouthful simply because it sounds like grovelling. No wonder we sometimes appear such an obsequious people. It would be so refreshingly simple with just "*Para hadirin*".

I hope the Pakatan Rakyat leaders who are still without titles will keep their status intact, but then if they become increasingly more entrenched in government, who knows what might get to their heads? I can say, however, that I can't conceive of a Datuk Nurul Izzah or a Datuk Seri Lim Guan Eng. Stomaching that would be even harder. Most unpalatable would be — when and if he ever retires — a Tun Lim Kit Siang! He is a people's icon; if he crosses over, it would be a monumental loss.

SEND IN THE DATUKS

MalaysianDigest.com, November 4, 2010

I had a good cackle the other day — over a caption that appeared in an article of a mainstream newspaper. It was for photographs of four Malaysian singers who had appeared as the opening acts for George Benson when he performed in Kuala Lumpur on October 29.

The caption named them as "Datuk Sheila Majid, Datuk Siti Nurhaliza, Datuk David Arumugam and Datuk Khatijah Ibrahim". Another one whose picture was not included but mentioned in the article is "Datuk Yusni Hamid".

Five Datuks performing as a prelude to Benson's entrance. Wow! He might have been bowled over if he had known. But then again, it might not have mattered a mite to a citizen of the American republic that upholds egalitarianism.

To him, it might have seemed that Datuks in Malaysia are a dime a dozen and that only Malaysians seem to take such titles seriously. If Cliff Richard, Elton John, Paul McCartney and Mick Jagger performed on the same stage and their photographs appeared in a British newspaper the next day, the caption would not read: "Sir Cliff, Sir Elton, Sir Paul and Sir Mick". You can bet they would be simply referred to as Richard, John, McCartney and Jagger. Or just by their first names.

Hey! If you're an artist, you don't need to be referred to as "Sir", right? It's your art that defines you, no? And those fans out there watching the concert — would they care a hoot if you're a Sir or Datuk? Does having the title make your voice sound better? Hmmm ... maybe to Malaysians, it does.

A couple of months ago, I had to cackle too when I read that Melaka had created a new Datukship that is lower in class to the existing one. Called Darjah Pangkuan Seri Melaka (DPSM), it is given to people in government positions that are lower than those of the people receiving the Darjah Mulia Seri Melaka (DMSM). So if your boss is a director-general, he'll get the DMSM but you are entitled only to the lesser DPSM. Cackle out loud!

Other states, it seems, also have such a classification for the Datukships they give out. They call these Class I and Class II. Imagine that, even Datuks fall into Class I or Class II. Cackle out louder!

But not to worry. As the Melaka Chief Minister quipped, they are still called Datuk anyway.

Hey, but next time someone tries to be pompous and says, "Do you know who I am? I'm a Datuk", you can ask them, "Class I or Class II?".

Still, it must be grand to be a Datuk since so many people want to be one. Some would even pay good money to get the title. In a recent report, the purchasing fee for one case was quoted at RM300,000. That's quite a sum to pay. Or maybe not if you can afford it. I wonder if you could write it off as business expenses.

It seems Malaysia has so many Datuks now that the joke going round has been modified. It used to be that if you were to throw a stone in Bukit Bintang, you would hit a Datuk; now if you were to throw one in Oxford Street, which happens to be in faraway London, you would hit a Datuk too.

What would happen if, in the near future, there are so many Datuks that the title becomes devalued? If we can see it happen on a concert stage, why not in a wider context? Then Datuks would come to be taken for granted. And once they reach critical mass, their significance — God forbid! — might even disappear. They might come to be treated like one of us.

Not so much prestige, status and recognition as before. Not so special any more the feeling of being a Datuk. Everyone around the wedding dinner table is one. Imagine the dinner conversation:

"Datuk, please have the last piece ... Datuk ..."

"Are you talking to me?"

"Yes, Datuk."

"I'm Datuk Seri."

"Oh, so sorry, Datuk Seri, please have the —"

"Thank you, Datuk, you go ahead. I've had enough."

"So have I, Datuk Seri. Perhaps the Datuk beside you would like to have it?"

"Datuk Apanama, would you like to have it?"

"No, Datuk Seri, I'm superstitious, I don't want to end up an old maid."

"Oh, of course, Datuk, I'm sorry. I still think of Datuks as men."

"I beg your pardon, Datuk Seri! Can't you tell from my looks that I'm a woman?"

Suddenly, there's a commotion at the next table. The real identity of one of the guests has been exposed — he is not a real Datuk! Horror of horrors! What's worse, he has been masquerading as one for years and fooling his business associates, some of whom are now seated at that table!

"You are worse than scum, Datuk!" yells one of the business associates furiously.

"He's not a real Datuk, don't call him that!" yells another.

"Oops, sorry, habit *laa*."

"Let's throw him out for deceiving us all these years!" yells yet another business associate.

"Yes!" yell several business associates. "He doesn't belong here!"

A well-built young man in a suit and bowtie saunters by. One of the business associates calls to him, "Hey, waiter."

The young man glares back and replies, "Excuse me, I'm not a waiter. I'm a Datuk!"

"Really?" says the business associate, surprised. "You're so young, you don't even look 30."

"So what? I'm 28. And I'm a sportsman."

"Why are they giving out Datukships to people so young?"

"Hey, at least I got mine for serving the country. How did you get yours?"

"Are you insulting me, you young *ciku*?"

Before you know it, the whole wedding ends in pandemonium! The poor couple who are getting married will remember it as the Dinner of Duelling Datuks. So will the bride's parents, who are both Datuks, and the bridegroom's parents, who are also both Datuks.

How wonderful it is that we have a class of people who are higher than us commoners. Without them, life would be so much duller, and certainly less funny. Even with a Datuk to his name, David Arumugam sounds more cool. And now when he sings 'Dapatkah?', it sounds so much more meaningful. Not bad for a *kucing lorong* eh? Kakakakaka ...

HOW DID WE TOLERATE THE ISA FOR SO LONG?

Penang Economic Monthly, November 2011

Is the Internal Security Act (ISA) really going to leave us? In name as well as in spirit? Will its body be laid to rest forever and its soul consigned not to purgatory but to hell, where it will be burned to nothingness and never more be resurrected?

Or will the government of Prime Minister Najib Razak design the two laws proposed as its replacement such that the repressiveness inherent in the ISA will live on, and the ruling regime can use it to its political advantage?

These are the questions on the minds of Malaysians who have, at one time or another, spoken out against the ISA or campaigned for its abolition over the years. For no law has had such power in shaping aspects of its people's personality and the socio-political culture they live in than this law that authorises detention without trial.

Even in recent times, you could hear Malaysians in private conversations lowering their voices and looking over their shoulders whenever they spoke about something that seemed slightly "sensitive" — for fear of being overheard and hauled away by some Special Branch officer who might be hiding behind a potted plant.

Has the situation changed since Najib made the announcement on September 15 that the ISA would be repealed?

For now, perhaps, because it would look odd if the Government hauled anyone in under any circumstances. But what it will be after

March 2012, when the repeal of the Act would have been tabled in Parliament together with the proposal of the two new laws replacing it, it's hard to predict – unless we have some inkling of the substance of the latter two.

But why are we getting two laws to replace one? That's been the nagging question and bone of contention. Are we being given a bazaar offer – sell one, get two free?

It looks like one of them could be used for preventive detention, which would probably cover so-called "threats to national security", and the other for anti-terrorism. If so, these are no different from the terms of the ISA, in which case the fundamental liberties of Malaysians that have been unfairly curbed by the ISA will continue to be curbed.

Will the two new laws give the Home Minister the same absolute powers he enjoys with the ISA? If so, what is there to ensure that he will not brand a political opponent a "terrorist" in order to shut him away? What mechanisms will be built into the two new laws to prevent the abuse of power?

To be sure, since the ISA's enactment in 1960, close to 11,000 people have been arrested under it. Although its original stated purpose was to deter Communism, its brief of acting against anyone believed to be a threat to national security is decidedly broad. Not surprisingly, therefore, detainees have included NGO personnel, student leaders, teachers and even theatre artists. Also a Malay who converted to Christianity, arrested for "disrupting Malay culture by being a Christian". How does one person's religious conversion amount to a security threat?

More drastically, in 2002, the then Deputy Home Minister Zainal Abidin Zin even threatened that the law could be used against those who gave a "racial" twist to the new policy of teaching Science and Mathematics in English in schools. This was then prime minister Mahathir Mohamad's pet policy, so woe betide anyone who tried to oppose it.

That happened at the height of the culture of fear, generated and intensified during Mahathir's premiership. In fact, the most notorious use of the ISA was under his watch, when Operation Lalang made its big swoop on more than a hundred Malaysians in 1987. Many of them were Opposition politicians and social activists who had spoken out against the Government. Operation Lalang remains a black mark for Malaysian democracy because it displayed how mighty the State could be for having a weapon like the ISA.

Apart from that, the decision on an arrest could sometimes be arbitrary, as we saw in the Tan Hoon Cheng case. The *Sin Chew Daily* journalist was arrested under the Act in September 2008 for no apparent reason.

Just prior to that, she had written a four-paragraph report of a speech made by Penang Umno leader Ahmad Ismail in which he called Chinese Malaysians "*pendatang*". The remark inflamed the Chinese. It bordered on sedition. But who got arrested instead? Irate Malaysians clamoured to know why. What crime had Tan committed in merely reporting what Ahmad Ismail said?

The then Home Minister Syed Hamid Albar came out to face the music. But instead of providing a rational answer, he came up with the most absurd reason. He said Tan's detention was meant for her own "protection" because, he declared, her life was "under threat".

The next day, loan defaulters were begging to be detained – in order to be protected from Ah Longs seeking blood! No wonder the Government had to release Tan after only a 20-hour detention, making her the shortest-serving detainee in the history of the ISA!

But, seriously, I have to say there has, however, been no such happy ending for all the other ISA cases, and I can't recall another blackly comic instance. I recall, instead, the gloom and severity of watching the eminent journalist A. Samad Ismail 'confess' on public television in 1976, three months after his arrest, that he was a Communist. After that, he was detained for another four years.

In 1981, he made a second 'confession' on television to attest that he had recanted. His deadpan expression and the way he merely mouthed the words without meaning what he said showed his innate resistance to the staged event. He would have known that acting as he did, astute viewers would see through the absurdist drama that was being played out. The words he seemingly read out looked like they were prepared by someone else.

It later became public knowledge that the man who orchestrated Samad's arrest and subsequent 'confessions' was none other than the then Home Minister Ghazali Shafie and that Samad had been coerced into making those appearances. Ghazali's use of the ISA to consolidate his power reinforced the belief that the law was increasingly being used against political opponents. Mahathir's was publicly perceived as doing that as well as silencing the citizenry.

The original purpose of deterring Communism has long been lost sight of. In any case, Communism in Malaysia is virtually dead. On that score, the ISA has gone way past its use-by date. Besides, we have ample provisions in our penal laws that can be upgraded to take care of terrorism. Before Zaid Ibrahim resigned as de facto law minister in 2008, he and his colleagues were already studying ways to address that through amending the Criminal Procedure Code and the Penal Code.

In fact, the current idea of having two new laws to replace the ISA is suspect. It cannot bode well for Malaysian democracy that in this day and age of increasing demands for civil liberties, our government is considering implementing more controls — even if it's in the name of "safeguarding peace and public order".

Detention without trial cannot be justified, and certainly not for an initial period of 60 days as is the case under the ISA. Even 14 days, the period allowed by detention laws in Australia and the United Kingdom, is too long. The ISA also allows for the detention to be extended to two years at the pleasure of the Home Minister, renewable after that for an indefinite number of terms. This is inhumane and cannot be allowed any more. How did we allow that to go on for 51 years?

The ISA must go. Detention without trial must go. Everyone must have a right to be proven guilty before he or she is put away. Between now and March 2012, it is not too late for the public to call on the Government to reconsider its proposal to introduce the two new laws. One law is bad enough. Two is doubly bad.

Malaysians have fought hard to get the ISA repealed. Many have risked arrest to demonstrate against it. On August 1, 2009, alone, about 15,000 took to the streets in Kuala Lumpur to call for the law's repeal, and nearly 600 were arrested. We have come this far to break the culture of fear. We must not regress. We must not let down the people who have struggled for our freedom, and allow the Government to deceive us.

If the Government cannot give us our fundamental right and our fundamental freedom, then it has no right to be our government.

WHAT THE
CHINESE WANT

Free Malaysia Today, May 2, 2010

Every time Barisan Nasional gets less than the expected support from Chinese voters at an election, the question invariably pops up among the petty-minded: Why are the Chinese ungrateful?

So now, after the Hulu Selangor by-election, it's not surprising to read in *Utusan Malaysia* a piece that asks: "*Orang Cina Malaysia, apa lagi yang anda mahu?*" (Chinese Malaysians, what more do you want?).

Normally, something intentionally provocative and propagandistic as this doesn't deserve to be honoured with a reply. But even though I'm fed up of such disruptive and ethnocentric polemics, this time I feel obliged to reply — partly because the article has also been published, in an English translation, in the *Straits Times* of Singapore.

I wish to emphasise here that I am replying not as a Chinese Malaysian but, simply, as a Malaysian.

Let me say at the outset that the Chinese have got nothing more than what any citizen should get. So to ask "what more" it is they want, is misguided. A correct question would be "What do the Chinese want?"

All their lives, the Chinese have held to the belief that no one owes them a living. They have to work for it. Most of them have got where they are by the sweat of their brow, not by handouts or the policies of the Government.

They have come to expect nothing – not awards, not accolades, not gifts from official sources. (Let's not lump in Datukships, that's a different ball game.) They know that no Chinese who writes in the Chinese language will ever be bestowed the title of Sasterawan Negara, unlike in Singapore where the literatures of all the main language streams are recognised and honoured with the Cultural Medallion, etc.

The Chinese have learned they cannot expect the Government to grant them scholarships. Some will get those, but countless others won't. They've learned to live with that and to work extra hard in order to support their children to attain higher education because education is very important to them. They experience a lot of daily pressure to achieve that. Unfortunately, not many non-Chinese realise or understand that. In fact, many Chinese had no choice but to emigrate for the sake of their children's further education or to accept scholarships from abroad, many from Singapore, which has inevitably led to a brain drain.

The writer of the *Utusan* article says the Chinese "account for most of the students" enrolled in "the best private colleges in Malaysia". Even so, the Chinese still have to pay a lot of money to have their children study in these colleges. And to earn that money, the parents have to work very hard. The money does not fall from the sky.

The writer goes on to add: "The Malays can gain admission into only government-owned colleges of ordinary reputation." That is utter nonsense. Some of these colleges are meant for the cream of the Malay crop of students and are endowed with the best facilities. They are given elite treatment.

The writer also fails to acknowledge that the Chinese are barred from being admitted to some of these colleges. As a result, the Chinese are forced to pay the exorbitant fees to attend private colleges. Furthermore, the Malays are also welcome to enrol in the private colleges, and many of them do. It's, after all, a free enterprise.

The writer claims that the Chinese live "in the lap of luxury" and lead lives that are "more than ordinary" whereas the Malays in Singapore, their minority-race counterparts there, lead "ordinary lives".

Such sweeping statements sound inane especially when they are not backed up by definitions of "lap of luxury" and "ordinary lives". They sound hysterical, if not hilarious as well, when they are not backed up by evidence. It's surprising that a national daily like *Utusan Malaysia* would publish something as idiosyncratic as that. And the *Straits Times*, too.

The writer quotes from a survey that said eight of the 10 richest people in Malaysia are Chinese. Well, if these people are where they are, it must have also come from hard work and prudent business sense. Is that something to be faulted?

If the writer had said that some of them achieved greater wealth through being given crony privileges and lucrative contracts by the Government, there might be a point, but even then, it would still take hard work and business acumen to secure such phenomenal success. Certainly, Syed Mokhtar Al-Bukhary, who is one of the 10, would take exception if it were said that he has not worked hard and lacks business savvy.

Most important, it should be noted that the eight Chinese tycoons mentioned in the survey represent but a minuscule percentage of the wider Chinese Malaysian population. To extrapolate that because eight Chinese are filthy rich, the rest of the Chinese must therefore live in the lap of luxury and lead more than ordinary lives would be a mockery of the truth. The writer has obviously not met the vast numbers of very poor Chinese. Even the middle-class ones don't enjoy luxury when so much of what they earn go towards their children's education.

The crux of the writer's article is that the Chinese are not grateful to the Government by not voting for Barisan Nasional at the Hulu Selangor by-election. But this demonstrates the thinking of either a simple mind or a closed one.

Why did the Chinese by and large not vote for BN? Because it's corrupt. Plain and simple. Let's call a spade a spade. And BN showed how corrupt it was during the campaign by throwing bribes to the electorate, including promising RM3 million to the Chinese school in Rasa.

The Chinese were not alone in seeing this corruption. The figures are unofficial but one could assume that at least 40 per cent of Malays and 45 per cent of Indians who voted against BN in that by-election also had their eyes open.

So, what's wrong with not supporting a government that is corrupt? If the government is corrupt, do we continue to support it?

To answer the question then, what do the Chinese want? They want a government that is not corrupt; that can govern well and proves to have done so; that tells the truth rather than lies; that follows the rule of law; that upholds rather than abuses the country's sacred institutions. BN does not fit that description, so the Chinese don't vote for it. This is not what *only* the Chinese want. It is something every sensible Malaysian, regardless of race, wants. Is that something that is too difficult to understand?

Some people think that the Government is to be equated with the country and therefore, if someone does not support the Government, they are being disloyal to the country. This is a complete fallacy. BN is not Malaysia. It is merely a political coalition that is the government of the day. Rejecting BN is not rejecting the country.

Let's be clear about this important distinction. In America, the people sometimes vote for the Democrats and sometimes for the Republicans. Voting against the one that is in government at the time is not considered disloyalty to the country.

By the same token, voting against Umno is also voting against a party, not against a race. And if the Chinese or whoever criticise Umno, they are criticising the party; they are not criticising Malays. It just happens that Umno's leaders are Malay.

It is time all Malaysians realised this so that we can once and for all dispel the confusion. Let us no more confuse country with government. We can love our country and at the same time hate the Government. It is perfectly all right.

I should add here what the Chinese don't want. They don't want to be insulted, to be called *pendatang* or told to be grateful for their citizenship. They have been loyal citizens; they duly and dutifully pay taxes; they respect the country's Constitution and its institutions. Their forefathers came to this country generations ago and helped it to prosper. They continue to contribute to the country's growth and development.

Would anyone like to be disparaged, made to feel unwelcome, unwanted? For the benefit of the writer of the *Utusan* article, what MCA president Chua Soi Lek means when he says the MCA needs to be more vocal is that it needs to speak up whenever the Chinese community is disparaged. For too long, the MCA has not spoken up strongly enough when Umno politicians and associates like Ahmad Ismail, Nasir Safar, Ahmad Noh and others before them insulted the Chinese and made them feel like they don't belong. That's why the Chinese have largely rejected the MCA.

You see, the Chinese, like all human beings, want self-respect. And a sense of belonging in this country they call home. That is all the Chinese want, and have always wanted. Nothing more.

SPEAKING FOR MYSELF

I'M INCLUDING HERE A FEW INTERVIEWS DONE WITH ME BY OTHERS BECAUSE WHAT I SAY IN THEM ALSO REFLECTS MY THOUGHTS AND BELIEFS. BESIDES, THESE INTERVIEWS PROVIDE SOME BACKGROUND INFORMATION THAT MIGHT HELP READERS UNDERSTAND WHERE I'M COMING FROM.

INTERVIEW:
KEE THUAN CHYE

By Wong Ming Yook
Transforming Truth, a Kairos publication, June 2001

Kee Thuan Chye is no stranger to the arts and literary world of Kuala Lumpur. He has worked many years in the New Straits Times and acted in the capacity of Literary Editor of that paper since 1991. Thuan Chye has helped generate a great deal of our interest in the literati of Southeast Asia by organising and planning workshops and seminars with writers, interviewing and reviewing them, and generally just bringing them into our contact and view. He has been both generous and energetic in such ways. I can say that at the least, I have been able to meet and talk to some writers via his good offices. He has been actively involved in writing himself, having published his works locally and abroad. Thuan Chye also has a penchant for acting, and fans of local sitcom Kopitiam would remember seeing him there in his role as the Fierce Major! He also had speaking roles in the films Anna and the King and Entrapment. Recently, Thuan Chye left his post at the NST to work for The Star as Associate Editor. This interview was made just after he had left.

Let's start with the most obvious question: When and why did you decide to leave the *NST* in favour of *The Star*?
Joining *The Star* was an option always at the back of my mind. I decided to leave the *NST* towards the end of 1999, when I felt my attempts to contribute towards improving the paper were of no avail. And I'm the sort

of person who can't help but want to contribute significantly to whatever organisation I'm attached to, and to see results arising therefrom.

How long exactly were you with the *NST*, and how has the paper (and you) changed and developed over the years? Do you feel you made a significant contribution to the *NST*? (How?)

I was with the NST for 21 years and a few months. That's really long in my reckoning. The paper has changed a lot. I've gone through six editors-in-chief (I survived five of them!). Its circulation has dropped by nearly half since the year I joined (1979). Now that I've left, I expect its circulation to rise again!

Did you always feel you wanted to be involved in journalism, or did you just stumble or drift into it? What does that word suggest to you, "journalist"? What sort of journalist do you see yourself as?

I wanted very much to be a reporter when I was in Form 5. I told my mother there was nothing I wanted more, never mind if I only got paid peanuts. But the interest began to wane when I entered university and became passionate about theatre. I was very active in writing and directing plays at Universiti Sains Malaysia (USM). So when it came to opting for a major, I couldn't bring myself to major in Mass Communications. I would have majored in Performing Arts except that I didn't want to do acting class! It's ironic in retrospect. As ironic as the fact that I eventually ended up in journalism. A series of things led to that. I graduated in Literature and applied to do my Masters, but I couldn't afford to do it without getting a position as a tutor. It was, however, given to someone else. Another irony because I was top of my class. He, of course, happened to be a Bumiputera.

So, I applied for a job at the university's Centre for Policy Research. It was a temporary job as a fieldwork co-ordinator for the Centre's many socio-economic surveys. I served several months until, through the machinations of a lecturer who took umbrage against my ticking him off for barging into my room "like a gangster" without knocking on the door, I got called before a tribunal chaired by the Vice-Chancellor. I held my own and staunchly defended myself. But for some reason I can't fathom, the V-C got offended and demanded I apologise to him. My immediate superior pleaded with me to tender the apology, saying that I would otherwise lose my job, but I refused. I maintained that I had not done anything wrong to the V-C. I still maintain that today.

The V-C went on to become a head of state, the lecturer in question is now a highly placed politician in Penang, and I got thrown out of my job. And that's what prompted me to write to *The National Echo* to seek an opening. I was hired as its Literary Editor. Yet another irony since I ended my career at *NST* in that same position!

What sort of journalism prevails in Malaysia today?
There is the mainstream kind — and nowadays "mainstream" doesn't carry positive connotations — and there is the *malaysiakini.com* kind. Both are bound by their respective agenda. They are not exactly on opposite sides of the coin, but the ways they present "the truth" somewhat differ. I'm still an idealist in a lot of ways but after 23 years in the profession, I've come to realise that there is no such thing as objective journalism. What facts you choose to present and how you present them is a reflection of your own bias — and that is exactly how the media operates, not only here but all over the world. In our case, there is a lesser degree of freedom to what the media can do because of the many sensitivities prevailing. The coverage of the recent Kampung Medan crisis is a good example of how gingerly the media responded to it initially. I believe as I always have that we practise too much self-censorship, but the realities of the newspaper industry are such, considering that the Printing Presses and Publications Act hovers over us, that one sometimes can't be too careful.

I am a constant advocate that the system must change — and the change must happen at the top — before we can become a more enlightened society. The authorities are often the ones who cause the problems, because of their own indecisiveness, inconsistency and irrational fears. This has led to a conditioning of Malaysian society, starting with children in schools, that is predicated on perpetuating a culture of fear and obeisance to authority. What I'm saying here is nothing new, of course. We Malaysians know all about it.

In my own small way as a journalist, I try to expose what I consider to be factors detrimental to the development of a progressive nation that provides justice and equality for all. I've sometimes had to pay the price for pushing the limits but I suppose, ultimately, a journalist has to ask himself or herself why he continues to be a journalist if he doesn't serve higher ideals.

I ask these questions because I want to lead into a discussion of your sense of vocation. "Vocation" is becoming a difficult word to define in these uncertain times. Some say a job is just a job; others feel it requires a deep sense of the rightness and fittingness of the individual for the task, and the task for the individual. What is your definition of a person's sense of "calling" or "vocation"?

Ideally, for any job, we need people with passion and commitment to do it. In journalism, there are many journeymen, the sort that just get by from day to day, do what's required and go home, and bread-and-butter journalists who do what they are told and are careful not to have their rice bowl broken. When a young person comes to me and says she wants to be a journalist, I often ask her if she has the passion for it, or the "calling" if you will. If she doesn't, I tell her to go do something else. Journalism is a vocation that requires passion and commitment more than many other professions because it carries a heavy social responsibility. You can't afford to be jaded. If you do and you continue in the profession, you are short-changing not only yourself but also the public. I guess this would also apply to professions like doctors, nurses, pilots, prime ministers. That sense of calling is hard to define but you feel it when you get excited over things you do at your job, and when you're away from it you feel lost or empty. You feel it when you are driven to learn as much as you can about everything pertaining to the profession. You feel it when you feel agitated seeing someone else do the job badly!

The word "calling" for Christians suggests a Caller, whom we recognise as God. Is there a Caller for you? How do you view religious faith?
Now that you've mentioned it, perhaps the reason why I'm such a dabbler (in journalism, theatre, writing, acting, directing) and, therefore, master of nothing is because I've never felt called, and I've never felt called because I don't subscribe to any religion!

I view religious faith with some ambivalence. I think it's fantastic for those who have it and believe strongly in whatever they profess, but I'm suspicious of organised religion because of the fanaticism it can engender if manipulated wrongly. Religion, with its power to harness spirits and emotions, can truly move mountains. Used positively, it is tremendous. I prefer something that professes a "way of life" rather than "religion". Which is why if someone dunked my head in water and threatened to drown me unless I chose a faith to follow, I would most likely opt for Buddhism, probably Zen Buddhism, which I can relate to for its embrace of irreverence and other unsolemn things that one usually doesn't associate with a religion. I very much like the Zen idea of

> *Sitting quietly, doing nothing.*
> *Spring comes, and the grass grows by itself.*

You're also involved in the arts and literary world in Malaysia, particularly in Kuala Lumpur. What is the extent of your involvement these days?
I've found it less appealing to be involved in theatre because of the huge investment of time and effort in it for marginal returns. Nowadays, I'm more inclined to consider it more economically viable to be in film or TV. But then, film and TV roles are few and far between. And with a face like mine, I find the range of opportunities limited. Let's be honest, I'm not going to get cast as a romantic lead — or just any lead, for that matter!

Writing-wise, I have a play that I finished writing a few years ago and is now waiting to be revised. I have also written a screenplay, which I somehow managed to do last year by cramming in whatever little time I had between work and chauffeuring my kids and doing household chores. I should sit down and write my novel in progress but that sounds like a formidable task and I sigh when I think of it. But an extract from it was accepted for inclusion in *New Writing 10*, which features works from the U.K. and the Commonwealth. It's published by Picador and is due for release anytime now. I'm thrilled to be in the company of leading British writers like Louis de Bernieres, Andrew Motion, Helen Simpson, Alan Silitoe, Janice Galloway ... sorry, I'm name-dropping but couldn't help it.

How important is the arts and literary world to you? These days, we like to talk of things being "commercially viable" before they are considered useful or good. The arts are very non-utilitarian subjects and therefore, not always "commercially viable". Do we still have something crucial to say to the immediate world? Look at the paucity of our local literary offerings — are we dinosaurs well on the way to extinction?

I don't believe everything has to be commercially viable, and for that reason the arts have an important place in human life — if not for anything, to remind us of that! I can't imagine a world without the arts. It's true that in these days of intense commercialisation, when the value of a thing is determined by its price tag and accumulating wealth is the number one priority, many people have less time for and interest in the arts. But there's also another side to the proposition. In Malaysia particularly, as the society gets more affluent, it becomes more aware of the need for cultural sustenance. This explains the growing audiences at theatre shows and musical concerts. It's now actually chic to be culturally aware, or at least to be seen to be so. To me, that's not a good reason to patronise the theatre or art exhibitions or musical recitals, but for the artist, it's better to play to full than empty houses. What I can't stand is the pretentiousness that accompanies this trend but that's another matter.

Literature, however, doesn't seem to be enjoying as much attention, particularly Malaysian literature in English. Malaysians are not flocking to bookstores to buy the latest Malaysian novel or poetry collection or play — if they get published at all! Basically, that's because there is such stiff competition from books from the West, and Malaysians, still suffering from the cultural cringe, would rather opt for these than the Malaysian offerings. The way out for Malaysian writers, as I see it, is to rise to the challenge of getting their books published in the West, in the so-called metropolitan centres of English. Then, they will be recognised by the folks at home.

As for having something crucial to say to the immediate world, I don't think there's any problem there. There's so much material, really, for Malaysian writers to delve into. The corruption at the core of Malaysian society, the fixation on success (Malaysia Boleh!) and the rise of crass materialism, the curbs on freedom, the contradictions inherent in Vision 2020 — these are just a few examples.

You're a published writer as well. Tell us something about your books and what you wanted to say in them.
I've had only four books out — two of them are plays (*1984 Here and Now* and *We Could **** You, Mr Birch*), one a collection of my writings in the press over the years (*Just In So Many Words*), and the fourth, a commissioned biography of a doctor in Sabah which I agreed to do to pay for my mother's coronary bypass (*Old Doctors Never Fade Away*).

My plays very much encapsulate the themes I have often dealt with — freedom to express, racial equality, social justice, political abuse of power, corruption, etc. Rather political stuff. My dream for Malaysia is that it will one day be open and generous and big enough to embrace all its races, cultures, languages, religions and accord them due place and recognition. I want my children to grow up in a land where they can speak without fear and in which they can feel a sense of belonging.

KEE-PING THE FAITH

By Jacqueline Ann Surin
theSun, September 17, 2005

Newspaper readers may know Kee Thuan Chye as the editor of The Star's *'Mind Our English' page, but before he became associate editor at* The Star, *he was an editor with the* New Straits Times. *"I've been in journalism since 1977, beginning with* The National Echo," *he says.*

But Kee is more than a journalist. He is a playwright and several of his plays, such as 1984 Here and Now, We Could **** You, Mr Birch *and* The Big Purge, *are political commentaries on the country. Not surprisingly, a few have been considered too risky to stage in Malaysia. The 51-year-old is also a theatre director and actor, and has acted on stage, in commercials, TV sitcoms and Hollywood movies* Entrapment *and* Anna and the King.

You wear several hats — journalist, editor, actor, director, playwright. Which of these roles is the most fulfilling for you?
I would say that all of them are fulfilling. But, if you were to ask whether it's a toss-up between the arts and journalism, that seems like a rhetorical question-*lah*. I mean, what contest would there be between the arts and journalism?

See, when I write my plays, I'm a free man. I can write what needs to be written. Of course, at the end of the day, I may not get the staging permit for it-*lah*. But, as a journalist, the constraints are certainly there. Everybody knows about that. Well, journalism for me has been fulfilling but it also has been very frustrating.

Can you talk about some of the frustrations?
I've been a journalist now for 28 years. I started with *The National Echo*. You know, it's ironic that when I was 16, I told my mother I wanted nothing better than to be a reporter! I also told her I didn't care if they paid me peanuts. But then later on, I got interested in law, I think from watching those courtroom dramas on TV at the time, but we couldn't afford for me to go to law school.

In fact, I wasn't thinking of going to university because of the expense. So, after Form 6, I took a job at MAS, and it lasted for two days [*chuckles*]. I'm from Penang, and the job was at Subang Airport. It was as a traffic clerk and it was quite boring work-*lah*. I suppose I didn't really give it a chance-*lah* [*chuckles*]. Then I asked the airport manager if I could be transferred to another department, and he said, "No."

And then I met somebody in KL who said to me, "If you have the chance to go to university, you should." So, I thought, well, maybe-*lah*, I'd try for USM since it was in my hometown. So, when the results came out, I did quite all right, and I applied and got in to do Humanities.

Originally, I had the intention of majoring in mass communications. But, after the first year — you know, you don't major until your second year — I found I couldn't bring myself to major in mass comm [*laughs*]. Just not my cup of tea any more, and I had become enamoured of the theatre after doing a lot of work at the Experimental Theatre. I wrote my own plays and directed them, and that became my passion.

So, that was your first exposure to theatre?
Er, in a concentrated sense-*lah*, ya.

So, since I couldn't bring myself to major in mass comm, I thought maybe I'd major in performing arts. And again, ironically, I decided not to do that because I couldn't stand doing the acting class [*laughs*].

Ironically, now if you were to ask me what I would like to do most, if I had the choice of doing something without having to worry about making a living, I would tell you I would like to be a full-time actor.

There've been quite a lot of ironic turns in my life [*grins*].

Eventually, I majored in literature.

But to come back to your question about journalism, I think it's been fulfilling for me because I've managed to do quite a few things that I feel strongly about. I've given my full commitment to being a journalist. And I've given my full commitment above all to doing my job as a professional.

And, sometimes it can be very hard-*lah* when you try to be a professional journalist. Because, you try to do it as you think journalism should be done, and it's sometimes not possible.

You do your job according to journalistic values, journalistic ethics, but that doesn't seem to be the norm, especially nowadays when journalism has metamorphosed into something else because of the new technologies that are coming in and also because of the competitive nature of the media business now.

I mean, there was a time when the editorial department was king, you know. And the advertising department was wary of encroaching on that territory. We kept advertising at bay. What was important was the editorial matter and the integrity of the paper. But nowadays, you find that there is such a close collusion between advertising and editorial.

I subscribe to the notion that journalism is not all about business. It's about telling it as it is. I suppose my views are pretty old-fashioned [*chuckles*]. And these ideals are probably not operable-*lah* in today's world of journalism.

I believe in the old notion that newspapers are meant to be watchdogs of society — critical, engaged, speaking out without fear or favour. When I was entertainment editor about 20 years ago, in my own way-*lah*, you know, I found ways to discuss issues of the day through culture and entertainment. I even ran a couple of articles that were critical of Mahathir [Mohamad]. And one was when he appeared on a programme called *Hal Ehwal Semasa*. Of course, it didn't go down well. Nowadays, there seems to be a tradition of not ever criticising the prime minister of the day, whoever he may be and whatever policy he may unveil.

I also remember, when I was a sub-editor, I ran a letter from a reader asking for multi-racial representation in an entertainment programme on TV. The next day, when I opened the paper, the letter had been yanked out [*looks incredulous*]. So, being young and idealistic, I marched to the chief editor's office and asked him, "What's the meaning of this? Why was it taken out?" And I wasn't even informed about it. And he gave me a two-hour lecture. He started by telling me, "If that letter had appeared in print, there would have been blood in the streets." I mean, this is rubbish-*lah*, of course. I mean, he was just exaggerating-*lah*. I'm not foolish enough to take that kind of thing [*chuckles*]. This was more than 20 years ago.

Once in the 1990s, I wrote a piece on the local literary scene in which I called for the repeal of the ISA (Internal Security Act) and a few other oppressive measures. Automatically, I got a memo-*lah* from my superior.

Over another disagreeable thing I did, he called me to his office, he said to me, "You don't have to work here, you know." I said, "How can you say that?" I mean, that was like a threat to me, you know [*chuckles*]. I don't think any superior should say that. So, he said, "Well, you think I'm a lousy editor. You think I'm a government ball-carrier." [*laughs*] It had come to that kind of thinking. So, I told him, "This is uncalled for."

After that, the order came for my pages to be henceforth closely scrutinised. And when everybody got one month's extra bonus, I got RM100. So, I wrote a cheque and returned the money.

It hasn't been easy for me in journalism. I used to get numerous memos from my bosses for doing what I did, which included obeying my conscience. But I have to make it very clear here that it's never been my intention to rock the boat, to create trouble, or what have you. I've always maintained that I do my job as a journalist. As a professional. And I do it like I think it should be done.

And, sometimes it's a very difficult dilemma that I face. I mean, it's a dilemma of doing your work as a journalist and obeying your employer's orders, right? What do you do in a situation like that? Do you go against your own principles or do you continue to pursue them and take the wrath of your superiors? Journalism is not like many other professions, it comes with social responsibility.

During the Anwar [Ibrahim] crisis ... now, I have to say categorically that I'm not an Anwar supporter but there were things done during that time that I felt were not just and I couldn't agree with them. So, in my own little way, what I did was ... I had a section called *Lit-Quotes* in my pages. Actually, they should carry quotes from literature-*lah*. But, I put in a lot of quotes on democracy, and oppression and authoritarianism and what not. And somebody told me later on that these quotes were actually photocopied by people and circulated during that time [*chuckles*]. Because, as you know, that was a time when a lot of people were very cagey and these quotes expressed what they themselves felt. But, eventually, the chief editor caught on to it. And he told me to stop it.

I think if we can't be a critical media, we should at least be a questioning media. We need to question.

And [*sounding pained*], I really feel sad for the new breed of reporters because they are getting a different idea of what journalism is. It's pleasing your boss, it's pleasing advertisers, it's pleasing the marketing department, it's pleasing the advertising department, it's not upsetting the government! That's not what journalism is about!

I also feel that a little disrespect for authority is always a healthy thing. Because authority is not always right. And if it is wrong, it should be pointed out.

It's like people say, "Oh, if you go against the government, you are not loyal to your country. You are a traitor." No! Loving your country is different from loving your government [*chuckles*]. You know, it's just the government of the day. But people fail to draw that line. And that's the sad thing, especially here, you know. It doesn't mean, if you criticise the government or you go against it because it did something which you thought was wrong that you, therefore, do not love your country. That's ridiculous.

You talk a lot about the problems you have faced. Is it any different where you are now, is it any better? If it is not any better in journalism today, why are you still in it? Because it pays the bills?

I'm doing creative things where I am now. I edit a page that deals purely with the English language. I'm also in charge of the Photo Section. As the Photo Section is mainly a service provider, my main concern is to upgrade the lot of the photographers, improve efficiency and the quality of their work. I've had to reinvent myself, which can be rejuvenating in the twilight of my career! I still fight — I fight for the photographers. And for better English!

When I'm given a job to do, I do it with commitment and integrity. I can say this at the risk of sounding like a brag because I don't bullshit. In the newsroom, I often speak straight from the shoulder. I think my current bosses know that and I hope they appreciate it. They know I'm not a yes-man or a ball-carrier.

Sadly, ours is a culture of *ampu-bodek*. If you're good at that, chances are you'll do well. And that's what partly keeps us from progressing at a faster rate. Because the capable ones who don't *ampu-bodek* get left behind, and those who are good at *ampu-bodek* may not be good at doing the real job.

These are your frustrations in journalism. What about in theatre? What kind of frustrations have you experienced?

I was rehearsing a play for about six weeks as an actor in a one-man play called *The Coffin is Too Big for the Hole*, [Kuo] Pao-kun's play, and we were denied the permit on the afternoon of opening night. We lost money because of that. People who came to the opening night show had to be turned away.

There was another play I was directing, and I also had been rehearsing for about six weeks. It was called *Madame Mao's Memories*. We also didn't get the permit for that. In both cases, no reasons were given. Apparently, the authorities are not compelled to give reasons.

Is it true that they now have a committee to vet playscripts?
Yes, for City Hall.

There's a whole committee to do it! I feel that's really demeaning! How could we be in a situation like this? How have we come to such a level? I mean, there's absolutely no trust at all in Malaysians being adult enough or open-minded enough to be able to discuss certain things? To watch plays that deal with issues?

Do you think the reason you didn't get permits for at least two plays was a form of retribution because of the views that you had as a journalist as well as a playwright?
I dare not even begin to speculate! I mean, it will just be speculation. I wouldn't know, right?

Either in the newsroom or in theatre, were you ever warned about going too far or that there would be repercussions if you continued to ...?
I did, of course, get memos and warnings from my bosses about my work but they never warned me about my theatre involvement. There were never any threats from any quarter. Advice, yes.

So, for the most part, you've been able to do what you've been doing with some amount of manoeuvring but without being threatened in any way?
Not directly-*lah*. But [*pause*], there may be some inference one could draw from the fact that [the decision to deny the staging permit for] *The Coffin is Too Big for the Hole* came after *1984 Here and Now* [was staged].

In your own experience, which has had more impact on society? Journalism or theatre? Which has been more effective for you as an agent of social change?
[*Laughs*] I think the reach of theatre is not wide enough. I mean, there's only so many people that you can get through to. There's no doubt that the mass media has a wider reach. But then again because of the

constraints, the effect is still somewhat limited-*lah*. I mean, if your editors are the ones who determine what can be published and they prefer to play safe, it's very hard. The potential for change that you want to bring about is really quite limited.

You do a play, a lot of the time, the people who come to see it are also, what they call, "the converted" in any case. So, you are not really changing minds, you know. Unless you write in Malay. But then if you wrote plays in Malay, your plays would actually be more closely scrutinised because the authorities are aware that it will reach out to larger audiences, so they are more cautious about that.

But, having said that, I write a play, I get it published. Sometimes, it gets picked up and it's taught at the universities.

As [*We Could **** You,*] *Mr Birch* was?

As *Mr Birch* was. I don't know about the other two. Quite a number of universities have taught it, are still teaching it. And sometimes, they invite me to go and give talks to the students. And that's one way of reaching out to them. I hope-*lah* that in their reading of the play, they might find some kind of awareness-*lah*.

How many plays have you written in total?

Oh, quite a number. But, some of them were when I was very young. Some of them quite forgettable, or rather, I'd like to forget them-*lah* [*laughs*].

Quite a number have also been broadcast over RTM. I sent [in] quite a lot during my undergraduate days. They were paying a princely sum of RM75 a play.

Wah, not bad for those days!

RM75, *ah*? It was enough to buy cigarettes and beer-*lah* [*laughs*].

Do you think there are any common challenges that you face in both journalism and in theatre?
Censorship.

Do you think that's getting worse?
[*Pauses to think*] Yes. We just said there's this committee that's vetting scripts. That's terrible.

What is even worse actually is self-censorship. And that is the biggest challenge for anybody, especially for journalists. Quite hard to overcome.

Have you ever self-censored?
I think I must have although I very much tell myself not to. You know, somehow or other, in an unconscious manner, having been so conditioned to what things are like, yes, I think I would have.

Without being conscious of it?
Yes.

Your play *1984 Here and Now* was seen as being rather controversial because it was about the state versus citizens, about racial inequality, the brain drain, and inter-racial relations. What compelled or inspired you to write it?
The contradictions that I saw in the country at that time. The inequality. The culture of fear. You remember how it was in the 1980s. And also, the arrogance of power. Um, Bills used to be just bulldozed through Parliament, you know. Of course, the institutionalisation of racial discrimination. That figures very prominently in the play. So does Big Brotherism.

Was there anything in particular that you or your family experienced that was the starting point for what you were writing, or was it an amalgamation of different experiences?
An amalgamation and I saw it more clearly when I came to KL. In Penang, it wasn't so sharp.

But in Penang itself, I did have personal experience of the effects of the pro-Bumiputera policy. When I graduated, I wanted to pursue my Master's. But I could not afford to do it unless I could get a tutorship in the university [USM]. So, I applied for it but I didn't get it.

But what I couldn't reconcile with was why I didn't get it when I was top in my Humanities class. I was also the winner of the Gold Medal for Top Literature Student.

So, it was obvious-*lah*, you know. That was my direct experience of that policy.

What about your children? Have they had to experience discrimination growing up?
Um, not in big ways, no. One is a girl about 15-plus, and the other a 14-year-old boy. I mean, ya, they do tell me some stories now and then but there have been no real major incidents.

Do you think things have changed in Malaysia since you wrote *1984* and since it was staged in Malaysia?
Ah, ya, it has, of course, because people are materially better off now. And I think the government got it right in the sense that they realised that economics was the basis of a lot of things. It was very important to make sure that people became well off, ya. And that would help to lessen the friction between the races. As long as you can keep the economy afloat and prosperous, you won't get these tensions. But, as you've seen on a couple of occasions when the economy dipped, these tensions have risen to the surface.

The drive is constantly on to make people happy through means that also distract them from the real issues. Hence, we've seen the rise of consumerism, the sprouting of megamalls, the providing of mass entertainment, huge celebratory spectacles. We partake of the fun and games like the Romans of ancient times did when their emperors gave them chariot races and gladiator fights. That way political leaders also get maximum exposure.

But the thing now is that what they've also done is they've made Malaysians more materialistic than ever. So much so that I think we are losing sight of things like spiritual development, moral development, intellectual development, values!

Do you sense that things are changing for the country because we have a new prime minister?
Changing in what sense, ah? Changing is a very big word. Which areas are you talking about?

Are things improving? Are we, at least, starting to look at spiritual, moral and intellectual development?
Our prime minister is trying to get us in that direction but at the same time, I'm sure he still has to juggle it with material prosperity, otherwise, problems are going to occur. Groups that are dependent on support and patronage will start knocking on his door.

By and large, Malaysians are still intellectually shallow. The push towards consumerism has made it worse. Shopping and having fun are what interest Malaysians more than the need to acquire culture. Even as I say that the media needs to address issues, I also realise that many people don't really want to discuss them or are not interested at all.

They're afraid or they don't care. Or they've been conditioned to accept things as they are. Our education system has been extremely effective in indoctrinating our children from the moment they enter school.

As for racial relations, on the surface, it now looks to have improved, ya. On the surface, it looks as if we are a happy family. But [long pause], at a deeper level, if you were to, for example, ask university students of a particular race, let's say a Malay student, to name you a non-Malay friend of theirs, or vice versa, you'd be surprised that they would be quite hard put to give you a name.

I think racial polarisation has still not been lessened. We are a far cry from the good old days when Malays would sit down with non-Malays to break bread together regardless where. Nowadays, if you invite your

Malay friends to your home to have a meal with you, I'm not quite sure that they will accept. There's a wariness.

So, race relations have not really improved?
I don't think it's improved in real terms. I mean, those non-Malays who have it good, the captains of industry and what have you, are still having it good. Any talk about the New Economic Policy, as you saw recently during the Umno Youth Assembly, still raises negative feelings and divides the races.

But why do we still have a policy like discounts for Bumiputeras buying houses? I mean, the irony here is that, if you have a house that costs a few million [*chuckles*], you have Bumiputera multi-millionaires buying these houses, and they are enjoying, what is it now, a 7 per cent discount? It doesn't add up, you know.

The metaphor I invoke is this: Our fathers and we helped to build this house. Why are we still considered tenants?

That feeling is still very much floating around among people like me. And that has not disappeared after all these years.

The sense that non-Malays are immigrants?
Yes, yes, that you are still an immigrant race. That there are certain things that you are not entitled to. Again, that doesn't add up as far as I'm concerned. There's something wrong with that equation. We were born in this country. We helped to build it.

Do you think art imitates life or is it the other way round?
That's a big question [*laughs*]. It can happen either way. Give me a specific example of what art you mean.

Well, your plays, for example.
My plays are a reflection of the reality I see around me. So, in that sense it would be art imitating life to a certain extent. I enhance it a bit, exaggerate it a bit. Such is the way of dramaturgy.

Does life imitate art? I mean if you were a prophet writing art, and your prophesies came true, then you might say, life imitates art [laughs]! I'm not a prophet. I'm an observer, and I put down, in as honest a way as I can, and in a way that I believe to be right, what I see around me.

I'm actually writing a new play.

Are you, now? What's it called?

It's called *The Fall of Singapura*. It's based on the *Sejarah Melayu*. Actually, only about two-and-a-half pages of the *Sejarah Melayu*. But I've extended it into a full-length play. It's near completion.

It's based on that famous story about *Singapura dilanggar todak* [Singapore attacked by swordfish]. I've taken that episode and meshed it with the episode of the fall of Singapura when Majapahit invaded it and destroyed it.

How is it that you're writing about Singapore?

It's not about Singapore! The play is about Malaysia! It's about modern-day Malaysia.

It is based on the episodes in the *Sejarah Melayu*, but I take a lot of liberties with it, just as I did with *Mr Birch*. You know, taking a historical episode and then doing all kinds of things with it. So, it's the same thing that I'm doing with this play. A lot of cheeky things, you know, but very much reflecting and questioning what is going on today.

So, what are some of the issues that you are questioning through this *Fall of Singapura*?

Erm, I'm not sure I should tell you [laughs]. Well, one of the things is the celebration of mediocrity-*lah*. I think we Malaysians are famous for celebrating mediocrity. I mean, I cannot understand the Mawi [*Akademi Fantasia 3* winner Asmawi Ani] phenomenon, you know. I didn't watch *Akademi Fantasia* but there was such a big hoo-ha over him winning. And he's now so big, he's suddenly sold 150,000 copies of his album. And then, I heard him sing on TV. And he can't sing [looks and *sounds incredulous*]! My whole family heard him, and they were, like, shocked, you know. And they are people with musical ears because they are musically trained.

How did this guy who can't sing become such a big phenomenon? What does it tell me? That it's another celebration of mediocrity?

It's not just that TV has this knack of generating hype, it's also the people who voted for him. There were other people who could sing much better than him. How come people didn't vote for them? [*laughs*]

I think it says so much about us. We don't have such a high regard for meritocracy, you know. Sometimes, I think we are too much influenced by our sentimentality-*lah*, sentiments for our *kampung*, the state we come from, religion, kinship, what have you. With that kind of mindset, how can we think about ourselves as would-be First Worlders?

Another issue in the play is our confusion about ourselves and the contradictions in our wanting to be progressive and yet adhering to our conservatism.

When is this play going to be completed?
I hope soon-*lah* [*chuckles*].

Are you going to self-publish? Or is it going to go to a publisher?
No, I think the best way is to have it staged first, so you can see better if there are any dramatic flaws. Then you can revise until you're quite satisfied that it should be published.

Are you thinking of directing it?
No.

Recently, your play The Big Purge was read [at the Soho Theatre, London] at the Typhoon Festival [an East Asian writing festival]. What is the play about? Why hasn't it been performed locally?
Well, that play was actually triggered by Operation Lalang [in 1987] and I dedicated it to the 100-over people who were detained under the ISA

as a result of Operation Lalang. It's a play about how the powers that be can manipulate events to their own political advantage, to frighten the people, to create a culture of fear.

I have two dimensions there. I have the *wayang kulit* [shadow play] world of the politicians, the powers that be. And the human dimension of the characters of the land, people who are affected by the policies and so on.

I also talk a lot about emigration, how people find it difficult to cope in that society and the only way out for them is to leave. It also deals a lot with racial tensions, racial relations.

Was this written right after 1987?
Yes, immediately after the thing [Operation Lalang] broke out, I started writing. I staged it in Essex [University, England] when I was doing my Master's [in Literature (Drama) in 1988]. But, it hasn't been done here. I did offer it to one theatre group but I think they were quite, er ... either they saw no merit in it or they felt that it was too risky-*lah*.

Do you hope that someday the play will be staged in Malaysia?
Yes! Certainly, sure.

What was the reception like in London?
Oh, very good! I was overwhelmed, actually! I didn't expect it to be so good and there was a discussion of the play afterwards and in the audience were people from London itself. It was a very mixed audience. There were some ex-Malaysians, some current Malaysians. But regardless of which nationality they belonged to, they could identify with the play. There were a lot of interesting questions floated and after that, the organisers said they were very pleased with it.

Do you think there is enough support for English creative writers and English-language theatre in Malaysia?
Aiyoh, I've spoken so much about that on other occasions. Do we have to go into that?

Of course not-*lah* [*sounding tired*]. We don't have the infrastructure for it. And for a long time, you know, English creative writing had to really work in isolation. There was no recognition for it, and it wasn't easy to get published, for obvious reasons. Because there wasn't a large enough market. There still isn't a large market for Malaysian English writing.

In the 1970s and 1980s, some of us felt really guilty continuing to write in the colonial language. It was an uneasy time for us. Even now, we could not dream of getting writing residencies in institutions of learning or writing grants.

And of course, you know, because [*pause*] there is — I don't know if it still exists — there used to be this doctrine that national literature was to be literature written in Malay, and literature written in other languages was known as "sectional" or "communal" literature.

I mean, that's also another demeaning thing-*lah*. If you write in your own mother tongue, you're only considered to be "sectional", you know [*laughs cynically*]. It's the same with the National Culture Policy which still remains to this day. It says that national culture must be based on Malay culture and Nusantara culture! Can you imagine it? Nusantara. That means they're including Indonesia. They're looking so far afield. And only incorporating "suitable elements" from immigrant cultures.

What are these "suitable elements"? I mean, it's really terrible, you know. If people say, "Okay-*lah*, I take what is suitable from you." How does that make you feel? And who are they to decide what is suitable and what is not? What do they mean by "suitable"? You mean, there are things in my culture that are not suitable?

These are things that I cannot reconcile with. I don't know if they will change in my lifetime or not.

Do you think there's enough appreciation for English literature in Malaysia?

I don't think a lot of people are very much into literature and again, because of the way our society is going — towards consumerism, towards science and technology. As I said earlier, the regard for intellectual development is not quite there. They have reintroduced English literature into the classroom at the lower forms. It's been going on for Malay literature. But for English, it's only just been reintroduced. A lot of teachers don't even know how to teach it. The students are quite lost! So, it will take a lot of time-*lah* for us to have any kind of interest or grounding in literature to appreciate it more deeply.

Why do you think it's important for society to have an appreciation of English literature?
Whether it's English literature or any kind of literature, it's important to have an appreciation of it because literature deals with life, it deals with a lot of moral issues, it deals with how people live, how they behave in certain situations.

And although literary works may be fictive, or fictional, there is a certain truth to them. And, as we read them, we empathise with the characters. We go through the journey that they go through and we hopefully understand something about life from their experience.

Who are the people who have inspired you in your writing and acting?
Very few people, actually. I'm not conscious of being influenced by anybody except when I was an undergraduate, I was very much into Samuel Beckett and Harold Pinter. I was very much taken by these playwrights after watching productions like *Waiting for Godot* and *The Birthday Party*.

They opened up an intriguing world for me. And I studied them more and more, and I was very much influenced by them. And I wrote absurdist plays in the kind of mould they were writing in.

And I suppose at the time, it was also quite appropriate for me to do so because I could empathise with their notions of a world gone topsy-turvy, in which language has lost its real meaning, and people lead existentialist lives in a meaningless world. That kind of thing-*lah*. Maybe I could identify with that because I wasn't getting any girlfriends [*laughs loudly*].

I understand that your children bear names from the three major races in the country. What are their names? Your 15-year-old daughter?
Soraya Sunitra Kee Xiang Yin.

And your 14-year-old son?
Jebat Arjuna Kee Jia Liang. I like the name Jebat. It's a strong masculine name. And Jebat was a true friend, unlike Hang Tuah who was blindly obedient. Blind obedience, I think, is stupid-*lah*. We have to be alert and questioning.

Was it a conscious decision to name your children this way?
Yes, it was certainly a conscious decision. It was a contribution to the development of Bangsa Malaysia. I find that [*pause*] to this day there's just a lot of lip service being paid to it. I hope that it will eventually come about-*lah*.

Do they have a hard time at school?
[*Chuckles*] Yes. In the beginning, they used to be quite fed-up. Because people would ask them, "What race are you, *ah*? Are you Malay, or what?"

But now, I think they are coming to terms with it. And I think they realise the significance of their names. And they are beginning to appreciate it.

My daughter, in fact, wrote an essay about her name last year. And, at the end of it, she mentioned that she was getting to be proud of it. And she also mentioned that she was proud of her country, and she supposed that having a Malaysian name would enhance that love for the country. And she also said that she got her love for the country from her father [*chuckles*] who often tells her that loving her country is not about waving flags! I was very proud of her.

I don't believe in all that hoopla of flying flags during Merdeka month. It's just a show. What's inside you is what really matters.

KEE TO DECIPHERING UMNO SEMIOTICS

By Helen Ang
Malaysiakini, November 15, 2007

Kee Thuan Chye is an author, actor-director and dramatist. He has written four major political plays: 1984 Here and Now, The Big Purge *[read at the Soho Theatre in London, 2005],* We Could ****You Mr Birch *and* The Swordfish, Then the Concubine *[adjudged one of the top five entries to the International Playwriting Festival 2006 organised by the Warehouse Theatre in the UK]. He's also a journalist of 30 years' standing, beginning his career at* The National Echo *in 1977.*

You're someone who works intimately with language and has broad experience of the mass media — which, in Malaysia, is the channel for communicating the dominant narrative. As such, I'd like to get your reading on the ideas behind some of the things said and done at the recently concluded Umno general assembly.

Let's start with Prime Minister Abdullah Ahmad Badawi saying: "The act of unsheathing and kissing a keris is part of our cultural heritage but its meaning has been twisted to spread fear among non-Malays, and the image of Umno and Malaysia has been smeared overseas."

The PM was referring to Youth chief Hishammuddin Hussein who, at the wing's assembly in 2005, started his so-called 'tradition' of brandishing the *keris*. He has since said he expects non-Malays to eventually become "desensitised" to his waving this "symbol", and in fact pronounced that naysayers should get used to it.

Deputy PM Najib Abdul Razak believes the act should be celebrated by all races. What do you make of the semiotics of the Umno *keris*? Is it a "symbol of protection for everyone" as Hisham and the local media would have us think?

I certainly don't think it is a symbol of protection for everyone. This kind of talk is typical of Umno politicians who often twist semantics for the purpose of fooling the people. Well, it can fool those who are easily swayed by superficialities but not the intelligent public. Many Umno politicians appear to be pretty superficial themselves and therefore tend to misperceive that the thinking of the *rakyat* is mainly of the lowest common denominator.

The *keris* is a striking visual image. When it was first brandished in 2005, it naturally sent fear waves among the non-Malays. The body language of the person wielding it and the words uttered in accompaniment and, more significantly, the tone in which they were uttered combined to even more dramatic effect.

In 2006, the second time it made its appearance, the event looked choreographed — with Hishammuddin raising the unsheathed *keris* heavenwards and his Umno Youth brethren raising their fists in unison alongside him, in rows of solidarity. It was fearsome, like a military phalanx. All the signs pointed to aggression.

Hishammuddin was theatricalising a moment, and it was theatre with a powerful message — all the more effectively communicated because it was televised 'live' and it went out to millions of viewers. And when you unsheathe a *keris* and hold it in that way, you're bound to incite certain sentiments among your followers and to provoke them to ask when you are going to use it, as Hashim Suboh did.

This inevitably recalls the moment of a day 20 years ago when Najib reportedly wielded a *keris* and vowed that there would be Chinese blood on its blade by the end of that day.

In Hishammuddin's theatrics, the context was clear. It was an Umno Youth assembly, which is a strictly Malay gathering. The aggressive stance, the iconic Malay *keris* and the invocation to uphold the Malay struggle — all these pointed to an ethnocentric concern. Other races were certainly not being defended; on the contrary, they were implied to be the enemy.

With weapon in hand, Hishammuddin was unequivocal in his assertion that Umno Youth wanted the return of policies favouring the Malays and would take action against those who opposed the movement's proposal to revive the NEP. He later said that the *keris* represented Umno Youth's "renewed spirit in empowering the Malays". So now for Hishammuddin to say that he would use the *keris* again in 2007 as a protector of all Malaysians — not just Malays — is disingenuous. Any intelligent Malaysian can see through the doublespeak.

What is even worse — and insulting — is what he said about "desensitising" non-Malays to the issue of the *keris*. Only a person with a supercilious attitude would behave that way. What he implies by that statement is that non-Malays must accept what he does, no matter how revulsed they are by it. It's like slapping someone in the face and then slapping him again and again, and telling him that he has to tolerate it each time until he gets used to it. What arrogance!

The arrogance surely stems from the idea of *Ketuanan Melayu* that has been the focus of Umno's propagation the last few decades. One could read into that "protection" doublespeak an implicit statement of Malay supremacy lording over the other races. This is the same kind of arrogance exhibited by Puteri Umno in its recent criticism of the People's Progressive Party (PPP). A mere wing of Umno had the gumption to tell a partner of the Barisan Nasional to "stop making noise".

This is the same kind of arrogance exhibited by Hishammuddin when he issued a warning to the MCA leadership last July to stop saying that Malaysia is a secular state. The leader of a Youth wing had the gumption to tell a senior partner of Umno's in the BN to shut up. On an issue of national significance, to boot. In supporting Hishammuddin's *keris* antics, Abdullah reveals himself to be contrary to what the mainstream media have hailed him as — "a prime minister of all Malaysians". It undoes what he had been trying to do throughout this year's Umno general assembly, which was to be conciliatory towards the other races by not bringing up issues that would be sensitive and threatening to them, particularly religion. No doubt Abdullah knows he cannot afford to alienate the non-Malay voters in light of the upcoming general election. He could have reminded the Umno delegates about this on the eve of the assembly when he briefed them on what issues to avoid. He could also have advised Hishammuddin to take that soft approach with the *keris* this time.

It was all rather predictable. Umno is inadvertently transparent that way!

In any case, how could Abdullah be considered a PM of all Malaysians when he was the one who stopped any further discussion of Article 11 of the Constitution; did little to clear the air about whether Malaysia is not a secular state; did nothing to quash a proposal by none other than the Chief Justice (then) to replace common law with Syariah law; rejected a proposal to set up an inter-faith council; told ministers within his own Cabinet to withdraw their memo to him calling for a review of laws that affect the rights of non-Muslims? One could go on.

Well, to go on to next in the hierarchy, Najib's address this year was themed 'Reaching for the Stars — Elevating a National Civilisation', doubtless to ride on the "Malaysians walking a few inches taller" hype generated by the first Malay to go into space. I note a resolute semantics when one man's "space tourist" is another man's "*angkasawan*", while a cynic's "joyride" is the administration's ambitious "space programme".

The use of "*angkasawan*" is blatantly deliberate; I find the English papers parroting this Malay word too. I'd read earlier that NASA does not see Sheikh Mustaphar Sheikh Abdul Shukor as an "astronaut" but rather a "space participant". Is the "*angksawan*" another case of Boleh creative accounting (adding and subtracting)?

Given the political reality we are in, a reality that has evolved under a campaign of institutionalised racial discrimination over the last 30-plus years, very few Malaysians would have expected the candidate for space to be other than a Malay. The non-Malay contenders were, to put it brutally, merely tokens. The final selection came as no surprise then. The more cynical among us would also have deduced that it was all part of the Umno agenda of creating "towering Malays". And there was not only one candidate, there were two. The second is now a spaceman-in-waiting, and to all intents and purposes, he will get his day in the stratosphere, because he will add to the list of "towering Malays".

(I like the use of the term "spaceman" to describe each of our two aspiring *angkasawan*; as my dear friend Azmi Sharom pointed out astutely in his column for *The Star* recently, Sheikh Muszaphar is a man and he was in space.)

More important, however, are the questions on a lot of people's minds: What did our spaceman really achieve? And what has our nation achieved? Did we build our own rocket? Did we find a new way of going to space?

I would say we found a new '*leng chai*' poster boy to set women's hearts aflutter ... but in any case, to look back, there was the less than enthusiastic reception of the Everest conquerors who were Indian. Whereas a Malay man swimming the English Channel was rewarded with a Datukship — a feat that even a 12-year-old girl and an 11-year-old boy (Thomas Gregory / 11 hr 54 min in 1988) accomplished minus the sort of state support and sponsorship given our Malaysian "hero" Abdul Malek Mydin (17 hr 40+ min).

Non-Malays who have accomplished greater feats tend not to be lionised as much. As you rightly pointed out, the Indians who scaled Mount Everest got short shrift. This also happens in the field of sports.

The Sidek brothers were elevated to legendary status for their success in badminton, totally overshadowing the non-Malay greats who had led the way long before them (Wong Peng Soon, Ong Poh Lim,

Ooi Teik Hock, Eddy Choong, Tan Aik Huang, Tan Yee Khan, Ng Boon Bee, etc).

When Mohd Hafiz Hashim won the All-England singles title in 2003, he was rewarded with a car, land, money and a hero's welcome home. When Koo Kien Keat and Tan Boon Heong won the All-England doubles title last March, they were rewarded with only a fraction of what Hafiz got. Not that such rewards are necessarily good. Sadly, Hafiz hasn't outdone himself since 2003.

I have a theory that our performance in sports started to decline with the inception of the NEP. Before that, we had great athletes like Jegathesan, Rajamani, Ishtiaq Mobarak and Nashatar Singh, and our football team was as good as South Korea's. But from the '70s onwards, things took a turn for the worse. I put it down to the decline in national morale. And, of course, also to the team selection criteria.

It all leads to further superficiality. That's what our leaders are good at — creating the myth of Bolehness by resorting to the accomplishment of superficial 'feats'. These would include having the tallest flagpole in the world, at one time the tallest building in the world, the paean to Bumiputeraism called Putrajaya (which now appears to be a white elephant), etc., etc. Is there a biggest *ketupat* in the world, too?

Most certainly, but could have been eaten by now.
But what it amounts to realistically is spending millions and billions of ringgit, which you and I contribute to whether we like it or not. To the movers of the cause, it doesn't matter what the cost is as long as it serves the Bumiputera-building exercise. I think that's unfair. Non-Bumis also deserve an even chance. We contribute too. I was disgusted when I visited Putrajaya at night a few weeks ago — all that money spent on maintaining it, all that energy to light up the streets and the buildings, and all for what?

I'll tell you what disgusted me even more recently. When I visited the Independence Memorial in Melaka last May and looked at the exhibits (pictures, write-ups, etc.), I found almost everything centred on the efforts of the Malays. The contributions of non-Malay nationalists were blatantly neglected or marginalised. A handful of Chinese and Indian leaders got mentioned in passing, but that was about all.

Unless I missed it, I didn't even see a single portrait of Tan Cheng Lock in there. And he was the leader of the MCA at the time. Not only that, his record shows that he was a true nationalist who was president of the All Malaya Joint Council for Action (AMCJA) which, together with Pusat Tenaga Rakyat (Putera), rallied for Merdeka long before Umno got wise to the idea.

I don't buy that 'National Civilisation' hogwash. "National" is just another abused word for "Bumiputera". But many non-Malays have been conditioned into believing the Umno propaganda, first from having their mindset programmed in school, then from being exposed to the spin-doctoring of the mass media daily and the grand-scale theatrical extravaganzas staged by the BN government occasionally.

When the general election comes around, they will probably vote like they have been doing over the decades.

A CULTURE OF
FEARING THE TRUTH

By Helen Ang
Malaysiakini, November 22, 2007

Let's examine the nuances of non-Malay support for the incumbency. Pundits are predicting that disgruntled Chinese will swing to the Opposition this time around. So it may actually turn out that a large percentage of the community will indeed buck the status quo. What I think is that while Chinese are prepared to secretly (they will refuse to tell anyone who they voted for) cast their once-every-five-years ballot in favour of the Opposition, their mindset in the remaining four years and 364 days will remain as you say, conditioned: fearful, refusing to engage and self-centred. But given the uneven electoral playing field and lack of proportional representation, popular disenchantment may, nonetheless, not translate into a diminished BN influence. Sadly true?

The gerrymandering that has been done has really made it harder for the Chinese to swing votes in many constituencies. I was in Balakong a couple of weeks ago and the residents there told me that their constituency used to be Opposition-controlled, but lately with the redemarcation exercise, the BN has been winning. There used to be about 70 per cent Chinese in the constituency but that has been diluted to about 50 per cent. The other 20 per cent has been moved to another constituency. They don't foresee the Opposition winning it back this coming election unless a huge majority of the remaining 50 per cent vote for them. Many Chinese, however, tend to vote BN.

Surely they can see that BN is a gross disservice to their community? Who are those still so blinkered?
Those in business, those who fear PAS, those who think BN will provide the peace and order to allow them to pursue their livelihood, those who don't want to rock the boat, those with vested interests and enjoy the patronage of the ruling establishment — these are the Chinese who will stand by it.

The BN needn't worry about not winning. It would be a great shock if they lost. But I think BN's greatest fear — more so Umno's, really — is not getting a two-thirds majority in Parliament. Without that, they can't have things their way. The *Ketuanan Melayu* agenda might not be so easily promoted. They will also find it difficult to settle for anything less when they've had it so good since elections were introduced in this country. A loss of the two-thirds could spark the beginning of a decline, which in the long term could result in Umno going through what the Indian National Congress or the Liberal Democratic Party of Japan have gone through.

I agree about the two-thirds majority being a matter of standing and 'face' for Umno. But what helps BN keep face is the thick layers of make-up that the mainstream media are prepared to paint on the coalition. The Bersih rally is the most recent example of the mainstream media's cosmetic enhancement to conceal the heavy-handed and unwarranted approach by the authorities. We can note that one of the reforms called for by Bersih is that opposing views have free and fair access to the mass media. Isn't an impartial media the essence of a democracy?
Yes, that's the essence of a democracy. This should have been one of the cornerstones of the '101 East' forum on Al Jazeera TV last week featuring lawyer Malik Imtiaz Sarwar, the Minister Nazri Abdul Aziz and Umno Youth deputy leader Khairy Jamaluddin. The forum discussed Bersih's November 10 march ending in the handing over of their memorandum to the King calling for fair and free elections. Yet, for all that Khairy said on the show about the reforms that have been

made by the Elections Commission such as the use of indelible ink, transparent ballot boxes, etc., he still ignored the main plot — how can elections be fair if the Opposition is virtually blacked out in the media and the usual airing they get is when something negative is reported about them?

I'm sure he's smart enough to know that free media access to all parties is the key issue, but he also appeared smart enough to deflect it by bringing up the cosmetic improvements.

Nazri, on the other hand, was far less brainy. In fact, he proved to be deficient at debating. And when he ran out of argument, he resorted to arrogance. He said, ostensibly without thinking, that there was no need to reform the political system, that the views of civil society didn't carry any weight. He implied that the Government was always right because "we are the representatives of the people". If the people have grouses, use the ballot box, which he kindly pointed out comes about once every five years. That's a pretty long time to wait to air your grouses. Why not air them at any time? Isn't that standard practice in a true democracy? He said what the public demands is not necessarily right. At the end of the day, he asserted, "We will decide."

So, clearly, as you're saying, we're not a true democracy, we're a flawed one premised on an even more flawed electoral system. And, yes, the BN, for which one can read Umno, decides on everything. But this is not something you'd grasp reading our local media. Is this 'oversight' due to over-regulating?

Khairy said the PM had announced that in the near future, the media would be allowed to regulate itself. "In the near future" sounds vague. But more importantly, what would be the real point of self-regulating if the media continues to have the Printing Presses and Publications Act around its neck? As we know, that Act requires all print media in this country to obtain a licence that has to be renewed annually — at the discretion of the Home Ministry. What an effective mechanism to encourage self-censorship, don't you think?

Can one blame newspapers, which survive or close down at the pleasure of the Home Ministry, for being cautious about what they publish? Obviously, no. But being cautious and being subservient are two different things. Hiding the truth, choosing not to report significant news because it may be damaging to the Government, putting a spin to certain events in the reporting of them to protect the Government — these are the practices of the subservient. But is there always a choice between being one or the other? There is, if newspapers don't get instructions from political leaders or their lackeys on what not to publish.

I've written this time and again. Newspapers toe the line set by their owners, who are the political masters of this country or their cronies. Correct?

Yes, many newspapers are owned by political parties, usually through a third party. And this does affect newspaper policies. Even so, the control was not as tight until Mahathir Mohamad came along. Curbing the press and causing it to cower started with him. His suspension of several newspapers in 1987 was a watershed. Since then, no newspaper — indeed, no radio or TV station either — has dared to criticise the PM. It has become a tradition!

But, surely, the PM can't always be above censure. He's here to serve the people. So are his ministers. They can't speak down from their high horse and declaim, "We will decide."

Nazri is not the only minister who exhibits arrogance. Some of his colleagues share the same trait. It shows in their intolerance of criticism. Which usually results in their inability to handle flak. Then they get defensive and start saying the most inane things.

One good example is Information Minister Zainuddin Maidin. From the things he's been saying in the past months, you can't imagine he was once a journalist. And a former chief editor, would you believe?

Zainuddin's bungling response to the Bersih march is now famous — or is it notorious? But let me first address what he said more than two weeks ago, just before the Umno general assembly, about young Malay writers being used by the English press to attack the Malays. He even named names — Azmi Sharom and Amir Muhammad. I know both of them well; they're not the sort who would allow themselves to be used by anyone. They wouldn't write what they didn't believe. Zainuddin's remark amounted to nothing less than an insult. He should apologise to Azmi and Amir.

As for his rebuke against Al Jazeera for its coverage of the Bersih demonstration, he will go down in history as saying that there is no point in holding protests because we have elections in Malaysia. How that logically connects, only he knows. In any case, there was a protest in Kuala Lumpur when Condoleeza Rice was in town and another last month against the actions of the Myanmar junta. Khairy himself was involved in both. In fact, he took centre stage. And both were presumably issued permits. So, what gives?

Besides, Bersih was not disputing that there are no elections, it only wanted a free and fair one. And even with elections, it doesn't mean that such protests are unnecessary. If the people feel unhappy about the way things are run in the country, they should have the recourse to make it known. One such recourse is holding a demonstration. I'm not drawing parallels between Malaysia and the Philippines, but if there had been no People's Revolution, no masses of people taking to the streets to express their disgust for a corrupt regime, Ferdinand Marcos would have continued to stay in power and possibly milked the country dryer.

The other day, I was watching Fahmi Reza's film *Sepuluh Tahun Sebelum Merdeka*, which documents big demonstrations, big rallies in our own Malaya of 1947. These were allowed then — 60 years ago, when we weren't even independent. Now we are an independent country and certain demonstrations are not allowed — especially those that don't belong to the right camp. It's ironic. What's the meaning of Merdeka then?

Actually, I think the Bersih demonstration only made the Government look bad after the fact because of the unseemly handling of the situation — after the water cannons used on the marchers, after Zainuddin's boo-boo, after Nazri and Khairy's confirmation of the Government's double standards, after the news spinning in the media for days afterwards.

If it had been given a permit in the first place and the media had given it neutral coverage, it wouldn't have attracted such unwarranted attention. An event that big could not have gone unnoticed. The sensible thing would have been to let it be recorded objectively. Malaysians would have read it and probably said, "Hmmm … okay, it happened", and gone on with their daily lives. Surely, it wasn't going to revolutionise their lives or change their mindset radically.

When something is a normal part of existence, we don't respond to it with extra excitement, we just take it as it comes. That is something that the Government should surely realise. For instance, if you ban a book because you don't want it widely distributed, the banning could actually make it even more popular. People become curious. And so, people became curious about Bersih.

Unfortunately, people's curiosity will not be assuaged by the mainstream media we now have. Aside from getting a true picture of events like Bersih's November 10, why else do we need a free media in Malaysia?
A free media will open the way for us to speak freely to one another as citizens of the nation, regardless of race. Then, we can have dialogue about ethnic issues with our Malay, Chinese and Indian compatriots and express our concerns candidly. As it is right now, if you're Chinese, don't you often feel you can't discuss, say, the NEP with your Malay friends and vice versa? No matter how close that friend is, there will be a barrier. After all, these are — as we are always reminded by our leaders and the media — "sensitive" issues. As long as we think that, we will be wary of not offending each other, an act that could lead to a loss of friendship. I have a Malay friend I consider to be my brother, but I would never engage him in face-to-face discussion of race issues

or tell him how disenfranchised I often feel. However, if there were a free media and any issue could be discussed openly, we would have a different world. I wouldn't have that same hang-up. It would be the norm to speak freely. I could have a dialogue with my Malay friends, colleagues, acquaintances. Or even just complain about inequalities. We could agree with each other or we could agree to disagree. They would know where I'm coming from, and I would know where they're coming from. We wouldn't be holding a knife or a *keris* behind our backs. It would be actually much healthier. Better than bottling up frustrations and resentments, as is the case now.

When we can speak freely and frankly, only then can there be a real and deep connection among the people of different races. Despite all the Government's propaganda, the so-called racial unity and harmony that we have now is merely superficial. Polarisation is still the order of the day. Central issues are unresolved. All it takes is for things like the economy to take a turn for the worse and the unresolved tensions will flare up and threaten peace and stability.

There is really no need to fear a free media. We are 50 years old as a nation. If our leaders are mature and responsible, they will advise their respective tribes to be rational and take part in fruitful discourse rather than resort to violence. Besides, we have the law. One excellent test case was the discussion of Article 11 of our Constitution, organised by the Article 11 Coalition and Aliran. That should have been a forum for rational exchange of ideas. Instead, we gave in to the violence-mongers. The authorities didn't put them in their place and warn them against taking the law into their own hands. Instead, the authorities pampered them, let them have their way, let them get away with their threats.

I feel very strongly about this, so I'm going to have my say here, too. The Chinese are too fearful and apathetic, too short-sighted and self-serving! That's why they will not stand up for Article 11 and Lina

Joy, but compliantly bend to the expediency that she's a Malay-Muslim "problem". She's not! She's a Malaysian issue, and affects every single one of us.

You are right, but there are those who will tell you that if we discuss such issues openly, the consequences may be disastrous. I think they are exploiting this to keep us in line, keep us fearful and therefore thankful for their protection. If we go by the rule of law and our police act according to the law, those who threaten violence can be contained. Unless, of course, they are organised by powerful parties.

To come back to your question: why, indeed, do we need a free media? At the very least to expose corruption, malpractices and inexplicable practices. For instance, a free media would surely conduct a thorough investigation into the case of the Perak state building in Belum that collapsed — to get at the 'real' truth. And that's just for starters. The media should indeed give us a regular dose of investigative journalism, but it would be pointless instituting that when there will always be some party blocking you from telling the truth. We have heard it said many times before that ours is a culture of fear. Truly, it's also fast becoming a culture of fearing the truth.

KEE THUAN CHYE UNMASKED

By Jee Wan
Malaysiakini, August 6, 2010

Kee Thuan Chye, a stubbornly patriotic writer, journalist, editor, playwright and occasional actor, allows a peep into what makes him tick and what does not, particularly where Big Brother is concerned.

What started your involvement in politics?
My political awakening occurred right after I graduated from Universiti Sains Malaysia when I personally suffered the effects of the New Economic Policy (NEP). I wanted to pursue my Masters but I wasn't able to afford it unless I could get a tutor's position. I applied, but didn't get it even though I was top in my class. It was given to someone else. So I had to go out and work.

Eventually, I was hired by *The National Echo* as Literary Editor. Part of my duties included writing editorials. And during that time, I was able to write quite scathingly about political matters.

I remember one of my editorials criticised Mahathir Mohamad for warning that Malaysia would "shoot" the Vietnamese boat people if they tried to land on our shores. He later insisted that he said "shoo", but I could already see then what kind of a guy we were dealing with.

I became more politically sensitised when I moved from Penang to Kuala Lumpur in the late 1970s, from *The National Echo* to the *New Straits Times*. In the capital, I began to see more sharply the contradictions in our society. At the time, the social re-engineering that had come into place after 1969 was beginning to show its effects. They became more pronounced in the early 1980s when Mahathir Mohamad became prime minister. Working at the *NST* made me see more clearly that things were going towards an authoritarian direction. I got numerous memos from my editor-in-chief for trying to push the parameters and opening up public discourse on "sensitive" issues. The most pressing issue then was race and how it had been politicised to divide the people. Mahathir was also showing signs of being increasingly dictatorial; he would tolerate no criticisms of him in the media.

What I couldn't express through the newspaper I eventually expressed in a play. Entitled *1984 Here and Now*, it spoke out frankly against Big Brother and institutionalised racial discrimination. It played to full houses in 1985 because it brought up issues of the day that people were afraid to discuss publicly. Those who came were surprised that it had obtained a permit to be staged.

I have since gone on to write more political plays. One of them, *The Big Purge*, brazenly satirises Mahathir and Operation Lalang.

What was your most difficult assignment?
My most difficult assignment has been my entire journalistic career in the mainstream media!

Except in *The National Echo*, I've had to battle my bosses and, as a result, been punished, marginalised, shut out. It's not something I would recommend to anybody — because if you work for a company, you should ideally not be fighting it. But I've always felt that journalism is not like a lot of other professions. As a journalist, you also have a responsibility to the public. To inform them of the truth. And certainly not to spin — in order to save someone's skin or to spew propaganda or to create the illusion that all is well with the country when it's not. The last-mentioned is the most sinful type of spin!

A newspaper is not a public relations rag; it should uphold journalistic ideals and principles. If you work in a newspaper that goes against these ideals, what do you do? Accept it, shut up and just do what you're told? Then you would not be fulfilling your responsibility not only to your readers but the society at large. What's worse is doing what you're told to do even though you know it's wrong.

What are the challenges of being a political writer?

One of the challenges is making yourself clear in your writing so that you are not misunderstood. Another is being consistent in your stand on certain things. Unlike the current Malaysian government, you can't afford to perform flip-flops! You are accountable for whatever you say, and a piece of writing that you wrote 20 years ago can come back and haunt you if the stand you took on a particular issue then turns out to be the direct opposite of your current stand. Of course, opinions and beliefs can change over time, but you'll still be flayed for the turnaround. This is an occupational hazard of political writers. In this regard, they are considered to be less than human!

You also have to be careful that you don't libel anyone, which means you have to be sure of your facts and have evidence to support what you say.

In Malaysia, the additional challenges for a political writer are the numerous laws that discourage free speech. Every time you write a political piece, you have to be mindful that it is not seditious. Then your friends, out of concern, remind you that there is such a thing as the ISA so you'd better be circumspect. That's because Malaysians have been so conditioned by fear for so long.

If you are writing for a mainstream publication, you will be reminded you can't knock the prime minister or his senior ministers. You might be cited incidents when the editor-in-chief was summoned to the Home Ministry to explain why a seemingly innocuous article managed to get published in the paper. Or of the telephone calls he has been receiving from Putrajaya. You might even be reminded of the Printing Presses and Publications Act (PPPA) and the need for the paper to survive that, because it has to take care of so many people who would be out of a job if the paper lost its licence.

It's no wonder then that most who write for the mainstream media become experts in self-censorship.

I could never have survived as a political writer in the *New Straits Times* or *The Star*, which I joined in 2001. This thesis was tested (although it was not my intention to test it) in 2007 when I started a weekly political column in *The Star* called 'Playing the Fool'. In my inaugural article, I wrote that I would be speaking frankly on social and political issues, instead of bullshit and all that. The second one hit out at racial discrimination. But when it came to my third piece, the editors shook their heads and it got spiked. And after I'd written my fourth and it had gone upstairs for scrutiny, the instruction that came back down was to terminate the column! To be honest, I wasn't surprised.

Why do you still do it?
The desire to speak up. The need to speak up. The need to give my views on what I feel is wrong and how things can be made right, even if it won't count for much. And, highfalutin as it may sound, the desire for a better Malaysia. These are what make me do it.

You can't underestimate how strongly people want — nay, need — to speak up. Which is why any government that tries to stifle free speech hasn't figured it out right.

Many books have been banned or confiscated in Malaysia. How do yours remain elusive?
That's not for me to answer. But I would say that I'm a citizen who cares for his country and would not do anything to hurt it, so whatever I write is in its best interests, as far as I perceive it. That should not be something punishable, surely?

What's the most challenging part of writing *March 8: The Day Malaysia Woke Up?* What's the most gratifying?
Putting it together in a mere three months — from scratch! That was a challenge. But it had to be done fast because of the topicality of the

book's subject. It was most gratifying that I had friends who responded to my call for help by contributing articles and comments. I'm greatly indebted to them for that.

What's perhaps even more gratifying is that others who contributed were people I had never known or met before. I found out about them and approached them — and they responded positively and generously. It showed to me that they, too, cared for their country, that they wanted to see a better Malaysia, which is the central theme and intent of the book.

The other challenging things were practical or logistical, such as trying to fix interviews with busy people like politicians and ministers; chasing people to meet deadlines; editing very raw material; transcribing interviews.

What do you think has and hasn't changed in Malaysia's journalism industry over the years?
It has become more reactionary and conservative. When I started out in the 1970s, the controls were not so tight. Even when I joined the *New Straits Times* in 1979, there was a strong sense of editorial integrity and a greater degree of independence (or you could call it non-interference). It had a Chinese editor-in-chief in Lee Siew Yee, which is something that became inconceivable not long after. Everything began to be race-centred from the beginning of the 1980s. I think the ruling regime then had a lot to account for that. It also had a lot to account for muzzling the media. Editors-in-chief at the *New Straits Times* had to be politically *halal*. Approved appointees. This naturally changed the orientation and workings of the media. And if it was felt that the editor-in-chief didn't live up to political expectations, he'd be replaced. I'm told this was what happened to Munir Majid. Although I had numerous clashes with him, I respected and still respect him for being the best and broadest-minded editor-in-chief I've worked under.

What would be the three changes that you'd like to see in Malaysia?
First, a change of government at the next general election. So that we can hopefully start on a fresh, if not totally clean, slate and have a better

chance of seeing real reform. The current one is only making cosmetic changes, and it's not showing true commitment to reform because it is worried about too many factors, too many interest-groups.

The highest-priority change for me is the elimination of race in all our considerations and endeavours. Perhaps that could begin with the disbanding of all race-based parties to herald the decline, if not demise, of the sickening politicisation of race. I would extend this to religion as well. PAS should, therefore, disband or reconstitute itself. And let us uphold the principle of our founding fathers in envisioning Malaysia as a secular state.

The third change will cover everything that needs to be righted from the many wrongs committed by the ruling regime over the past few decades. You might call it a change-back, e.g. the judiciary changing back to being an independent one; the negotiated contract changing back to open tenders; the appointment of local councillors changing back to elected ones; and so on.

Ever thought of migrating? Why?
No. Because I have always considered Malaysia my home. It has everything going for it, except the lousy, dirty politics. Which is profoundly sad. I can't stay away from the country for long. When I was doing my MA in England in 1987–'88, I was impatient to come home.

In fact, in the 1980s, I was actively persuading my friends not to emigrate. But eventually, I saw the point of their wanting to leave. I wrote about it in an essay called 'All We Want Is an Even Chance', which got published in the *NST*, thanks to a forward-thinking editor. The decision to publish it was, however, questioned by higher-ups after it came out. The essay is also in my book *Just In So Many Words*.

What's your advice to anyone who aspires to be a political writer?
Open your eyes, think critically, be brave and write with good intentions.

LIST OF ABBREVIATIONS

ACA	Anti-Corruption Agency
BTN	Biro Tata Negara
CDA	Critical Discourse Analysis
DAP	Democratic Action Party
DMSM	Darjah Mulia Seri Melaka
DPSM	Darjah Pangkuan Seri Melaka
EC	Election Commission
EO	Emergency Ordinance
ETP	Economic Transformation Programme
FLOM	First Lady of Malaysia
GAS	Gerakan Anti-Samy
GLCs	Government-linked Companies
GPSM	Peninsular Malaysia Malay Students Front
GST	Goods and Services Tax
GTP	Government Transformation Programme
Hindraf	Hindu Rights Action Force
IGP	Inspector-General of Police
IPCMC	Independent Police Complaints and Misconduct Commission
ISA	Internal Security Act
KLSCAH	Kuala Lumpur and Selangor Chinese Assembly Hall
MACC	Malaysian Anti-Corruption Agency
MB	Menteri Besar
MCA	Malaysian Chinese Association
MCE	Malaysian Certificate of Education
MCMC	Malaysian Communications and Multimedia Commission
MCP	Malayan Communist Party
MIC	Malaysian Indian Congress
MP	Member of Parliament
NEM	New Economic Model
NEP	New Economic Policy
NGO	Non-Governmental Organisation
NST	New Straits Times
NUJ	National Union of Journalists

OSA	Official Secrets Act
PAS	Parti Islam SeMalaysia
PBB	Parti Pesaka Bumiputera Bersatu
PBS	Parti Bersatu Sabah
Pekida	Pertubuhan Kebajikan dan Dakwah Islamiah Malaysia
Perkasa	Persatuan Pribumi Perkasa Malaysia
PKFZ	Port Klang Free Zone
PKMM	Parti Kebangsaan Melayu Malaya
PKR	Parti Keadilan Rakyat
PM	Prime Minister
PPP	People's Progressive Party
PPPA	Printing Presses and Publications Act
PR	Pakatan Rakyat
PSC	Parliamentary Select Committee
PSM	Parti Sosialis Malaysia
PTP	Political Transformation Programme
Putera-AMCJA	Pusat Tenaga Rakyat-All-Malaya Council of Joint Action
PWTC	Putra World Trade Centre
RCI	Royal Commission of Inquiry
ROS	Registrar of Societies
SABM	Saya Anak Bangsa Malaysia
SNAP	Sarawak National Party
SPM	Sijil Pelajaran Malaysia
Suaram	Suara Rakyat Malaysia
Suhakam	Human Rights Commission of Malaysia
SUPP	Sarawak United People's Party
UCSI	University College Sedaya International
UEC	United Examination Certificate
UKM	Universiti Kebangsaan Malaysia
UM	Universiti Malaya
Umno	United Malays National Organisation
UPM	Universiti Putra Malaysia
USM	Universiti Sains Malaysia
UUCA	Universities and University Colleges Act

ABOUT THE AUTHOR

KEE THUAN CHYE is a Malaysian who wants a better Malaysia, one that is run by a clean government that respects the rights of citizens and the rule of law, that does not politicise the issues of race and religion. He was a full-time journalist for more than 30 years until 2009. He now writes political commentaries for online news websites. He is also an actor and a playwright, best known for his political plays, the latest of which is *The Swordfish, Then the Concubine*. He is also the author of *March 8: Time for Real Change*, published in 2010, an update of *March 8: The Day Malaysia Woke Up*, which he brought out in 2008.

Also available from Kee Thuan Chye ...

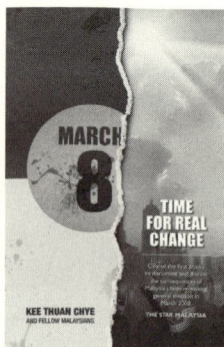

March 8: Time for Real Change
Publisher: Marshall Cavendish Editions
ISBN: 978-981-4328-33-3

With their votes, Malaysians dealt a blow to the Barisan Nasional government that had held almost absolute power for 50 years. Malaysians woke up to the true meaning and practice of democracy. This book is about that historic day and the change that came with it. There are also eyewitness accounts, interviews with key people, and articles never published before, written by fledgling and established writers.